"The discussion about what was P[...]
intended), full of all kinds of sugges[...]
esting detail, Ken Berding's look at t[...]
the most thorough examination of the issue of which I am aware. The lessons th[...]
emerge from understanding the type of suffering involved are instructive for all of [...]

—DARRELL L. BOCK, senior research professor [...]
New Testament Studies, Dallas Theological Semina[...]

"Some problems of New Testament interpretation are difficult. Others seem intracta[...]
The identity of Paul's thorn in the flesh is an example of the latter. Churchill mi[...]
have called it a riddle wrapped in a mystery inside an enigma. But fear not. Kenn[...]
Berding has left no stone unturned in his quest to discover the most probable s[...]
tion to this mystery—and his conclusion might well surprise you. With Churchill[...]
bulldoggedness, Berding has faced a perennial crux of interpretation head on a[...]
has succeeded magnificently. Don't miss this book!"

—DAVID ALAN BLACK, senior professor of New Testament and Gr[...]
Southeastern Baptist Theological Semin[...]

"Dr. Berding has provided readers an insightful interpretation of the meaning of 'th[...]
in the flesh' in 2 Corinthians 12:7. His interpretation of the phrase shows wh[...]
biblical-exegetical study should look like. He carefully attends to the literary [...]
text of the passage in the broader context of Paul's corpus, and draws upon insi[...]
from historical, cultural, and intertextual contexts. The identification of Paul's th[...]
has often been carried out without testing against a set of rigorous criteria, [...]
Ken has defended his thesis well through twenty criteria derived from meticu[...]
research. This book is a valuable and useful addition to the study of Paul and[...]
New Testament."

—DONGSU KIM, president of Saint Paul Academy of Theol[...]
adjunct professor of New Testament at Denver Seminary and M[...]

as written an absorbing book about Paul's thorn in the flesh that not
aders in understanding a contested New Testament passage but also
have a fuller, more human understanding of the great apostle whose
s may have been strikingly similar to those of contemporary Christians
n chronic illnesses."

—ECKHARD J. SCHNABEL, Mary F. Rockefeller Distinguished
rofessor of New Testament, Gordon-Conwell Theological Seminary

in the Flesh addresses a thorny problem in Pauline studies. The rele-
cularly in 2 Corinthians and Galatians, are thoroughly discussed along
is interpretations. These are evaluated in light of twenty criteria that
ed for. Three charts help readers process the various positions at a
ialists will appreciate the clear and accessible discussion of techni-
s will no doubt become the go-to volume for ongoing discussions
g yet controversial topic."

—MARK WILSON, director, Asia Minor Research Center;
rofessor extraordinary of New Testament, Stellenbosch University

r shies away from the hard questions, and always impresses with
his research and the originality of his answers. In this deep dive
ve matter that most are content to ignore or minimally investi-
s a creative and insightful proposal concerning the actual con-
the Apostle Paul. Leaving no stone unturned, Berding suggests
n the flesh' (2 Cor 12:7) was a long-term, intermittent, stabbing
by ancient onlookers to black magic, but regarded by Paul as a
mitted by God for the advancement of Paul's own spiritual for-
s produced a study that will benefit not only scholars, pastors,
o those who suffer from disability and chronic pain. The great
s eminently relatable to those whose bodily ailments leave them

feeling weak and marginalized. Physical suffering, Berding shows us, is central to the cruciform experience and instrumental in learning about God's grace. This book is highly recommended!"

—JOHN K. GOODRICH, professor of Bible, Moody Bible Institute

"Some may question whether anything more can be said about Paul's thorn in the flesh, other than it was some vague, mysterious ailment that Paul suffered from. Within the first few chapters, Ken Berding will convince you that this is indeed a question worth pursuing, and there is a lot more information that previous scholarship had not uncovered. No other book on this topic has conducted such a comprehensive analysis—from the literary context, the Old Testament background, the historical context, and church history. Grounded in sound exegesis, a thorough understanding of the secondary literature, and an examination of the issue from various angles, this book makes a compelling case for the specific ailment that constituted Paul's thorn in the flesh. Whether you are convinced by his conclusion or not—I was—Ken Berding's book is an essential read for anyone who wishes to better understand Paul's thorn in the flesh. It is the first book I will recommend to anyone interested in this topic."

—ADAM DAY, associate professor of New Testament Language and Literature, Tyndale Theological Seminary, The Netherlands

"*Paul's Thorn in the Flesh* is a careful and comprehensive study that judiciously tackles a problem whose answer has consistently eluded scholars. Kenneth Berding presents an intriguing solution based on Paul's life and theology, his cultural environment, and the literary and linguistic context of 2 Corinthians. This is an important work for those of us who have long wondered what Paul's 'thorn' could have been. Even more significantly, it challenges us to know more deeply the implications of the apostle's sharing in the sufferings of his Savior."

—MICHELLE LEE-BARNEWALL, senior affiliate professor of New Testament, Talbot School of Theology

"You are holding a landmark—a new standard against which all further treatment will be measured. Professor Berding has gifted church, academy, and healthcare with a fascinating, definitive treatment of Saint Paul's unsolved 'thorn in the flesh,' one of Pauline studies' most elusive and understudied enigmas. Nowhere in the history of New Testament studies has Paul's morbidity and mortality been so meticulously investigated. Employing every conceivable source—ancient pagan to contemporary neuroscience, ante-Nicene fathers to craniofacial pain support groups, and the sweep of canonical Scripture—Berding's close reading of texts, imaginative energy, and correlation with modern medicine is breathtaking. As a Pauline scholar, physician, and pastor, I am no longer agnostic: something physical, visible, excruciating, crippling, shameful, and mysterious was agonizing the apostle and collapsing his authority in Corinth. Yet, Paul's Gospel prevails. In the dazzling light of this breakthrough study, no disciple of Jesus Christ will be able to view *bodily affliction of any kind* as outside the purposeful reach of God's saving power."

—RICHARD DEIBERT, MD, associate medical director,
Tidewell Hospice, Sarasota, Florida; author of *Second Corinthians
and Paul's Gospel of Human Mortality* (Mohr Siebeck)

PAUL'S

NEW CLUES
FOR AN
OLD PROBLEM

THORN

in the
FLESH

PAUL'S

**NEW CLUES
FOR AN
OLD PROBLEM**

THORN

in the
FLESH

BY KENNETH
BERDING

LEXHAM
ACADEMIC

Paul's Thorn in the Flesh: New Clues for an Old Problem

Copyright 2023 Kenneth Berding

Lexham Academic, an imprint of Lexham Press
1313 Commercial St., Bellingham, WA 98225
LexhamPress.com

Print ISBN 9781683596837
Digital ISBN 9781683596844
Library of Congress Control Number 2022947468

Lexham Editorial: Derek Brown, Caleb Kormann, Jessi Strong, Mandi Newell,
  Katrina Smith
Cover Design: Alecia Sharp, Brittany Schrock
Typesetting: Justin Marr

CONTENTS

DETAILED OUTLINE |

ABBREVIATIONS

AB	Anchor Bible
ABR	*Australian Biblical Review*
ACNT	Augsburg Commentaries on the New Testament
AFP	*American Family Physician*
AsJT	*Asia Journal of Theology*
AnBib	Analecta Biblica
Ann. Indian Acad. Neurol.	*Annals of Indian Academy of Neurology*
ANF	*The Ante-Nicene Fathers*
ANTC	Abingdon New Testament Commentaries
Arch. Phys. Med. Rehabil.	*Archives of Physical Medicine and Rehabilitation*
BAR	*Biblical Archeology Review*
BBR	*Bulletin for Biblical Research*
BCOTWP	Baker Commentary on the Old Testament Wisdom and Psalms
BDAG	Danker, Fredrick W., Walter Bauer, William F. Arndt, and F. Wilbur Gingrich. *Greek-English Lexicon of the New Testament and Other Early Christian Literature*. 3rd ed. Chicago: University of Chicago Press, 2000 (Danker-Bauer-Arndt-Gingrich)

BECNT	Baker Exegetical Commentary on the New Testament
Bib	*Biblica*
BJP	*British Journal of Pain*
BNTC	Black's New Testament Commentaries
BSac	*Bibliotecha Sacra*
BTB	*Biblical Theology Bulletin*
BTL	Biblical Theology for Life
BZNW	Beihefte zur Zeitschrift für die neutestamentliche Wissenschaft
CBQ	*Catholic Biblical Quarterly*
ClAnt	*Classical Antiquity*
Clin. Geriatr.	*Clinics in Geriatric Medicine*
CRINT	Compendia Rerum Iudaicarum ad Novum Testamentum
CTR	*Criswell Theological Review*
Curr Neurol Neurosci Rep	*Current Neurology and Neuroscience Reports*
Curr Pain Headache Rep	*Current Pain and Headache Reports*
DBI	*Dictionary of Biblical Imagery*
DPL	*Dictionary of Paul and His Letters.* Edited by Gerald F. Hawthorne and Ralph P. Martin. Downers Grove, IL: InverVarsity, 1993
ECL	Early Christianity and Its Literature
ETAM	Ergänzungsbände zu den Tituli Asiae Minoris
EvQ	*The Evangelical Quarterly*
ExpTim	*Expository Times*
FRLANT	Forschungen zur Religion und Literatur des Alten und Neuen Testaments
Headache	*Headache: The Journal of Head and Face Pain*
HUCA	*Hebrew Union College Annual*
ICC	The International Critical Commentary
Int	*Interpretation*

IRM	International Review of Mission
IVPNTC	The IVP New Testament Commentary Series
JBL	Journal of Biblical Literature
JBR	Journal of Bible and Religion
JETS	Journal of the Evangelical Theological Society
J. Disabil. Relig.	Journal of Religion, Disability & Health
J. Man. Manip. Ther.	Journal of Manual & Manipulative Therapy
J. Moral Theol.	Journal of Moral Theology
J. Neurol.	Journal of Neurology, Neurosurgery, and Psychiatry
J. Oral	Journal of Oral & Facial Pain and Headache
J. Philos.	The Journal of Philosophy
JPT	Journal of Pentecostal Theology
JSHJ	Journal for the Study of the Historical Jesus
JSNT	Journal for the Study of the New Testament
JSNTSup	Journal for the Study of the New Testament: Supplement Series
JSOT	Journal for the Study of the Old Testament
JSPL	Journal for the Study of Paul and His Letters
JTS	Journal of Theological Studies
JTSA	Journal of Theology of Southern Africa
Lancet Neurol.	The Lancet Neurology
LCL	Loeb Classical Library
LNTS	Library of New Testament Studies
LSJ	Liddell, Henry George, Robert Scott, Henry Stuart Jones. A Greek-English Lexicon. 9th ed. with revised supplement. Oxford: Clarendon, 1996
Mayo Clin. Proc.	Mayo Clinic Proceedings
MeyerK	Meyers Kritisch-exegetischer Kommentar über das Neue Testament
MH	Medical History
MNS	Mnemosyne Supplements

NAC	New American Commentary
NCBC	New Cambridge Bible Commentary
Neot	*Neotestamentica*
Neurosurg. *Clin. N. Am.*	*Neurosurgery Clinics of North America*
NIBC	New International Biblical Commentary
NICNT	New International Commentary on the New Testament
NICOT	New International Commentary on the Old Testament
NIGTC	New International Greek Testament Commentary
NIVAC	The NIV Application Commentary
NovT	*Novum Testamentum*
NovTSup	Supplements to Novum Testamentum
NPNF	Select Library of the Christian Church: Nicene and Post-Nicene Fathers
NTM	New Testament Monographs
NTS	*New Testament Studies*
OBT	Overtures to Biblical Theology
OECS	Oxford Early Christian Studies
OTE	*Old Testament Essays*
PBM	Paternoster Biblical Monographs
PGM	*Papyri Graecae Magicae: Die griechischen* *Zauberpapyri.* Edited by Karl Preisendanz. 2nd ed. Stuttgart: Teubner, 1973–1974
PKNT	Papyrologische Kommentare zum Neuen Testament
PNAS	*Proceedings of the National Academy of Sciences of* *the United States of America*
PNTC	The Pillar New Testament Commentary
PPS	Popular Patristics Series
Postgrad. *Med.*	*Postgraduate Medicine*
PTMS	Pittsburgh Theological Monograph Series

R&T	Religion & Theology
RBS	Resources for Biblical Study
RevExp	Review & Expositor
RGRW	Religions in the Graeco-Roman World
RRA	Rhetoric of Religious Antiquity
SEÅ	Svensk Exegetisk Årsbok
SemeiaSt	Semeia Studies
SetF	Scientia et Fides
SHBC	Smyth & Helwys Bible Commentary
SNTSMS	Society for New Testament Studies Monograph Series
TDNT	Theological Dictionary of the New Testament. Edited by Gerhard Kittel and Gerhard Friedrich. Translated by Geoffrey W. Bromiley. 10 vols. Grand Rapids: Eerdmans, 1964–1976
TOTC	Tyndale Old Testament Commentaries
TTCLBS	T&T Clark Library of Biblical Studies
TynBul	Tyndale Bulletin
TZ	Theologische Zeitschrift
VCSup	Supplements to Vigiliae Christianae
WBC	Word Biblical Commentary
WUNT	Wissenschafliche Untersuchungen zum Neuen Testament
ZECNT	Zondervan Exegetical Commentary on the New Testament
ZNW	Zeitschrift für die neutestamentliche Wissenschaft und die Kunde der älteren Kirche

INTRODUCTION |

I magine with me a first-century house-church meeting. The apostle Paul is addressing a new group of Jesus followers that has recently sprung up as an extension of Paul's ministry in Ephesus. Paul is passionately exhorting the assembled group about their need to view one another as brothers and sisters in the family of God. He is twenty minutes into his talk when suddenly—and without warning—Paul's face grimaces, his hand moves rapidly to the side of his face just in front of his ear, he collapses into a sitting position, his breathing quickens as he leans forward, eyes shut, fighting to hold back the groans working their way out of his throat. The matron of the house rushes forward along with a half dozen others. She cries out, "Brother Paul, are you OK? What's happening? What's wrong?"

Paul holds up his available hand and temporarily halts their questions. His new friends wait apprehensively. The only sounds in the room are Paul's muffled groans. Tears wet his cheek. An agonizing thirty seconds pass. Paul's breathing slows. After another thirty seconds, Paul releases a long sigh and looks up apologetically at his friends. "I am so sorry."

"Sorry? Don't worry, Paul. Are you all right? What happened? Is it over?" Questions tumble out.

Paul answers haltingly. "God allowed this ... to keep me humble. Like Job."

1

The house matron shushes everyone and takes over. "But what was it? Tell us what happened, Paul. What did you just experience?"

"Terrible pain in my face."

"Where on your face?"

"Just in front of my ear ... but extending throughout the one side of my face ... inside the skin and much deeper down ... "

"What kind of pain?"

"I'm hesitant to talk about it."

"That won't do, Paul. You're our teacher and brother. Tell us about your pain. What kind of pain was it?"

"Piercing pain. Stabbing pain. Like someone driving a stake into my face."

Wince. They begin looking around at each other—uncomfortably. Finally, one woman articulates what everyone knows the others are thinking: "Somebody is attacking you, Paul. Someone doesn't want you here. Someone with power is casting a curse on you."

Paul turns his gaze upward, reflectively. "You could be right. It wouldn't be the first time. Dozens of curses have been unleashed upon me over the years. I don't know whether this pain is related to a curse—but, whatever it was, it was some sort of satanic attack. Satan and his evil angels often seek my harm, as they try to harm anyone who serves our Lord Jesus Christ. Still, I don't want you to worry. I have no fear of Satan's messengers, and neither should you. I'm prepared for weaknesses or insults or distresses or persecutions or difficulties for Christ's sake if God should so permit."

"But why would he allow it? Why would God permit such terrible pain like you've described?"

"I already told you. God sometimes allows such attacks to keep me humble."

One of the men in the back of the room mumbles—perhaps a little too loud—"Humble ... that's for sure."

Mrs. Matron sends the mumbler a look with daggers in it. She turns back to Paul. "Is this going to happen again?"

"Yes, I'm afraid so. It could happen again today. Sometimes it occurs repeatedly, though I never know when I'll be struck. Sometimes attack periods recede for months at a time. I must ask your forgiveness in advance. Three times over the years, I have asked the Lord to take it away from me. His only answer has been to remind me that his grace is enough for me. He never allows the pain to entirely overcome me, as excruciating as it might be in the moment—and let me assure you, it is terribly painful. I have to trust that God will continue to be faithful, and will never allow me to be tested beyond my ability, but will always provide a way of escape so that I can endure these attacks of the Evil One."

After a bit more discussion, Paul resumes his talk about the church being the family of God. Paul's message is marked by the power of the Holy Spirit, but some in the room wonder why God would allow one of his faithful servants to face such humiliation in front of them all. Some wonder whether Paul really was one of those faithful servants in light of what they just witnessed.

———

What was Paul's thorn in the flesh? Many people deem this question unanswerable. The bias against finding a solution to this intriguing historical question is powerful (see chapter 1). But in our haste to pronounce the puzzle unsolvable, might we have missed some clues? Or, even if we have accurately identified some relevant clues, have we failed to connect them with other clues previously identified by interpreters who have worked on this fascinating historical enigma?

Select almost any commentary on 2 Corinthians and read what has been written about 2 Corinthians 12:7. A handful of observations get drawn out, followed by a tentative solution based upon a few criteria. But what would happen if we brought together all the clues that have been identified by past interpreters, and then added more into the mix that haven't yet been adequately explored? What if we drew up a list of twenty criteria? Would we not then be in a place to propose a more satisfying solution? I think that we have come to that place, and the time has come for us to reopen this conversation.

The essence of my argument is a list of twenty criteria, each of which I will support on the pages ahead. When taken together, these criteria limit the possibilities of what Paul's thorn in the flesh could have been. As we work together through each relevant verse, inter-textual connection, and cultural background, it will be easier to follow the overall argument if we keep this list of criteria in mind. I propose that the following are the twenty criteria necessary for establishing a plausible solution to the riddle of Paul's thorn in the flesh:

Twenty Criteria

1. Viewed by others as black magic attacks

2. Viewed by Paul as attacks by an angel of Satan, though permitted by God

3. Paralleling Job's sufferings (especially Job 1–2), which included skin/flesh

4. Impacting Paul's physical flesh

5. Comparable to the jabbing of a sharp-pointed object

6. Excruciating, not simply annoying

7. Impacting Paul's face (as a part of his head)

8. Viewed by Paul as educational discipline by God

9. Viewed by others as humiliating and weak

10. Unusual, not like the pains of others

11. Long-term, but intermittent

12. Paralleling the sufferings of Jesus

13. Exacerbated by stress

14. Negatively impacting Paul's rhetorical ability

15. Known to the Corinthians, not a secret

16. Analogous to Paul's other sufferings

17. Connected to the heavenly ascent

18. Involving the ear

19. Involving the eye

20. Visible bodily damage

I will argue on the pages ahead that any proposed solution to the historical puzzle of Paul's thorn in the flesh must attempt to account for these twenty criteria.

How will the argument progress?

In chapter 1, I expose an unnecessarily strong bias against pursuing a plausible solution to this historical perplexity. I also include a brief discussion of how presuppositions impact interpretation, including a few key presuppositions related to the study of Paul's thorn in the flesh, and lay out my own presuppositions pertaining to the matters under discussion.

In chapter 2, I summarize the history of interpretation of Paul's thorn in the flesh. We will observe that a physical explanation continues—rightly—to be the dominant interpretive position for much of that history, despite a litany of other creative solutions that have been proposed along the way. At the end of this chapter, I expose the problems with listing out opinions.

Chapters 3–10 form the heart of the argument.

In chapter 3, I argue that Paul's combination of the words "a thorn in the flesh" and "an angel of Satan" would have caused Paul's first-century readers to think of black magic attacks. Ancient magicians regularly fashioned figurines (ancient "voodoo dolls," as they are sometimes called today) and stuck them with sharp objects such as pins, nails, or thorns. Those magicians also inscribed curses upon tablets that they pierced, and stabbed animals on behalf of people who wanted to bind their adversaries with magic. I argue that people who heard Paul's "thorn" and "angel of Satan" language would have connected Paul's sufferings with such attacks of magic. Suggesting this as a historical-cultural background fits well with what we know about Paul's encounters with evil spirits in the book of Acts as well as in his own letters. I close chapter 3 by reflecting on two theological issues raised by positing this as a relevant background.

In chapter 4, I draw out a set of literary and conceptual features shared by 2 Corinthians 12 and Job (especially Job 1–2). This will support my contention that the story of Job runs as a subtext beneath Paul's explanation of his own suffering. This literary and conceptual dependency of Paul upon the story of Job is significant because Job (analogous to Paul, I argue) was struck (or "stung") with painful sores in his literal skin and flesh.

In chapters 5–7, I analyze Paul's thorn in the flesh in the immediate literary context of 2 Corinthians 12:7, working outward in three concentric circles. In chapter 5, I consider the first and smallest circle, the sentence (2 Cor 12:7). I evaluate the words "thorn" and "flesh" and their relationship to one another, the expression "an angel of Satan," the idea of given-ness, the facial connotations of the Greek word *kolaphizō*, and the educational-disciplinary nature of God permitting the thorn.

In chapter 6, I draw out clues appearing in the second concentric circle, the paragraph (2 Cor 12:1–10). I explain the fourteen-year duration and intermittent nature of the thorn. I observe how the thorn was connected to the heavenly ascent (vision/revelation) described by Paul in 12:1–4. I evaluate Paul's note about seeing and hearing in 12:6, the excruciating nature of his suffering, the importance of "weakness(es)" for understanding Paul's thorn (12:5, 9, 10), and clarify how Paul's special misery belongs in a class alongside other sufferings Paul endured.

In chapter 7, I widen into the third concentric circle, the discourse (2 Corinthians 10–13). I note that Paul's body was perceived as weak (10:10), draw out the weakness/humiliation/shame theme that pervades these chapters, and observe a collocation of facial terminology—a focus on the face that differs from other places in Paul's letters. I support the contention that Paul's malady was known to the Corinthians and observe that the themes of stress and spiritual warfare are both significant and relevant. I close by asking whether Paul's rhetoric was weak or strong, and how a particular understanding of Paul's thorn in the flesh might address this unusual question.

In chapter 8, I identify clues from the suffering of Jesus that might bear upon the nature of Paul's thorn. I begin the chapter by noting how intimately Paul identified with the suffering of Jesus in his letters, especially in 2 Corinthians. I argue that Paul's unique identification with the sufferings of his Lord brought spiritual encouragement to Paul in the midst of his own physical suffering, particularly as he encountered piercing pain. I observe that Jesus was pierced on the head with a crown of thorns, pierced with nails and a spear, struck on the head and slapped in the face, resulting not only in pain, but also in shame—all in fulfillment of Old Testament piercing passages. Paul's identification with the sufferings of Jesus suggest that when Paul himself experienced piercing pain, he likely would have considered his pain as analogous to the piercings that his Lord endured.

In chapter 9, I probe the question of how people in the post-apostolic church interpreted Paul's thorn in the flesh. I argue that the comments of Irenaeus, who viewed Paul's thorn in the flesh as a bodily ailment, and Tertullian, who similarly viewed it as a bodily ailment—but more specifically as a pain of the ear or head—are more valuable than any other of the church fathers who commented on Paul's thorn. This is because Irenaeus and Tertullian wrote during a period (roughly one hundred and fifty years after Paul wrote about his "thorn") when oral transmission should still be highly valued. The other primary authors who commented on the nature of Paul's thorn in the flesh wrote three centuries after Paul, and accordingly should be differentiated in terms of their historical value from Irenaeus and Tertullian.

In chapter 10, I dive into the difficult question of whether there is anything in the book of Galatians that assists us in determining the nature of Paul's thorn in the flesh. It has been necessary for me to take up this question because so many interpreters in the past have answered this question in the affirmative, while some have been skeptical. I end up answering this question with a hesitant affirmative. I draw out clues from Galatians 4:13–15, and briefly inquire into what Galatians 3:1 and 6:17 might add to the discussion.

I start chapter 11 by explaining how it is possible for various influences (literary, historical-cultural, ethical) to simultaneously layer. I do this with the aim of addressing a question that might arise during the study. I spend the remainder of the chapter exploring other possible literary and conceptual relationships to Paul's thorn in the flesh in the Bible, and explain why I factored them out of an overall solution.

In chapter 12, the book shifts from argument to application. In chapter 12, I restate the twenty criteria that have already emerged from the study and summarize primary reasons each criterion was included on the list. (Note: If you desire a short summary of core arguments that appear in chapters 3–10, the place to find such a summary is chapter 12.)

In chapter 13, I present comparative charts that display how the twenty criteria relate to other past proposals for the nature of Paul's thorn in the flesh. I then employ the same chart format to illustrate that there are seven medical conditions (centering, for the most part, on the trigeminal nerve) that fit the criteria better than any of the other alternatives included on the charts. This final chart prepares the reader for the following chapter.

In chapter 14, I identify and describe seven medical conditions that closely fit the criteria.

1. Trigeminal Neuralgia (Type 1)

2. Posttraumatic Trigeminal Neuropathic Pain

3. Herpes Zoster (Shingles) in the Trigeminal Nerve + Post-herpetic Neuralgia

4. Short-lasting Unilateral Neuralgiform Headache Attacks

5. Episodic Paroxysmal Hemicrania

6. Episodic Cluster Headaches

7. Primary Stabbing Headaches, or Migraines with Primary Stabbing Headaches

The chapter concludes with an explanation of the trigeminal (facial) nerve, and its central role in the solutions offered. Finally, in order to bridge the relevance gap with those who have never heard of such medical conditions, I have included a handful of testimonials from people who suffer from intense piercing pain in the trigeminal nerve.

In chapter 15, I draw out a few implications of this study beyond the simple identification of Paul's thorn in the flesh. In particular, I focus on how this study enhances our understanding of the *person* of Paul.

There are many new points of argument in this book, including: the facial associations of *kolaphizō* in 2 Corinthians 12:7, along with other facial indicators in 2 Corinthians 10–13; the historical setting of magical curses, voodoo-doll-like images, and the piercing of animals; some of the suggested intertextual relationships with Job; and the connection with stress, to mention only a few. But some of the criteria have also been drawn from observations made by others, including the honor-shame impulse in the text, possible links to Paul's rhetorical ability or inability, the possible involvement of head, ears and/or eyes, and the combination of a chronic condition with intermittency, among others. I am deeply grateful for all the insights I have gleaned from those who have closely looked at 2 Corinthians 12:7 before me.

Since I anticipate that many intelligent people who have never had the opportunity for advanced academic training as New Testament scholars or historians will be interested in this question, I have chosen to write this book in a register that will be a bit easier to access than are some scholarly books. In practice, this means that I do not assume that all my readers will be familiar with the technical jargon that often gets employed by biblical scholars, historians, linguists, and medical practitioners, and thus I try to use more direct and accessible language (though some technical language appears occasionally, especially in footnotes). My decision to accommodate non-specialists in this way does not mean that I have attempted to avoid any of the difficult questions, some of which, admittedly, are technical in nature. Nor does it mean that the observations I offer are simplistic. Nevertheless, I have made every effort to explain matters in ways that anyone who is serious about thinking through the details of this perplexing historical question can join in.

Even if one is not persuaded by the solution(s) proposed here, this study includes many new lines of inquiry that need to be evaluated by future historians and biblical scholars who attempt to uncover a solution to this famous historical conundrum.

CHAPTER
ONE

WHY WE'RE SKEPTICAL

The topic of Paul's thorn in the flesh is, on the one hand, like a puzzle to be solved—what could have caused Paul such agony?—and, on the other hand, the source of a powerful spiritual lesson—"My grace is sufficient for you, for power is made perfect in weakness" (2 Cor 12:9). Perhaps the combination of its mystery and profundity is why the riddle of Paul's thorn has been attended by keen interest by some, but profound skepticism by others. Since presuppositions have played a significant role in how interpreters have historically approached this interpretive problem, in this chapter I will clarify how presuppositions impact the study of Paul's thorn in the flesh.

A key factor in interpreting texts, ancient or otherwise, is the recognition that every interpreter floats or sinks in a personal pool of presuppositions. A presupposition is "any preconception of reality that is part of our thinking as we come to interpret the Bible."[1]

---

1. Jeannine K. Brown, *Scripture as Communication: Introducing Biblical Hermeneutics* (Grand Rapids: Baker, 2007), 122–23.

All people wade their way through life with individual presuppositions, whether or not they recognize and acknowledge their presence. Presuppositions impact the way we view the world around us, including texts. Thomas Kuhn, in his celebrated book, *The Structure of Scientific Revolutions*, comments, "What a man sees depends both upon what he looks at and also upon what his previous visual-conceptual experience has taught him to see."[2] It is beneficial, even necessary, to become aware of one's assumptions, biases, and proclivities in interpretation. Awareness of one's presuppositions can actually help someone float when approaching the task of interpretation. To carry forward the analogy, people sink into their presuppositional pools when presuppositions become prejudices.[3] The current interpretive climate vis-à-vis Paul's thorn in the flesh can best be described as unreceptive, even antagonistic. As a historical puzzle, it is habitually deemed unsolvable. Possibly more than any other biblical problem I have encountered, scholars are discouraged from attempting to further the conversation on Paul's thorn in the flesh (that is, unless they need to say something about it in a commentary they have agreed to write). This might be why, heretofore, there has been no scholarly book-length study written on this topic, only an occasional article or portion of a commentary that introduces a handful of relevant observations followed by a possible solution. Let us consider some of the places where presuppositions might play a role in the study ahead.

The first place where presuppositions are significant for this study, as has just been mentioned, regards the question of whether it is even worth exerting effort to try to identify what Paul referred to as a "thorn in the flesh" (*skolops tē sarki*). Many interpreters view this historical difficulty as intractable. A profound pattern of bias emerges when we pull together comments from biblical

---

2. Thomas S. Kuhn, *The Structure of Scientific Revolutions*, 2nd ed. (Chicago: The University of Chicago Press, 1970), 113.

3. See discussions in Grant R. Osborne, *The Hermeneutical Spiral: A Comprehensive Introduction to Biblical Interpretation* (Downers Grove, IL: IVP Academic, 2006), 516–17, and Anthony C. Thiselton, *The Two Horizons* (Carlisle: Paternoster, 1980), 304–6.

interpreters who have given thought to this question. Here is a sampling of such comments:

Plummer writes: "But nothing approaching to proof is possible, and of the numerous conjectures as to what the form of this suffering was, one may be true of the σκόλοψ [thorn], while something quite different may be true of the ἀσθενεία [weakness]. Unfortunately, we have to confess that in neither case can we be at all certain as to what is true ... When all the arguments for and against these and other guesses have been considered, the fact remains that we still do not know, for the evidence is insufficient."[4]

Dodd, while preferring a physical explanation, perhaps even malaria, finally pronounces: "Diagnosis is impossible."[5]

Bultmann thinks that Paul's suffering was probably physical, but deems irrelevant any attempt to say more: "For the rest, it is not to be diagnosed. The diagnosis is irrelevant to the context..."[6]

Bruce states bluntly "...no certainty is possible."[7]

Similarly, Garrett writes, "...this question is, finally, unresolvable."[8]

Kruse calls the lack of clues in the text a plain fact. He writes, "However, the plain fact is that there is simply insufficient data to decide the matter."[9]

Martin is openly agnostic: "We will probably never know the truth (or, at least, never know for sure we have the truth)."[10]

---

4. Alfred Plummer, *A Critical and Exegetical Commentary on the Second Epistle of St. Paul to the Corinthians*, ICC (Edinburgh: T&T Clark, 1915), 349–50.

5. C. H. Dodd, *New Testament Studies* (New York: Scribner, 1954), 68.

6. Rudolf Bultmann, *The Second Letter to the Corinthians*, trans. Roy A. Harrisville (Minneapolis: Augsburg, 1985), 225.

7. F. F. Bruce, *The Epistle to the Galatians*, NIGTC (Grand Rapids: Eerdmans and Exeter: Paternoster, 1982), 208.

8. Susan R. Garrett, "Paul's Thorn and Cultural Models of Affliction," in *The Social World of the First Christians: Essays in Honor of Wayne A. Meeks*, ed. L. Michael White and O. Larry Yarbrough (Minneapolis: Fortress, 1995), 83.

9. Colin G. Kruse, *The Second Epistle of Paul to the Corinthians: An Introduction and Commentary* (Leicester: Inter-Varsity Press and Grand Rapids: Eerdmans, 1987, repr. 1995), 206.

10. Ralph P. Martin, *2 Corinthians*, WBC (Waco, TX: Word, 1986), 416.

Harris deems the quest to identify the thorn as eternally impossible: "Although Paul has not identified the 'thorn,' commentators have not been slow to attempt the impossible. Paucity of data and the ambiguity of Paul's language have frustrated—and will always frustrate—all efforts to reach finality in this enigmatic question."[11]

Danker similarly reckons that the thorn "will be an eternal mystery."[12]

While Fee thinks that Paul's ailment was probably a physical problem, he is certain that there is no way of knowing what it was: "Finally, even though we have no way of knowing what the infirmity was, Paul continued to be plagued by a physical problem, even after seeking relief from God."[13]

Hughes waxes eloquent about the impossibility of finding a solution: "The problem of Paul's 'thorn in the flesh' is another one of those questions which, on the evidence available, must remain unanswered. Over the centuries many solutions have been proposed, frequently with excessive confidence, but the plain fact is that it is impossible to escape from the realm of conjecture, which is by its nature the realm of inconclusiveness. ... The great diversity of solutions which have been offered from the early centuries onward is sufficient warning to those who may think that they have answered the problem—not, of course, that we regard the formulation of conjectures as illegitimate; but we do feel that in this instance history has proved that no amount of induction, however ingenious, is going to dispel the uncertainty with which the subject is enveloped."[14]

Kistemaker calls all proposed theories mere guesses: "Whether Paul's affliction happened to be external or internal, the outcome

11. Murray J. Harris, *The Second Epistle to the Corinthians: A Commentary on the Greek Text*, NIGTC (Grand Rapids: Eerdmans, 2005), 858.

12. Frederick W. Danker, *II Corinthians*, ACNT (Minneapolis: Augsburg, 1989), 193.

13. Gordon D. Fee, *God's Empowering Presence: The Holy Spirit in the Letters of Paul* (Peabody, MA: Hendrickson, 1994), 353.

14. Philip Edgcumbe Hughes, *Paul's Second Epistle to the Corinthians: The English Text with Introduction, Exposition and Notes* (Grand Rapids: Eerdmans, 1962), 442–43.

remains the same: our theories are mere guesses, for we do not know what ailed the apostle."[15]

Garland sounds almost fatalistic: "In the end we must accept the fact that we will never know for certain what Paul's stake in the flesh was."[16]

Roetzel claims that speculation about the thorn is "fruitless" and a "barren exercise."[17]

Longenecker's dogmatic assertion fittingly concludes our examples: "Paul does not tell us, and so there is no way for us to know."[18]

As you can see, the prejudice against identifying Paul's thorn is powerful. In light of such a strong prejudgment in the scholarly community, I made a decision early in my study to avoid (for the most part) commentaries while I dug deep into intertextual connections, historical backgrounds, and observations from the immediate context. I spent more than a year simply looking and re-looking at the relevant texts and noting anything that appeared pertinent while laying down rough drafts. Most often, I did this before looking at secondary literature, though in a few select cases, I read seminal articles on specialized ancillary topics. After fleshing out basic arguments, I immersed myself in the secondary literature to discover what I missed, where various arguments were weak, and what I needed to adjust in what I had already attempted to work out mostly on my own.

In addition to the general bias against solving this puzzle, we need to be aware that our presuppositions also play a role in our openness (or lack thereof) to particular aspects of the arguments that lie ahead. For example, I will present evidence that Paul's thorn in the flesh was a painful nerve condition that felt like the repeated stabbing of something sharp into the flesh of his face. However, since most of us have no personal experience with such pain, and furthermore since we

---

15. Simon J. Kistemaker, New Testament Commentary: Exposition of the Second Epistle to the Corinthians (Grand Rapids: Baker), 416.

16. David E. Garland, 2 Corinthians, NAC (Nashville: Broadman & Holman, 1999), 521.

17. Calvin J. Roetzel, 2 Corinthians, ANTC (Nashville: Abingdon, 2007), 111.

18. Richard N. Longenecker, Galatians, WBC (Dallas: Word, 1990), 191.

frequently judge the plausibility or lack of plausibility of a proposal by drawing analogies to our own experiences, many will judge this proposal implausible, albeit without adequate reason. Most people I know have never met anyone who suffers from acute chronic face pain, despite the fact that the Facial Pain Association claims that in the United States alone 4.3 million people experience craniofacial nerve pain. A minority of those 4.3 million experience acutely painful conditions that feel like the repeated stabbing of a pointed object.[19] In contrast, many biblical interpreters' personal experience of pain in the face does not extend beyond tension headaches or toothaches. The idea that someone might experience repeated, long-term, jabbing, shock-like pain in the face could easily be deemed implausible by a person who has never experienced anything more painful than acne. One's experience with craniofacial pain, or lack thereof, is likely to impact the persuasiveness of the argument ahead. This is an issue of presuppositions and needs to be kept in mind as you read.

Another problem of presuppositions in this study is that many of us approach texts with anti-supernatural assumptions. I will mount an argument that Paul's jabbing face pain would have been viewed by observers as attacks of black magic. I will describe a widespread belief in evil spirits and their perceived ability to harm humans that was pervasive in the first-century communities in which Paul ministered. This belief would have been prevalent in the world of Paul; many people lived in fear that someone might cast a curse upon them, or otherwise attack them through the practice of magic. Paul himself also shared this worldview, though he believed that the attacks he experienced were attacks by a fallen angel of Satan that were permitted by God. Many historians of early Christianity do their scholarly work on the assumption that such pre-modern ideas are unfounded superstitions. Since such ideas are false, we are told, belief in angels and demons should be factored out of any inquiry into the nature of Paul's thorn in the flesh. The influence of

---

19. "Patient Guide: Understanding Trigeminal Neuralgia and Neuropathic Face Pain," Facial Pain Association, https://fpa-support.org/support-network/guide/.

writings such as Hume's famous essay, *Of Miracles*, continues to be felt in the books and articles of many who deny that we can talk historically about anything supernatural.[20] An interpreter of the Bible who carries this prejudgment into a historical study of Paul's thorn in the flesh is likely to be biased against any solution that factors the supernatural into its conclusions.[21] The problem with such modernistic presuppositions, ironically, is a historical one. If both Paul—who described his thorn as "an angel of Satan"—and his audience would have agreed on the reality of supernatural powerful beings of the spirit world, then twenty-first-century skepticism toward such a worldview is likely to skew an interpreter's judgments regarding whether an argument is plausible or not.[22]

I will also present a case for an intertextual relationship between 2 Corinthians 12:7, including its surrounding context, and the book of Job. Biblical scholars will have little trouble accepting in principle the suggestion that a passage in Paul was influenced by an Old Testament book like Job, since intertextuality is an important area of study in contemporary biblical scholarship. Since, however, I anticipate that some thoughtful people who otherwise would not read academic books will be interested in the topic of Paul's thorn in the flesh, and thus may be reading this book right now, I need to remind such

---

20. See David Hume, "Of Miracles," in *In Defense of Miracles: A Comprehensive Case for God's Action in History*, ed. Douglas Geivett and Gary R. Habermas (Downers Grove, IL: IVP Academic, 1997), 29–44. See also the excellent responses to Hume by the various authors in that volume. For other insightful responses to Hume, see John Earman, *Hume's Abject Failure: The Argument Against Miracles* (Oxford: Oxford University Press, 2000) and Craig S. Keener, *Miracles: The Credibility of the New Testament Accounts*, vol. 1 (Grand Rapids: Baker, 2011), 107–208.

21. See also Graham H. Twelftree, "The Historian and the Miraculous," *BBR* 28 (2018): 199–217. Derek R. Brown writes, "Consequently, interpretations which take the reference to Satan in 2 Cor 12:7 to mean evil in a generic sense insufficiently account for Paul's understanding of Satan" (Derek R. Brown, *The God of This Age: Satan in the Churches and Letters of the Apostle Paul*, WUNT 2, Reihe 409 [Tübingen: Mohr Siebeck, 2015], 185).

22. John G. Gager wrestles with the question of whether such ancient curses "worked" (John G. Gager, ed., *Curse Tablets and Binding Spells from the Ancient World* [Oxford: Oxford University Press, 1992], 22–24). Without conceding an actual belief in the supernatural, Gager (in dialogue with Roger Tomlin) suggests that it is better from the standpoint of good historiography to concede that ancient curses worked in some sense, since such were the beliefs of those attacking and being attacked by curses, and for some reason they kept doing it.

readers that quotations, allusions, reminiscences, and echoes of earlier Scripture fill the pages of the New Testament. Paul maintains a deep and intractable connection to the Jewish writings that came before him, and in particular, to the writings of what we now call the Old Testament. I will marshal a new argument—not new in the sense that no one has previously noticed the connection between the two passages, but new because robust arguments have not yet been detailed— for a literary and conceptual connection between 2 Corinthians 12:7 (in its literary context) and the book of Job. If someone has not spent much time looking into the breadth and depth of biblical interconnectivity, the suggestion that Paul is literarily dependent upon Job, including the shared connection of stinging or jabbing pain in the flesh, could potentially function as a bias that could prevent someone from acknowledging the plausibility of this kind of argument.

Another presupposition that might negatively influence one's appropriation of the argument ahead stems from the fact that many reading this book have grown up in literate (non-oral) cultures. I will mount an argument that Irenaeus's comment (written about 125 years after Paul wrote 2 Corinthians) that Paul suffered something in his physical body, and Tertullian's more specific comment that Paul's suffering was in his head or his ear (around 150 to 160 years after Paul wrote) should be granted significant weight, since they occurred in cultures that highly valued oral transmission. General presuppositions of instability in orality, such as those that undergird the practice of much of biblical form criticism, have kept us from granting these comments the distinction that they deserve.

One further presupposition relates to how one weighs the relative value of historical evidence and consequent conclusions drawn from it. Among my university students, I have encountered many who have not yet grasped that the historian's task is one of probabilities falling on a spectrum of lesser to greater plausibility. Incontrovertible proof is not attainable in the study of most particulars from ancient history; the goal is to accumulate evidence and sort through clues that point toward an overall explanation that provides a substantively greater plausibility than explanations previously proposed. In this sense, the task of a historian is similar to that of a jurist in a courtroom who carefully listens to clues in a quest to determine what did or did not occur. But unlike a courtroom setting, the work of a historian does not require a conclusion to be demonstrated beyond a reasonable doubt for it to have validity, only for it to provide considerably greater explanatory power than previous explanations.[23] Those who desire incontrovertible proof will be more comfortable in a science laboratory than they will in evaluating ancient historical documents.

One final presupposition relates to the unity, or lack thereof, of what we currently refer to as Paul's *Second Letter to the Corinthians*. Various partition theories have been suggested, with the most widely accepted separating chapters 10–13 from chapters 1–9. Occasionally, I will suggest a line of reasoning that rests upon connections between earlier and latter parts of the letter. If one carries into a study of 2 Corinthians the presupposition that 2 Corinthians is two (or more) letters, rather than a single unified letter, the force of an argument drawn from the earlier portions of 2 Corinthians may be somewhat diminished. One who holds to the unity of 2 Corinthians is more likely to be influenced by arguments drawn from earlier chapters. I should state in advance that this issue will not play a significant part in my overall argument, and so should not create much tension for those who hold to some sort of partition theory. Nevertheless, this is an issue of presuppositions that needs to be kept in mind while reading this book.

Regarding each of the topics mentioned above, let me be candid about my own presuppositions:

---

23. "The historian can rest-satisfied even when his explanation is not absolutely probable (i.e., probable *per se*), provided he has shown that it is significantly more likely than any of the comparable alternatives. Due to the paucity of the data and the difficulties in their interpretation, which are typical and insuperable features prevalent throughout his domain, the historian can legitimately claim that his job has been successfully accomplished when he succeeds in convincing us that the evidence indicates that the explanatory hypothesis espoused by him is more probable than any alternative that has been (or can reasonably be) envisaged" (Nicholas Rescher and Carey B. Joynt, "Evidence in History and in the Law," *The Journal of Philosophy* 56 [1959]: 564).

General Interpretive Presuppositions: I believe that every text, including difficult texts like 2 Corinthians 12:7, need occasionally to be revisited with the goal of uncovering clues and connections that have been missed in the past. In this regard, one of my presuppositions is that careful literary, historical, and canon-conscious work can overcome a significant amount of one's interpretive biases, even though no amount of study will ever entirely free one from the influences of his or her presuppositions.

Face Pain: I believe that one's life experiences can sometimes blind an interpreter from accurately interpreting a text. At other times, life experiences crack open a door to a set of questions that help him or her ask probing questions that otherwise might never have been asked. The reader should be apprised that I have some personal experience with face pain, though the nature of Paul's specific pain may have been something rather different from what I have experienced. Positively, this aspect of my own experience has aided me in asking questions that I probably would never have previously asked. It has also prodded me to keep digging deeper. Negatively, I have had to remain vigilant during my period of study to make sure that I have fairly weighed arguments and allowed those arguments to speak either for or against my proposal. This is also an aspect of my presuppositional pool.

Supernaturalism: I believe in the existence of God, the existence of angels (both good and evil), and the possibility that demons can attack humans (even God-fearing humans like Paul or Job) with physical pain, but only with God's permission. Despite this being an aspect of my presuppositional pool, the study ahead does not require any reader to accept the reality of the supernatural. All that is required is the acknowledgment that Paul himself was a supernaturalist, and that most of his contemporaries were supernaturalists. In other words, the assertion that Paul's audience would have perceived Paul's stabbing pains as resulting from black magic attacks should not be discounted simply because a modern interpreter is a non-supernaturalist. Furthermore, I think that the assertion that Paul himself would have attributed his pain to the agency of a demon who had God's permission to attack him with pain should also not be discounted simply because a modern interpreter does not share Paul's worldview. Proper historical study requires that the interpretation of a historical character be carried out with sensitivity to that character's own worldview. But the reader should know that, like Paul, I am a supernaturalist, and, furthermore, that this is one aspect of my presuppositional pool.

The reader also should be apprised that I lived in the Middle East for seven years (and speak one Middle Eastern language with proficiency). Many people in the country where I used to reside are powerfully influenced by folk religious beliefs, particularly regarding magic. I have known people who have sought out local magicians for help in combatting their fear of malicious spirits. Living so many years in a culture where attentiveness to the supernatural world was commonplace may have had some influence on me accepting a non-metaphorical reading of Paul's words when he wrote about an "angel of Satan" in connection to his thorn in the flesh.

Intertextuality: I believe that the New Testament authors in general, and Paul in particular, deeply depended upon the writings that formed what Christians came to refer to as the Old Testament. I believe that we need to stay sensitive to the influence of earlier authors upon later authors such as Paul who knew and extensively drew upon the writings of earlier authors.[24]

Basic Stability of Oral Traditions: I believe that oral traditions in cultures such as the Mediterranean cultures during and after the time of Paul were more stable than most recent interpreters have been willing to grant—and accordingly, that the comments of Irenaeus and Tertullian should be admitted greater weight than they have typically heretofore been afforded.[25]

---

24. For a quick start on how the New Testament authors use the Old Testament, I recommend reading the introduction in G. K. Beale and D. A. Carson, eds., *Commentary on the New Testament Use of the Old Testament* (Grand Rapids: Baker, 2007), xxiii–xxviii, then moving on to Kenneth Berding and Jonathan Lunde, eds., *Three Views on the New Testament Use of the Old Testament* (Grand Rapids: Zondervan, 2008) and following the footnotes.

25. For some helpful directions in this regard, see Kenneth E. Bailey, "Informal Controlled Oral Tradition and the Synoptic Gospels," *AsJT* 5 (1991): 34–54. Regarding the role of

Historical Evidence: I am committed to seeking out every clue I can discover, and to evaluating carefully any and every clue I come across in the quest to uncover the nature of Paul's thorn in the flesh. I do not consider my conclusions incontrovertible, but I am persuaded that the conclusions presented here hold considerably greater explanatory power than most proposals that have been previously tendered.[26]

Unity of 2 Corinthians: I am unconvinced that partition theories are more likely than the supposition of a unified letter of 2 Corinthians, though the letter may have been written over a period of weeks during which Paul could have received new information about the situation in Corinth.[27] James Scott notes that "a historical reconstruction that can operate with the unity of 2 Corinthians has the advantage over partition theories, since it works with fewer unknowns."[28] I proceed in this study with the presupposition that 2 Corinthians is most likely a single letter, and should be read as such.[29]

---

communities in forming memories, see Maurice Halbwachs, *On Collective Memory*, ed. and trans. Lewis A. Coser (Chicago: University of Chicago Press, 2008).

26. For more on the nature of a biblical historian and the task of historiography, see V. Philips Long, "The Art of Biblical History," in *Foundations of Contemporary Interpretation*, ed. Moisés Silva (Grand Rapids: Zondervan, 1996), 281–428 (especially ch. 5, 388–408).

27. E. Randolph Richards has estimated that Paul and his secretary would have needed twelve days *minimum* to prepare a long letter like 2 Corinthians (E. Randolph Richards, *Paul and First-Century Letter Writing: Secretaries, Composition and Collection* [Downers Grove, IL: InterVarsity Press, 2004], 161–65). This time period takes into account the first meeting between Paul and his secretary, the drawing up of a preliminary draft by the secretary (even exempting second or third drafts), the time it would have taken simply to write the words on the page, the drafting of a copy for Paul himself, and the preparation of a final draft to be dispatched to the recipients. It is not at all unlikely that, during the process of composition, additional information came to Paul that added emotional fuel to the rhetorical fire we observe in the final chapters of the letter. For the suggestion of the coming of such new information, see D. A. Carson and Douglas J. Moo, *An Introduction to the New Testament*, 2nd ed. (Grand Rapids: Zondervan, 2005), 434–35.

28. James M. Scott, *2 Corinthians*, NIBC (Peabody, MA: Hendrickson, 1998), 7.

29. For a summary of common arguments for the literary unity of 2 Corinthians, see discussion in George H. Guthrie, *2 Corinthians*, BECNT (Grand Rapids: Baker, 2015), 23–32. For a defense of the letter's unity employing systemic functional linguistics, see Christopher D. Land, *The Integrity of 2 Corinthians and Paul's Aggravating Absence*, NTM 36 (Sheffield: Sheffield Phoenix Press, 2015).

CHAPTER

TWO

WHAT OTHERS THINK |

P aul's thorn in the flesh (2 Cor 12:7) has been of interest to his readers for the past two thousand years. As a historical puzzle, it has enticed interpreters and sometimes made them a bit crazy. It has also engendered a long list of suggestions for the nature of Paul's thorn. This chapter will list the various positions people have suggested for what Paul's thorn in the flesh might have been.

It would be easy to get the impression from this chapter that there is no agreement whatsoever about the nature of Paul's thorn. That is because a *list of opinions* is the most convenient way to lay out the various suggestions for what Paul's thorn in the flesh might have been, and is the approach taken in most commentaries on 2 Corinthians. Here I have included just such a list to help anyone who might find a list of opinions beneficial as a starting point for study. But this approach masks five important observations. That is, there are five things that someone is likely to miss if he or she simply surveys suggestions people have made about what Paul's thorn in the flesh might have been. Thus, immediately following the list, I will explain why the making of such a list is problematic.

WHAT WAS PAUL'S THORN IN THE
FLESH? A LIST OF SUGGESTIONS

In light of the direction the current study will take, I will divide proposals for the nature of Paul's thorn in the flesh into two categories:
(1) Physical Pain or Ailment Proposals, and (2) Other Proposals. At
least one representative of each proposal will be listed.[1]

PHYSICAL PAIN OR AILMENT PROPOSALS

1. *An undefined bodily pain or ailment*: A majority of
   interpreters have thought that a bodily pain or ailment is the best explanation for the nature of Paul's
   thorn in the flesh.[2] Some of these interpreters have
   made no comment on the specific nature or location
   of the bodily ailment, and others have intentionally
   opted to leave the nature of the ailment undefined.
   Examples: Irenaeus,[3] Gregory of Nazianzus,[4] Ambrose,[5]
   Victorinus,[6] Kierkegaard,[7] Dodd,[8] Bultmann,[9] Black,[10]

---

1. See also summaries in Gerhard Delling, "σκόλοψ," TDNT 7:409–13; J. B. Lightfoot, *Saint Paul's Epistle to the Galatians: A Revised Text with Introduction, Notes, and Dissertations* (London: Macmillan, 1921), 186–91; Hughes, *Paul's Second Epistle to the Corinthians*, 442–46, and Margaret E. Thrall, *2 Corinthians 8–13*, vol. 2 of *A Critical and Exegetical Commentary on the Second Epistle to the Corinthians*, ICC (London and New York: T&T Clark, 2000), 809–10.

2. Lightfoot commented more than a century and a half ago: "Lastly, having thus travelled round the entire circle of possible interpretation, criticism has returned to the point from which it started. *Bodily ailment* of some kind has been felt by most recent writers to be the only solution which meets all the conditions of the question" (Lightfoot, *Galatians*, 189).

3. See my discussion of Irenaeus in ch. 9.

4. Gregory of Nazianzus, "Select Orations" 42.26 and 43.82, NPNF[2] 7:394, 7:422.

5. Ambrose, *St. Ambrose: Select Works and Letters*, NPNF[2] 10, 342.

6. Among other clues, Victorinus writes: "he teaches that the Galatians themselves understood Paul to have been weak in the flesh, not in the spirit" (Stephen Andrew Cooper and Marius Victorinus, *Marius Victorinus' Commentary on Galatians* [Oxford: Oxford University Press, 2005], 316).

7. Søren Kierkegaard, "The Thorn in the Flesh," *Edifying Discourses* 4 (Minneapolis: Augsburg, 1962), 2:164.

8. Dodd, *New Testament Studies*, 68.

9. Bultmann, *Second Letter to the Corinthians*, 225.

10. David Alan Black, *Paul, Apostle of Weakness: Astheneia and Its Cognates in the Pauline Literature*, rev. ed. (Eugene, OR: Pickwick, 2012), 99–100.

Russell,[11] Thomas,[12] Harris,[13] Yong,[14] Glessner,[15]
Wallace,[16] Moss[17]

2. *A pain or ailment of the head*: Tertullian ("head or ear"),[18]
   Jerome,[19] Johnson,[20] Heckel,[21] Thrall[22]

---

11. Ronald Russell, "Redemptive Suffering and Paul's Thorn in the Flesh," *JETS* 39 (1996): 559–70.

12. John Christopher Thomas, "'An Angel from Satan': Paul's Thorn in the Flesh (2 Corinthians 12.7–10)," *JPT* 9 (1996): 43–47, and John Christopher Thomas, *The Devil, Disease, and Deliverance: Origins of Illness in New Testament Thought* (London: Sheffield University Press, 1998, repr. 2005), 61–73.

13. Harris, *Second Epistle to the Corinthians*, 859.

14. Amos Yong, *The Bible, Disability, and the Church: A New Vision of the People of God* (Grand Rapids: Eerdmans, 2011), 82–90. Yong leans toward failing eyesight as the most likely solution, but ends up keeping it general.

15. Justin M. Glessner, "Ethnomedical Anthropology and Paul's 'Thorn' (2 Corinthians 12:7)," *BTB* 47 (2017): 15–30.

16. James Buchanan Wallace, *Snatched into Paradise (2 Cor 12:1–10): Paul's Heavenly Journey in the Context of Early Christian Experience*, BZNW 179 (Berlin: Walter de Gruyter, 2011), 273.

17. Candida R. Moss, "Christly Possession and Weakened Bodies: Reconsideration of the Function of Paul's Thorn in the Flesh (2 Cor. 12:7–10)," *J. Disabil. Relig.*, 16.4 (2012): 319–33. Moss writes that she "is less interested in the precise nature of Paul's condition than in the rhetorical function that the thorn plays in Paul's argument against his opponent" (320). Nevertheless, she proceeds throughout the article to describe it "broadly in terms of ancient medical theory" (320).

18. See my discussion of Tertullian in ch. 9.

19. "[T]radition records that he often suffered from severe headaches, and that this is the angel of Satan that was appointed for him, to buffet him in the flesh lest he become puffed up" (Jerome, *St. Jerome's Commentaries on Galatians, Titus, and Philemon*, trans. Thomas P. Scheck [Notre Dame: University of Notre Dame Press, 2010], 172). However, elsewhere Jerome mentions a thorn in someone, but not in relation to Paul, but regarding a woman who has an enemy. "So the Lord stirred up against Paula Hadad the Edomite to buffet her that she might not be exalted, and warned her frequently by the thorn in her flesh not to be elated by the greatness of her own virtues or to fancy that, compared with other women, she had attained the summit of perfection" (Jerome, *St. Jerome: Letters and Select Works* 108.18 [NPNF² 6:204]). This could suggest a non-physical use of the expression by Jerome in a different context. See also Jerome's comments about Jovinianus in *Adv. Jov.* 2.3 (388–89).

20. Eleanor Anglin Johnson, "St. Paul's 'Infirmity,'" *ExpTim* 39 (1927–28): 428–29. Johnson claims it was a migraine, in particular, and that it affected the eyes.

21. Ulrich Heckel, "Der Dorn im Fleisch: Die Krankheit des Paulus in 2Kor 12,7 und Gal 4,13f," *ZNW* 84 (1993): 65–92. Heckel, following the Tübingen neurologist L. Dichgans, even suggests that Paul's suffering could have been trigeminal neuralgia (see pp. 90–92), which is more particularly face-oriented than general head-oriented. Heckel's study anticipates some of my own conclusions.

22. Thrall, *2 Corinthians 8–13*, 817–18.

3. *A pain or ailment of the eyes*: Lewin,[23] Farrar,[24] Plumptre,[25] Nisbet,[26] Merrins,[27] Leary,[28] Akin,[29] Hisey and Beck,[30] Togarasei,[31] Witherington[32]

4. *Epilepsy*: Ziegler,[33] Lightfoot,[34] Krenkel,[35] Wrede,[36] Dibelius,[37] Windisch,[38] Schweizer,[39] Landsborough,[40] Dawson,[41] Collins[42]

---

23. Thomas Lewin, *The Life and Epistles of St. Paul*, vol. 1, 5th ed. (London: George Bell and Sons, 1890), 186–89.

24. F. W. Farrar, "St. Paul's 'Stake in the Flesh,'" excursus X in *The Life and Work of St. Paul*, vol. 1 (New York: E. P. Dutton, 1879), 652–61.

25. E. H. Plumptre, *The Second Epistle to the Corinthians*, ed. Charles John Ellicott (London: Cassell, 1883), 117–18.

26. Patricia Nisbet, "The Thorn in the Flesh," *ExpTim* 80 (1969): 126.

27. Edward M. Merrins, "St. Paul's Thorn in the Flesh," *BSac* 64 (1907): 672–92.

28. T. J. Leary, "A Thorn in the Flesh—2 Corinthians 12:7," *JTS* 43 (1992): 520–22.

29. Daniel Akin, "Triumphalism, Suffering, and Spiritual Maturity: An Exposition of 2 Corinthians 12:1–10 in its Literary, Theological, and Historical Context," *CTR* 4 (1989): 138.

30. Alan Hisey and James S. P. Beck, "Paul's 'Thorn in the Flesh': A Paragnosis," *JBR* 29 (1961): 125–29.

31. Lovemore Togarasei, "Paul's 'Thorn in the Flesh' and Christian Mission to People with Disabilities," *IRM* 108 (2019): 136–47.

32. Ben Witherington III, *Conflict and Community in Corinth: A Socio-Rhetorical Commentary on 1 and 2 Corinthians* (Grand Rapids: Eerdmans), 462–63.

33. W. C. L. Ziegler, *Theologische Abhandlungen*, vol. 2 (Göttingen: Vandenhoeck & Ruprecht, 1982), 128.

34. Lightfoot, *Galatians*, 190–91.

35. Max Krenkel, *Beiträge zur Aufhellung der Geschichte und der Briefe des Apostels Paulus*, 2nd ed. (Braunschweig: C. A. Schwetschke, 1895), 70–75.

36. William Wrede, *Paul*, trans. E. Lummis (London: Philip Green, 1907), 22–23.

37. Martin Dibelius, *Die Geisterwelt im Glauben des Paulus* (Göttingen: Vandenhoeck & Ruprecht, 1909), 47.

38. Hans Windisch, *Zweite Korintherbrief*, MeyerK 6 (Göttingen: Vandenhoeck & Ruprecht, 1924), 386–87.

39. Albert Schweitzer, *The Mysticism of Paul the Apostle*, 2nd ed., trans. William Montgomery (London: Adam & Chaarles Black, 1953), 152–54.

40. D. Landsborough, "St Paul and Temporal Lobe Epilepsy," *J. Neurol.* 50 (1987): 659–64.

41. Audrey Dawson, *Healing, Weakness and Power: Perspectives on Healing in the Writings of Mark, Luke and Paul*, PBM (Eugene, OR: Wipf & Stock, 2008), 195.

42. Adela Yarbro Collins, "Paul's Disability," in *Disability Studies and Biblical Literature*, ed. Candida R. Moss and Jeremy Schipper (New York: Palgrave Macmillan, 2011), 173–76.

5. *Malaria*: Ramsay,[43] Allo,[44] Wilkinson[45]

6. *Maltese fever*: Alexander[46]

7. *Speech impediment*: Whitby,[47] Eadie,[48] Clarke,[49] Mangan,[50] Barrett[51]

8. *Weak voice*: Nash[52]

9. *Deafness*: Knapp[53]

10. *Rheumatoid arthritis*: Renan[54]

---

43. William M. Ramsay, *St. Paul the Traveler and Roman Citizen*, rev. Mark Wilson (Grand Rapids: Kregel, 2001), 90–92.

44. E. Bernard Allo, *Seconde épître aux Corinthiens* (Paris: J. Gabalda, 1937), 311, 320–321.

45. Wilkinson, *Bible and Healing*, 221–26.

46. Wm. Menzies Alexander, "St. Paul's Infirmity," *ExpTim* 10 (1904): 469–73 and *ExpTim* 15 (1904): 545–48. The modern name for Maltese fever is brucellosis.

47. Daniel Whitby, *A Paraphrase and Commentary on the New Testament*, vol. 2 (London: Black Swan, 1703), 236–37.

48. John Eadie, "Paul's 'Thorn in the Flesh'," in *The Weekly Christian Teacher*, vol. 1 (Glasgow: A. Fullerton, 1838), 334–35.

49. W. K. Lowther Clarke, *New Testament Problems: Essays, Reviews, Interpretations* (London: SPCK, 1929), 136–140. Clarke includes "nerves" and "splitting headaches" as contributing to Paul's "inability to express himself clearly, partial aphasia, or to use one word, a stammer.'"

50. Edward A. Mangan, "Was Saint Paul an Invalid?" *CBQ* 5 (1943): 68–72.

51. C. K. Barrett, *The Second Epistle to the Corinthians*, BNTC (Peabody, MA: Hendrickson, 1973), 315.

52. Charles Harris Nash, "Paul's 'Thorn in the Flesh' in Its Bearing on His Character and Mission," *RevExp* 28 (1931): 33, 41, 47, 50.

53. Margaret L. Knapp, "Paul the Deaf," *The Biblical World* 47 (1916): 311–17.

54. Ernest Renan simply called it "rheumatism" (Ernest Renan, "The Portraits of Saint Paul: Letter to M. Mézmièrez of the French Academy," in *Recollections and Letters of Ernest Renan*, trans. Isabel F. Hapgood [New York: Cassell Publishing Company, 1892], 152–54).

11. *A socially-debilitating disease or disfigurement*: Marshall[55]

12. *Shingles*: Chilton[56]

13. *A flaring skin condition*: Maloney,[57] Pascual with others[58]

In addition, Hughes lists (without citation) the following: "gallstones, gout, rheumatism, sciatica, gastritis, leprosy, lice in the head, deafness, dental infection, neurasthenia . . ."[59]

---

55. Peter Marshall, *Enmity in Corinth: Social Conventions in Paul's Relations with the Corinthians* (Tübingen: J. C. B. Mohr, 1987), 240–43, 515–16, 523, 586–87; see also Peter Marshall, "A Metaphor of Social Shame: ΘΡΙΑΜΒΕΥΕΙΝ in 2 COR. 2:14," *NovT* 25 (1983): 315–16.

56. Bruce Chilton, *Rabbi Paul: An Intellectual Biography* (New York: Doubleday, 2004), 60–61, 125–27, 279–80. Chilton appears to regard herpes zoster (shingles) as primarily an eye disease, which it is not (he refers to it simply as "a chronic visual disease" and a "scarring condition of the eye" on p. 61) and suggests that the condition is generated by stress rather than aggravated by stress ("an ailment produced by a virus that is activated by anxiety" on p. 61). Chilton, after quoting Gal 4:13–15 on pp. 125–26, writes on p. 126: "Paul used his own injuries, most visible in his face, to drive home the message he announced in Derbe. He portrayed Christ Jesus as crucified before the Galatians' very eyes (Galatians 3:1), because—as they could see and he insisted (Galatians 6:17)—he bore the marks of Jesus (the stigmata, he said) on his own body." The strength of this suggestion is that shingles (and sometimes its attendant condition, post-herpetic neuralgia) produces jabbing, electric-shock-like pains. See my discussion of shingles and post-herpetic neuralgia in ch. 14.

57. Elliott Maloney, "When I Am Weak, Then I Am Strong: Understanding St. Paul's 'Thorn in the Flesh,'" *The Priest* (September, 2018): 20–26. For specific possibilities, on p. 24 he lists: "recurring inflamations such as shingles (herpes zoster, called simply 'herpes' by medical writer Hippocrates), lupus vulgaris (a chronic tubercular infection of the skin) and erysipelas (bacterial reddening inflammation of the skin)."

58. Antonio Macaya Pascual, et al., "Paul's Thorn in the Flesh: A Dermatological Weakness?" *SetF* 10 (2022): 9–27. "The aetiology of Paul's thorn cannot be known with certainty, but we think that cutaneous diseases like lupus erythematosus, angio-edema, panniculitis, vasculitis or herpes should be added to the list of candidates to be Saint Paul's 'thorn in the flesh.'"

59. Hughes, *Paul's Second Epistle to the Corinthians*, 446.

OTHER PROPOSALS

1. *Trials in ministry from human opponents in general*: Basil of Caesarea,[60] Chrysostom,[61] Erasmus,[62] Barré,[63] Loubser,[64] Louw and Nida,[65] Brown,[66] Guthrie[67]

2. *Opposition from false apostles in Corinth*: Mullins,[68] Binder,[69] Hagel[70]

3. *Accusations in Corinth that Paul was an angel of Satan because he had persecuted the church*: Thierry[71]

---

60. Basil of Caesarea, *Asketikon* Longer Response 55.4. The translation is from Anna M. Silva, *The Asketikon of St. Basil the Great* (Oxford: Oxford University Press, 2005), 269. Silva also points out another passage from Basil indicating Paul's ongoing illness and suggests an allusion there to 2 Cor 12:7.

61. John Chrysostom, *Homilies on the Epistles of Paul to the Corinthians* 26.2 (cited in *ACCS*, 7:305). This citation suggests that Chrysostom thought that Paul's thorn was *people* who opposed Paul's preaching ("Alexander the coppersmith, the party of Hymenaeus and Philetus, all the adversaries of the word"), but at the end of his life, in letters he wrote to the deaconess Olympia, while still maintaining that illness was not the issue, he focused on the various physical tortures unleashed upon Paul. Chrysostom wrote: "If illness did not befall him, trials no less formidable than illness did buffet him, causing him to suffer great pain in his flesh: 'For a thorn in the flesh was given to me by a messenger of Satan,' he says, 'in order to buffet me'—indicating by this the blows, the bonds, the chains, the prisons, being led away, being savagely attacked, being struck often with whips by public torturers" (John Chrysostom, *Letters to Saint Olympia*, trans. David C. Ford, PPS 56 [Yonkers, NY: St. Vladimir's Seminary Press, 2016], 165; cf. 113).

62. "But in his annotation on 2 Cor 12:7 (LB V1 793) Erasmus ... explains Paul's phrase as referring to malicious slanderers, which here fits the context better" (James M. Estes, *Correspondence of Erasmus: Letters 2082 to 2203*, trans. Alexander Dalzell [Toronto: University of Toronto Press, 2011], 18 n77).

63. M. L. Barré, "Qumran and the 'Weakness' of Paul," *CBQ* 42 (1980), 225–27.

64. J. A. Loubser, "Exegesis and Proclamation: Winning the Struggle (Or: How to Treat Heretics) (2 Corinthians 12:1-10)," *JTSA* 75 (1991): 77.

65. Johannes P. Louw and Eugene Albert Nida, *Greek-English Lexicon of the New Testament* (New York: United Bible Societies, 1996), 230.

66. Brown, *God of This Age*, 182–86.

67. Guthrie, *2 Corinthians*, 591–92.

68. Terence Y. Mullins, "Paul's Thorn in the Flesh," *JBL* 76 (1957): 299–303.

69. Hermann Binder, "Die angebliche Krankheit des Paulus," *TZ* 32 (1976): 1–13.

70. Lukas Hagel, "The Angel of Satan: 2 Corinthians 12:7 Within a Social-Scientific Framework," *SEÅ* 84 (2019): 193–207.

71. J. J. Thierry, "Der Dorn im Fleische (2 Kor. Xii 7–9)," *NovT* 5 (1962): 301–10.

4. *Rejection of Paul's claim to apostleship*: McCant,[72] Woods[73]

5. *Opposition from Judaizers*: Barnett[74]

6. *General persecution*: Severian,[75] Theodoret,[76] Keener[77]

7. *Temptations (of various kinds)*: Calvin,[78] Henry[79]

8. *Sexual temptations*: Aquinas,[80] à Lapide,[81] many medieval interpreters[82]

9. *Temptations to anger*: Holmes-Gore[83]

---

72. Jerry McCant, "Paul's Thorn of Rejected Apostleship," NTS 34:4 (1988): 550–72.

73. Laurie Woods, "Opposition to a Man and His Message: Paul's 'Thorn in the Flesh' (2 Cor 12:7)," ABR 39 (1991): 44–53.

74. Paul Barnett, *The Second Epistle to the Corinthians*, NICNT (Grand Rapids and Cambridge: Eerdmans, 1997), 568–70.

75. Severian, though, also mentions that "many people think this was some kind of headache," then adds, "but in reality Paul is referring to the persecutions which he suffered, because they came from diabolical powers" (Severian of Gabala, *Pauline Commentary from the Greek Church*, [cited in *ACCS*, 7:305]).

76. "By 'messenger of Satan' Paul means the insults, attacks and riots which he had to face" (Theodoret of Cyrus, *Commentary on the Second Epistle to the Corinthians* 349 [cited in *ACCS*, 7:305]).

77. "[T]he thorn may have been the persecutions mentioned in the surrounding context" (Craig S. Keener, *Galatians: A Commentary* [Grand Rapids: Baker, 2019], 374, and Craig S. Keener, *1–2 Corinthians*, NCBC [Cambridge: Cambridge University Press, 2005], 240).

78. "My opinion is, that under this term is comprehended every kind of temptation, with which Paul was exercised." John Calvin, *Commentary on the Epistles of Paul the Apostle to the Corinthians*, vol. 2 (Grand Rapids: Eerdmans, 1948), 373.

79. Matthew Henry, *Matthew Henry's Commentary on the Whole Bible: Complete and Unabridged in One Volume* (Peabody, MA: Hendrickson, 1994), 2291.

80. Thomas Aquinas, *Commentary on the Letters of Saint Paul to the Corinthians*, trans. F. R. Larcher, B. Mortensen, and D. Keating, ed. J. Martensen and E. Alarcon, Biblical Commentaries 38 (Lander, WY: Institute for the Study of Sacred Doctrine, 2012), 601. This seems to be his preferred interpretation (over pelvic pain, which he also mentions), since he makes a connection with Paul's battle with the flesh in Romans 7. He also mentions on p. 604 that external afflictions can be "in bodily persecution … from place to place" or in "distress, i.e., in the anxieties of soul."

81. R. P. Cornelii à Lapide, *Commentaria in Scripturam Sacram* (Paris: Apud Ludovicum Vivès, Bibliopolam Editorem, 1891), 503–5.

82. Lightfoot, *Galatians*, 188, comments: "Throughout the middle ages it seems to have been very generally received." In addition to Aquinas and à Lapide, he adds Bellarmine and Estius as other representatives.

83. V. A. Holmes-Gore, "St. Paul's Thorn in the Flesh," *Theology* 32 (1936): 111–12.

10. *Temptations to despair or to diminish apostolic activities:* Luther[84]

11. *The pains of an unsettled conscience over his former persecution of the church:* Schlatter,[85] Janzen[86]

12. *Grief over the unregenerate state of Jewish countrymen:* Menoud[87]

13. *Weak self-presentation and speech:* Jegher-Bucher[88]

14. *Paul's cruciform, sacrificial manner of life:* Hood[89]

15. *Depression after ecstatic visions:* Clavier[90]

16. *Demonic reminders of his former persecution of the church:* Yoon[91]

---

84. Lightfoot suggests the following timeline for Luther's changing views: "In his shorter and earlier commentary on the Galatians (1519) Luther explains it of 'persecution'; in his later and fuller work (1535) he combines spiritual temptations with persecution; and lastly in the Table-talk he drops persecution and speaks of spiritual trials only, xxiv. P7 (vol xxii., 1092 of the Halle edition)" (Lightfoot, *Galatians*, 189n1).

85. Adolf Schlatter, *Paulus, der Bote Jesu: Eine Deutung seiner Briefe an die Korinther*, 2nd ed. (Stuttgart: Calwer Verlag, 1956), 667.

86. Janzen, "Paul's 'Robust Conscience' and His Thorn in the Flesh," *Canadian Theological Review* 3 (2014): 71–83.

87. Philippe-H Menoud, "The Thorn in the Flesh and Satan's Angel (2 Cor. 12:7)," in *Jesus Christ and the Faith: A Collection of Studies*, PTMS 18 (Pittsburgh: Pickwick, 1978), 24–26.

88. Verena Jegher-Bucher, "'The Thorn in the Flesh'/'Der Pfahl im Fleisch': Considerations about 2 Corinthians 12.7–10 in connection with 12.1–13," in *The Rhetorical Analysis of Scripture: Essays from the 1995 London Conference*, ed. Stanley E. Porter and Thomas H. Olbricht, JSNTSup 146 (Sheffield: Sheffield Academic Press, 1997), 388–97.

89. Jason B. Hood, "The Temple and the Thorn: 2 Corinthians 12 and Paul's Heavenly Ecclesiology," *BBR* 21 (2011): 367–70.

90. H. Clavier, "La santé de l'apôtre Paul," in *Studia Paulina in honorem Johannis De Zwaan Septuagenarii*, ed. J. N. Sevenster and W. C. van Unnik (Haarlem: De Erven F. Bonn N.V., 1953), 78–80.

91. David I. Yoon, "Paul's Thorn and His Gnosis: Epistemic Considerations," in *Paul and Gnosis*, ed. Stanley E. Porter and David I. Yoon (Leiden: Brill, 2016), 23–43.

17. *Demonic attacks during Paul's heavenly ascent*: Price,[92] Oropeza,[93] Morray-Jones,[94] Gooder,[95] Litwa[96]

18. *Ongoing demonic harassment*: Tabor,[97] Abernathy,[98] Bowens[99]

WHAT'S WRONG WITH THIS LIST?

I have already registered concern with constructing a list. But what could be problematic about making such a list? Here are five issues that are masked when presented with a list such as the one you have just surveyed.

First, the view of the earliest Christian writers (starting from the second century) was that Paul suffered physical pain. Some of those authors claimed that the pain involved the head. Nor is there any clear example of a specific alternative to the bodily ailment view until the end of the fourth century, that is, two hundred or so years after the physical view was first mentioned. This observation is important,

---

92. Robert M. Price, "Punished in Paradise (An Exegetical Theory on II Corinthians 12:1–10)," *JSNT* 7 (1980): 33–40.

93. B. J. Oropeza, *Exploring Second Corinthians: Death and Life, Hardship and Rivalry*, RRA 3 (Atlanta: SBL Press, 2016), 670–74. It still could have been pain, according to Oropeza, but felt in a temporary body Paul had during his heavenly vision/ascent.

94. Christopher R. A. Morray-Jones, "The Ascent into Paradise (2 Cor 12:1–12): Paul's *Merkava* Vision and Apostolic Call," in *Second Corinthians in the Perspective of Late Second Temple Judaism*, ed. Reimund Bieringer et al., 245–85, CRINT 14 (Leiden and Boston: Brill, 2014), 276–77.

95. Paula R. Gooder, *Only the Third Heaven? 2 Corinthians 12:1–10 and the Heavenly Ascent*, LNTS 313 (London: T&T Clark, 2006), 196–203.

96. David M. Litwa, "Paul's Mosaic Ascent: An Interpretation of 2 Corinthians 12.7–9," *NTS* 57 (2011): 238–57.

97. James D. Tabor, *Things Unutterable: Paul's Ascent to Paradise in Its Greco-Roman, Judaic, and Early Christian Contexts* (London: University Press of America, 1987), 87–88.

98. David Abernathy, "Paul's Thorn in the Flesh: A Messenger of Satan?" *Neot* 35 (2001): 69–79.

99. Lisa M. Bowens, *An Apostle in Battle: Paul and Spiritual Warfare in 2 Corinthians 1:1–10*, WUNT 2, Reihe 433 (Tübingen: Mohr Siebeck, 2017), 123–80. She summarizes on p. 180: "As a result of hearing such unspeakable things as well as the number and extraordinary quality of his revelations, Paul experiences an attack from the satanic realm which seeks to prevent him from accessing any further revelations."

and the implications of this insight will be explored in chapter 9. But you would not know that the physical pain/ailment view was the earliest and most prominent recorded view in the early centuries of the church, or be able to weigh the importance of this observation, if you merely surveyed a list of positions such as I have just presented.

Second, listing positions masks the fact that a majority of modern interpreters have opted—and continue to opt—for bodily suffering (of some kind) as the general solution for Paul's thorn in the flesh. This certainly does not necessitate that other suggestions should be ignored. It is always beneficial to carefully consider alternative proposals as they arise. I am simply taking this opportunity to offer a reminder that among interpreters during the modern period, a physical explanation has predominated. Let me add that, in my opinion, there are good reasons for the majority position, many of which will be detailed below.

Third, most advocates of particular positions offer little argumentation for the specific "position" they adopt. In the majority of cases, only a few observations get presented, after which an interpreter pronounces that there are simply not enough clues to offer a confident determination. Such a comment is then followed with a statement like, "But if I were forced to choose, I would choose X position." Thankfully, there are a few exceptions to this pattern, but it is a recognizable pattern nonetheless. Someone new to this discussion who began by perusing the lengthy list of positions such as appears above might suppose that each position is undergirded by substantial argumentation. Such is not the case. In the majority of instances, the proffered position is little more than a slight preference over other positions, as many interpreters openly acknowledge.

Fourth, the listing-of-positions approach fails to alert the reader that an accident of translation was a key factor in spawning a number of non-physical interpretations from the fifth until the fifteenth century. When "sharp-pointed object in the flesh" (a literal English translation of the Greek *skolops tē sarki*) got translated as *stimulus carnis meae* into Latin, the subsequent use of that Latin translation opened the door to psychological and spiritual interpretations (such as sexual temptations or spiritual distress).[100] This is because *stimulus* in Latin is more commonly used metaphorically for "incitement" or "stimulation" than is the Greek *skolops*.[101] Don't forget that the Latin translation of the Bible was the preferred version for both western priest and scholar for more than a thousand years, so such a translation carried the potential of wielding a far greater influence than was justified.[102]

Fifth, when positions are simply listed, we often fail to pay attention to the non-exegetical reasons an interpreter might adopt a position. For example, the leading alternative to the physical ailment view is that Paul's thorn was a person or people who opposed Paul. John Chrysostom (late fourth to early fifth century) is often cited as the earliest proponent of this view.[103] But some needed observations go by the wayside when Chrysostom is simply listed as an advocate for the relational-opposition viewpoint. Chrysostom first acknowledged his awareness of the head-pain view before stating his own view—and thus himself became a witness to the presence of that view—commenting that there "are some then who have said that he [Paul] means a kind of pain in the head that was inflicted by the devil." But it is crucial to observe that Chrysostom argued against the physical view for *theological* reasons: "but God forbid! For the body of Paul never could have been given over to the hands of the devil." So instead of the physical pain view, he suggested that Paul's thorn was "Alexander

---

100. Cf. Lightfoot's similar discussion of the related expression *per infirmatatem* for *di' astheneian* in Gal 4:13 (Lightfoot, *Galatians*, 174).

101. See Heckel, "Der Dorn im Fleisch," 68–69; Collins, "Paul's Disability," 167; Abernathy, "Paul's Thorn in the Flesh," 69; Plummer, *Second Epistle of St. Paul to the Corinthians*, 350.

102. Though I have not been able to identify a clear influence, it might be worthwhile for someone in the future to explore whether Philo's equating of thorns with passions might also have influenced later Christians (who sometimes looked to Philo for allegorical interpretations of the Old Testament) to interpret Paul's thorn in the flesh in a non-physical manner. See Philo's comments in this regard in *The Works of Philo: Complete and Unabridged*, trans. Charles Duke Yonge (Peabody, MA: Hendrickson, 1993), 79.

103. Note that Basil of Caesarea used it similarly but without argumentation shortly before Chrysostom in *Asketikon* Longer Response 55.4. The translation is from Silva, *Asketikon of St. Basil the Great*, 269.

the coppersmith, the party of Hymenaeus and Philetus, all the adversaries of the word."[104] That is, Chrysostom took a different position from the common physical position because he could not accept the premise that God would allow the devil to touch the physical body of the great apostle. One would never notice the influence of this theological assumption on Chrysostom's view if Chrysostom were simply listed as an early proponent of the people-in-opposition view.

Similarly, external circumstances, not just theological, can exert an influence on the plausibility of a particular viewpoint in a given age. Minn suggests, for example, that "the explanation of *skolops* as persecutions or persecutors may have originated in the horrors of the Diocletian persecution," and "the theory about carnal desires being the Apostle's great trial spread widely in the epoch of the hermit movement and the consolidation of monasticism."[105] Such possible influences as persecution or monasticism in swaying an interpreter to adopt a particular position on Paul's thorn are imperceptible in simple lists.

Still, the sheer number of suggestions for the nature of Paul's thorn in the flesh can feel dizzying. Does the multiplicity of views mean that a plausible solution is unattainable? I will argue on the pages ahead that there are clues—some already observed and some yet to be observed—that aid us in narrowing the possibilities of what Paul's thorn in the flesh could have been. Those clues are the focus of the following chapters and the majority of the book ahead.

---

104. Cited in *ACCS*, 7:305.

105. H. R. Minn, *The Thorn that Remained: Materials for the Study of St. Paul's Thorn in the Flesh: 2 Corinthians XII. vv. 1–10* (Auckland: Institute Press, 1972), 25.

UNCOVERING THE CLUES |

We have now come to the heart of our discussion. What clues can we unearth about Paul's famous condition? What clues can be discerned by attending to historical and cultural backgrounds, by carefully observing intertextual connections, and, of course, by paying close attention to the literary context in which 2 Corinthians 12:7 finds itself? This central section of the book will draw out clues from piercing curses and ancient "voodoo dolls," clues in connection with the book of Job, clues from the literary context—focusing successively upon sentence (2 Cor 12:7), paragraph (2 Cor 12:1–10), and discourse (2 Cor 10–13)—clues from the suffering of Jesus, clues from comments made by Irenaeus and Tertullian, clues in Galatians, and concludes by evaluating potential clues that probably should not be factored into a solution.

CLUES FROM THE HISTORICAL CONTEXT

ANCIENT PIERCING CURSES
AND VOODOO DOLLS

The central claim of this chapter is that any ailment Paul would have described using the combination of the words "a thorn in the flesh" and "an angel of Satan" would have been perceived by a first-century resident of Corinth (or by most anyone else in the Greco-Roman world) as an attack of black magic. The reason for this claim is that piercing language, and physical instruments used for cursing that jabbed, nailed, and stung—including thorns—were commonplace among magical practitioners in the Greek and Roman world. This strange world of magic included the nailing of curse tablets, and the stabbing of animals and ancient "voodoo dolls."[1] If such

---

1. Following specialists in the field, I employ "voodoo doll" with no intention of making any sort of connection to the religious rites of Haiti, but rather to draw upon an English expression that provides a starting analogy for someone encountering ancient Greek and Roman curse dolls. Compare Christopher A. Faraone, "The Agonistic Context of Early Greek Binding Spells," in

a background to Paul's thorn in the flesh is deemed plausible, it will necessitate that we appeal to a narrower range of possible ailments from which Paul could have suffered. This chapter will demonstrate that the thing from which Paul suffered fits well into a cultural milieu in which "nailing" curses were common, curse tablets were pierced before being delivered to their intended destinations, and ancient voodoo dolls or animals were stabbed with the intention of binding someone's actions, or, on occasion, simply to do harm. What do we mean by "magic" during the time of Paul? Clinton E. Arnold writes:

> In the world of Paul's time, magic was not a form of entertainment consisting of the skilled use of illusory tricks. It was far more serious and corresponds closely with what we might today call sorcery, witchcraft or the occult. Magic was based on the belief in supernatural powers which could be harnessed and used by appropriating the correct technique. Magic can therefore be defined as a method of manipulating supernatural powers to accomplish certain tasks with guaranteed results.[2]

Naomi Janowitz helpfully encourages her readers to ask what people who wrote about magic during the Roman period (the period we are studying) meant when *they* used the term. She notes the variety of ways writers of that period described magic and focuses on one set of commonalities.

> The debates [about magic by writers of the Roman period] prefigure most of the elements of modern discourse about magic, but not in the same proportion. Fraud was a part of the equation, but more important was any use of supernatural power which was suspect in the eye of the beholder. While the specific content of the various authors' ideas of what is magic

---

Magika Hiera: Ancient Greek Magic and Religion, ed. Christopher A. Faraone and Dirk Obbink (Oxford: Oxford University Press, 1991), 25n31.

2. Clinton E. Arnold, "Magic," in *Dictionary of Paul and His Letters*, ed. Gerald F. Hawthorne and Ralph P. Martin (Downers Grove, IL: InterVarsity Press, 1993), 580.

varied quite widely from author to author, we have found striking consistency in the criteria used to talk about the issue of
"magic." Did an action harm someone? Who did it? What kind
of effect did it have? Was it done via evil powers? People from
various religious traditions shared these criteria across the
board. This is the closest we can get to some notion of "late
antique magic."[3]

OMNIPRESENCE OF MAGIC

The first thing to highlight about magic is that most everyone in the
ancient world believed in it.[4] Even those who complained (Pliny
the Elder, Galen) about charlatans believed in magic to some degree.[5]
Pliny, one of the more skeptical, once commented, "There is no one
who does not fear to be spellbound by curse tablets."[6] The ubiquity
of magic in the ancient world—not only the belief in magic, but the
actual practice of magic—set the stage for whatever else we might
say about it.[7]

---

3. Naomi Janowitz, *Magic in the Roman World: Pagans, Jews and Christians* (London:
Routledge, 2001), 26.

4. Fritz Graf, *Magic in the Ancient World*, trans. Franklin Philip (Cambridge: Harvard
University Press, 1997), 1. Glessner cites the work of G. P. Murdock who observed that "without
exception, every society (in the sample) which depends primarily on animal husbandry for
its economic livelihood regards spirit aggression ... as either the predominant or an important
secondary cause of illness," but also notes that "causation of illness by witchcraft and sorcery is most characteristic and deep-seated in the circum-Mediterranean region" (Glessner,
"Ethnomedical Anthropology," 22)

5. On Pliny, see Gager, *Curse Tablets*, 253, citing E. Tavenner, *Studies in Magic from Latin
Literature* (New York, 1916). On Galen, see Paul T. Keyser, "Science and Magic in Galen's
Recipes (Sympathy and Efficacy)," in *Galen on Pharmacology: Philosophy, History and Medicine,
Proceedings of the Vth International Galen Colloquium, Lille, 16–18 March 1995*, ed. Armelle Debru
(Leiden: Brill, 1997), 175–98.

6. *Natural History* 28.4.19. Cited in Gager, *Curse Tablets*, 253. But note the comment by
Laura M. Zucconi, *Ancient Medicine: From Mesopotamia to Rome* (Grand Rapids: Eerdmans,
2019), 305: "Pliny the Elder, though, recognized within Roman culture a tension between, on
the one hand, the magical thought processes of incantations and rituals and, on the other, the
treatments grounded in the logical application of the rules of nature derived from philosophy."

7. In our modern society, we are accustomed to drawing a hard line between medicine and
magic. That is, one is viewed as scientific, and the other superstitious. Such a presupposition,
however, was not shared by people in the ancient world. There was substantial overlap between
the healing medicine and healing magic. See Christopher A. Faraone, "Magic and Medicine

People used magic to protect themselves from the evil spirits that they assumed roamed every street, hill, and field. They used magic to ward off illnesses and disasters that they knew must lurk behind every corner. But they also used magic to get what they wanted. Do you want someone to fall in love with you? There is a magical spell for that. Do you want your favorite charioteer to win the upcoming contest? Magic will help. Do you want your business to succeed? You are unlikely to succeed in business without some help from magic.

There was also a dark side of magic. You may not only want your business to succeed, you may want the rival business across the street to fail. Not only do you root for your favorite charioteer, you might use magic to cause the wheels of his chief rival to fall off during an upcoming race.[8] You may not only hope that the girl who captured your heart will love you, but, as payback for her multiple rejections of your advances, you may try to use magic to forcibly *make* her love you.

Scholars have been working hard over the past decades to publish and translate magical texts from the ancient world. These include a collection of magical papyri from Egypt, descriptions of the activities of witches and other practitioners of magic in the general literary remains, and, perhaps most significantly, binding curses in physical form (Greek: *katadesmoi*; Latin: *defixiones*). These execration tablets (often made from lead) have been found in locations all over the ancient world.[9]

Daniel Ogden has included a handy list of the properties of these binding curses in his sourcebook on magic in the Greek and Roman world:

- Some sixteen hundred, the majority in Greek, survive from all periods of antiquity from ca. 500 BC onward.

- They are found throughout the Graeco-Roman world, from Egypt to Britain.

---

in the Roman Imperial Period: Two Case Studies," in *Continuity and Innovation in the Magical Tradition*, ed. Gideon Bohak, Yuval Harari and, and Shaul Shaked (Brill, 2011), 135–58.

8. Graf, *Magic in the Ancient World*, 156.

9. Graf, *Magic in the Ancient World*, 3.

- They seek, often explicitly, to "bind" or "restrain" their victims.

- The desired restraint or confusion of the victim is often reflected in or induced by the use of reversed, twisted, or jumbled forms of writing, conventions, or imagery.

- They are often inscribed on lead, which is then rolled or folded and nailed, in additional symbolic acts of twisting and restraint.

- In their imagery and application they have much in common with "voodoo dolls," which are already found in the archaic period.

- Their curses are to be enacted by ghosts and/or underworld powers.

- To this end they are typically deposited in graves, in underground bodies of water, such as springs or wells, or in chthonic sanctuaries. They can also be deposited in the victim's home or workplace.

- The majority of curses, where their subject can be discerned, fall into one of the following categories: legal; choral or athletic competition; trade; love and sex; and prayers for justice.

- Curses are often made between rivals in a competitive context, as Faraone ("The Agonistic Context") has observed.

- Earlier tablets tend to be concise. Later ones are usually much more prolix and enhanced with various paraphernalia; *voces magicae*, vowel patterns, palindromes, appeals to protracted lists of syncretized gods or demons and images.[10]

---

10. Daniel Ogden, *Magic, Witchcraft, and Ghosts in the Greek and Roman Worlds: A Sourcebook* (Oxford: Oxford University Press, 2002), 210. This list has been reproduced exactly

In addition to the curse tablets and other magical texts (including the papyri), magicians used *kolossoi* to activate their curses. These voodoo dolls were often fashioned out of flexible and malleable materials so that the person enacting a curse could twist, dismember, or pierce the representative figure. Faraone lists thirty-four archeological finds of such dolls or groups of dolls.[11] Various materials were used to make them, including lead, bronze, and clay (both baked and unbaked). In the ancient literature, we read also about wax, wool, and dough dolls.[12]

A meticulous labor of love by modern translators—translating less-than-uplifting ancient magical texts, including curse tablets—has allowed us an insider's look into how magic was practiced in cities such as Corinth and Ephesus. This hard-earned labor illuminates something about the world of Paul that can help us understand his thorn in the flesh. That is, there are four aspects of these curse tablets and voodoo dolls that are relevant to our discussion. (1) The action of piercing was commonplace in (and upon) these inscriptions, and were enacted upon ancient "voodoo dolls" to affect the target of the curse. (2) One common target of such magic was a person's head. (3) One common aim of curses was to hinder the effectiveness of someone trying to speak or speak effectively (such as in a court of law). (4) Thorns, along with other piercing instruments like pins and nails, were among the instruments employed.

Because this world of curses and ancient voodoo dolls is foreign to most readers, I will include enough ancient Greek and Roman magical texts to demonstrate the relevance of this background for understanding Paul's thorn in the flesh. Paul himself understood that his thorn was caused by an angel of Satan even while acknowledging that it was permitted by God. Nevertheless, in the Greco-Roman world where magic was taken seriously, those who observed Paul suffering

---

but without internal references to other sections of Ogden's book.

11. Christopher A. Faraone, "Binding and Burying the Forces of Evil: The Defensive Use of 'Voodoo' Dolls in Ancient Greece." *ClAnt* 10 (1991): 200–5.

12. Ogden, *Magic, Witchcraft, and Ghosts*, 245.

from stabbing pain and listened to him describe that pain as a *thorn in the flesh* and an *angel of Satan* would likely have assumed that Paul was under attack through the use of magic.[14] I am not arguing that the malady Paul labeled a thorn in the flesh was *in fact* mediated by one or more

13. A 2nd–4th century AD Voodoo doll. Artist is unknown. This work is part of the collections of the Louvre (Department of Greek, Etruscan, and Roman Antiquities). Photo is by Marie-Lan Nguyen, Wikimedia Commons, CC-BY 2.5, https://commons.wikimedia.org/wiki/File:Voodoo_doll_Louvre_E27145b.jpg. Note that some scholars of ancient magic have categorized the spell that accompanies this doll simply in the love category, but I read it to be about control, binding, and sexual slavery.

14. There are also many references to magic and magicians, curses and charms in Jewish writings of antiquity. See Gideon Bohak, *Ancient Jewish Magic* (Cambridge: Cambridge University Press, 2008).

magicians (though it is likely that on some occasions magicians sought to do him harm), only that people would have perceived this to be the case if Paul was using such words to describe whatever he was suffering.

PIERCING IN (AND ON) ANCIENT CURSE TABLETS, VOODOO DOLLS, AND ANIMALS

As was noted by Ogden in his summary, a curse tablet was written on lead, either rolled or folded, and then pierced by one or more nails or other sharp instruments. As Gager points out, the purpose of the nail could not have been simply to keep others from seeing the contents of the curse, because in most cases the tablet would end up in a location where no one was likely to find it. "The use of nails ... must have some special meaning," writes Gager. What is that meaning? Gager suggests that "the root meaning probably derives from the ordinary function of nails, which is to fasten, to fix, to tie down, and thus to bind."[15] People tried to control others ("fix" them; "bind" them) to do what they wanted them to do. Curse tablets were nailed to accomplish this through magic.[16]

Even the words most closely associated with such rituals in the ancient literature point out their function, as Versnel comments: "Their implicit or explicit purpose is another and far more important element; the victim must be 'bound' (according to Greek terminology) or 'nailed down' (as the Latin puts it)—which may include a wide variety of different meanings from 'making powerless and unable to

---

15. Gager, *Curse Tablets*, 18. Elsewhere, Gager comments: "the effectiveness of the process was dependent to a certain degree on public knowledge that 'a fix' had been placed on a particular suspect" (Gager, *Curse Tablets*, 176).

16. Clinton E. Arnold, *Powers of Darkness: Principalities & Powers in Paul's Letters* (Downers Grove, IL: InterVarsity Press, 1992), 28, writes, "A lead curse tablet typically consisted of a magical formula with a curse written on a leaf of lead. Usually the tablet was rolled up and pierced by a nail to symbolize the 'fix' on a victim. The tablet would then be deposited in a place where it was thought to have easy contact with the underworld, such as a grave, tomb or well. This procedure would then effect the curse, which would be carried out by supernatural means against the victim." Magali Bailliot, though, adds to the common fixing observation: "However, these verbs were also used in a physical sense. *Defigere* is related to *fixum, fixere*: 'to embed', 'sink into', 'pierce'" (Magali Bailliot, "Rome and the Roman Empire," in *Guide to the Study of Ancient Magic*, ed. David Frankfurter, RGRW 189 [Leiden: Brill, 2019], 194).

take action' to 'making ill' (often with a detailed enumeration of the bodily parts to be afflicted) to 'killing' (only rarely)."[18]

Following are examples of texts that highlight such piercing magic.

First is the text of two second-century AD tablets discovered in a Gallo-Roman grave, the tablets themselves pierced with a nail. (Warning: animal lovers should skip over the following three curses.) These curses appear to be communicating: "as it happened with these animals, so may it happen to my opponent at court."

> (*First tablet*) I denounce the persons written below, Lentinus and Tasgillus, in order that they may depart from here for Pluto and Persephone. Just as this puppy harmed no one, so (may

17. Artist unknown (Roman). Tablet (Lamella) Cursing Slaves, about 100 BC. The J. Paul Getty Museum, Villa Collection, Malibu, California, Gift of Dr. Federico Zeri, 77.AI.97.

18. H. S. Versnel, "Beyond Cursing: The Appeal to Justice in Judicial Prayers," in *Magika Hiera: Ancient Greek Magic and Religion*, ed. Christopher A. Faraone and Dirk Obbink (Oxford: Oxford University Press, 1991), 61. Similarly, Esther Eidinow says that it often goes beyond simply binding and moves into the conceptual world of judicial punishment (Esther Eidinow, "Binding Spells on Tablets and Papyri," in *Guide to the Study of Ancient Magic*, ed. David Frankfurter, RGRW 189 [Leiden: Brill, 2019], 370–71).

they harm no one) and may they not be able to win this suit; just as the mother of this puppy cannot defend it, so may their lawyers be unable to defend them, (and) so (may) those (legal) opponents (*Second tablet*) be turned back from this suit; just as this puppy is (turned) on its back and is unable to rise, so neither (may) they; they are pierced through, just as this is; just as in this tomb animals/souls have been transformed/silenced and cannot rise up, and they (can)not ... (the rest is unreadable).[19]

Similarly, here is a curse tablet where we learn of a cat being pierced: "Let them be turned away from this trial in the same way that this cat is turned away and cannot get up. Let it be thus for them as well. Let them be pierced through like the cat."[20]

In a different context, Livy mentions that after the Romans established a particular alliance, the Roman priest cut a pig with a short knife and pronounced, "Let him who breaks the alliance be killed like this pig."[21]

Ovid imagined that a Thessalian witch had fashioned a wax or woolen doll and then stuck pins into it to make him sexually impotent. "She places binding spells [*devovet*] on people from afar, molds voodoo dolls out of wax, and pushes fine needles into their pathetic livers. ... Or did a witch bind [*defixit*] my name with red wax and drive fine needles through the middle of my liver?"[22]

One dramatic piercing story is the late sixth century AD account by Sophronius about a certain Alexandrian Christian named Theophilus who was on the receiving end of a binding curse that rendered him a tetraplegic, and also left him with terrible pain in each paralyzed limb. As the story is told, Theophilus had a dream in which he was instructed by two saints to get someone to carry

---

19. Gager, *Curse Tablets*, 143–44.
20. Graf, *Magic in the Ancient World*, 137.
21. Graf, *Magic in the Ancient World*, 208.
22. Ovid, *Heroides* 6, in Ogden, *Magic, Witchcraft, and Ghosts*, 126.

him to the seaside and pay a fisherman to cast his nets into the sea for him. Sophronius recounts:

> After a short time he tossed the net and pulled out a very small box, secured not just with locks but muzzled with lead seals. ... With much effort they opened the box before everyone's eyes and discovered a terrible and disturbing sight ... a carved image in human form, made of bronze and resembling Theophilos, with four nails driven into its hands and feet, one nail for each limb. ... One of them gave the command to pull the nails out, if it could be done. He took the statue and grabbed the nail stuck into the right hand and with much effort succeeded in drawing it out. Once it was out, Theophilos's right hand was immediately restored and he ceased suffering the great pain and the related condition of paralysis. And it became clear to all what abominable magic the charlatans had used against him in cooperation with those most evil demons, by throwing it (the box) into the deep waters so that it would not be recovered. ... They hastened to remove the remaining nails. ... As they removed them, the ill man was released from his bonds and suffering, until all of them were drawn out. Thus the sick man was relieved of the entire diabolical business. When they removed the nail on the left hand of the statue, the suffering man was able immediately to stretch it out. And when they pulled out the nails driven into its feet, the sick man was able to move with no pain at all.[23]

We do not need to believe that this event actually happened to acknowledge the worldview lying behind a text in which the author assumed that his readers would be impacted by reading about a magician-induced piercing.[24]

---

23. Gager, *Curse Tablets*, 263.

24. Faraone, "The Agonistic Context," 9. Faraone comments about this story: "Although certainly no one would vouch for the historicity of this particular incident, the need for verisimilitude in the details of such miracle stories suggests that the underlying assumptions about

ATTACKS ON THE HEAD

Sometimes curses were directed toward particular parts of the body, the head being the most common. Here is one example:

> I bind (?) Philônidês, son of Xenodikos. I demand that he
> be punished and that vengeance be exacted on the man who
> caused me to be expelled from the household of Dêmêtrios, due
> to my headaches and other pains. Thus may oblivion seize the
> binding spell that he pronounced against me. Let Philônidês,
> rendered harmless and incapable of harming others, be forever
> voiceless and destitute. Now, quickly.[25]

Here is a portion of a papyrus that includes instructions for a curse against a thief:

> Take gallows wood and carve a hammer. With / the hammer
> strike the [eye] while saying the formula: "I conjure you by
> the holy names: hand over the thief who made off with it. ...
> Hand over the thief who stole it. As long as I strike the eye
> with this hammer, let the eye of the thief be struck, and let
> it swell up until it / betrays him." While saying these things,
> strike with the hammer.[26]

From a papyrus fragment, we learn that if someone wants to inflict an illness, that person is instructed to take:

> the blood of a weasel and write on a triangular potsherd and
> bury it in the house: THRAX TRAX BRAX. ... Take unsmoked
> beeswax and make a little manikin. Write the characters / on
> a tiny piece of papyrus and place it inside the beeswax. Also
> write the three "ō's" and the letters that follow on the head of
> the manikin, and the bonds of the victim (?). ... / Prick the

---

the paralyzing but nonfatal effects of voodoo dolls were common knowledge, at least in the early Byzantine period."

25. Gager, *Curse Tablets*, 203–4.

26. PGM V. 70–95 in Hans Dieter Betz, *The Greek Magical Papyri in Translation: Including the Demotic Spells* (Chicago: University of Chicago Press, 1986), 102.

left one into the left eye of the manikin and the right one into the right. Hold the figure upside-down on its head / and put it into a new pot. Leave the pot in the dark.[27]

Maltomini understands the prick of the eye to mean "the left *part*" and "the right *part*" of the manikin, respectively. In other words, the magician should prick the manikin up until the left eye and subsequently the same on the right side, up to the eye. But the specific intention of the author is unclear.[28] Either way, the magician is stabbing the face of the wax figurine with the intention of inflicting illness.

Sometimes ancient curses were specific to body parts, but the head and face often gets special attention. Faraone comments:

A first-century BCE Latin curse, for example, lists the "neck, mouth, cheek, teeth, lips, chin, eyes, forehead and eyebrows" (*DT* 135a) and another the "head, forehead, eyebrows, eyelids, pupils, nostrils, lips, ears, nose, tongue and teeth." An earlier, second-century BCE Greek curse likewise includes this eclectic list: "hair, face, forehead, eyebrows, eyes, eyelids, nostrils, mouth, teeth, ears, throat and shoulders."[29]

Wilburn describes an assemblage that:

consisted of three nesting lead cylinders, each of which was sealed with resin. The third container enclosed a lead tablet inscribed with *charaktēres*, including a stylized *theta*, perhaps standing for "deceased," and an image of a human face. Two nails pierced the tablet, including one that was driven through the inscribed human face. The tablet enclosed a small poppet, identifiable as human by its head and shoulders.[30]

27. PGM CXXIV. 5–26 (Betz, 321).

28. PGM (Betz, 321n4).

29. Faraone, "Magic and Medicine," 148–49.

30. Andrew T. Wilburn, "Figurines, Images, and Representations Used in Ritual Practices," in *Guide to the Study of Ancient Magic*, ed. David Frankfurter, RGRM 189 (Leiden: Brill, 2019), 497–98.

One amulet from the first or second century AD mentions "half-of-the-head," which could point in the direction of a migraine (often on one side of the head), or another unilateral face/head condition like trigeminal neuralgia, post-herpetic neuralgia, or one of the trigeminal autonomic cephalalgias, which almost always occur on one side of the face. (See chapter 14 for more detailed descriptions of these conditions.) This text is also interesting in that the Ephesian Artemis is the one who *stops* the demon from entering the head.[31] Keep in mind that Paul probably wrote 2 Corinthians shortly after spending almost three years in Ephesus.[32] Here is the short text: "For half-of-the-head. Antaura came up out of the sea, she shouted out like a deer, she cried aloud like an ox. Ephesian Artemis meets her: 'Antaura, where are you taking yourself?' 'Into the half-of-the-head.' 'You certainly will not go into the ... '"[33]

---

31. Artemis was sometimes referred to as "the scorpion Artemis." E.g., *PGM*, XXVIIIa: "scorpion of Artemisia"; XXVIIIb: "scorpion of Artemisos"; XXVIIIc: "Artemisian scorpion" (Betz, 265). Elsewhere, Artemis is referred to as "the arrow-pouring goddess, and straight-shooting" (see Ogden, *Magic, Witchcraft, and Ghosts*, 246.) Furthermore, a well-known text related to Artemis from second-century Ephesus speaks of a plague that had swept a client-city near Ephesus (perhaps Sardis), the cause being witchcraft via hidden, magical, wax figurines. Here is how the spell will be counteracted: "(Artemis) will dissolve the death-bringing sorcery of the disease, melting with fire-carrying torches in nocturnal flame the forms of wax, the terrible tokens of the sorcerer's craft" (translation from Fritz Graf, "Magic and Divination: Two Apolline Oracles on Magic," in *Continuity and Innovation in the Magical Tradition*, ed. Gideon Bohak, Yuval Harariand, and Shaul Shaked [Brill, 2011], 121). When Paul commented on a thorn in the flesh, might people in his day have connected this comment with the goddess of Ephesus?

32. Interpretation of the occasion of a letter should focus not only on what is happening with the recipients, but also on the place of sending. Paul has recently completed nearly three years of ministry in Ephesus, a place that Arnold claims was well-known for its magic. See Clinton E. Arnold, *Ephesians: Power and Magic: The Concept of Power in Ephesians in Light of Its Historical Setting* (Grand Rapids: Baker, 1989), 14–20. Paul's time in Ephesus would likely have factored in his thinking as he was writing 2 Corinthians. Second Corinthians indicates that Paul is writing his letter after having recently left Ephesus, and he may have recently also passed through one area well known for witchcraft and anticipating traveling through another. "Thrace was considered to be the home of many magicians, as was Thessaly, which was notorious for its witches" (Janowitz, *Magic in the Roman World*, 13; for a list of primary sources for Thrace and Thessaly, see Janowitz's endnote 24 on p. 102, as well as ch. 6 of the same volume). Paul might not only have been thinking about the spiritual warfare he encountered in Ephesus; witchcraft was a present reality to him even as he traveled through from Ephesus toward Macedonia with the goal of reaching Corinth.

33. Ogden, *Magic, Witchcraft, and Ghosts*, 266.

HINDERING SPEECH

Libanius was one of the noted orators of the fourth century BC. Libanius experienced terrible pains in his head during his later years. Then, after dreaming that he was being attacked by magic, his friends searched his lecture hall and found a several-months-dead chameleon with its head forced behind its back legs and one leg placed over its mouth. Libanius, although initially skeptical that magic was the cause of his ailment, eventually conceded that this magical attack must have been the source and the reason he had been unable to continue giving his speeches. Apparently, he recovered shortly after the chameleon was discovered.[34]

Observe that binding curses could be very specific. In a lead tablet that also displays five nail holes and suggests that it is a binding curse related to an upcoming court case, the following words are found.

> And Phereklês, I bind the tongue and soul and evidence that he gives for Theagenês. Seuthês, I bind the tongue and soul and speech that he is practicing and his feet and hands and eyes and mouth. Lamprias, I bind the tongue and soul and speech that he is practicing, and his hands and feet and eyes and mouth. All of these I bind, I hide, I bury, I nail down. If they lay any counterclaim before the arbitrator or the court, let them seem to be of no account, either in word or in deed.[35]

In the following example, three people are cursed successively, and all the curses are similar to one another. Three times the tablet issues the command, "stab their tongue," which seems to indicate some sort of hindering of their spoken testimony. I will only include the middle portion:

> I have seized Hipponôidês and Sôkratês and bound their hands and feet and tongues and souls; and if they are in any way about to utter a harsh or evil word about Philôn, or do something

34. Gager, *Curse Tablets*, 121–22; Graf, *Magic in the Ancient World*, 164–65.
35. Gager, *Curse Tablets*, 131–32.

bad, may their tongues and souls become lead and may they be unable to speak or act; but rather stab their tongue ... [36]

Here is a portion of a papyrus instructing the magical practitioner how to speak the binding curse:

> Piercing [the package] through the characters / with the pen and tying it, say, "I bind NN with regard to NN [thing]. Let him not speak, not be contrary, not oppose; let him not be able to look me in the face nor speak against me; let him be subjected / to me, so long as this ring is buried. I bind his mind and his brains, his desire, his actions, so that he may be slow [in his dealings] with all men."[37]

Who would want to deny that there were many who wanted Paul to stop speaking? Since Paul himself would have been viewed from the outside as a magician (in light of his many miracles and exorcisms), people who wanted him stopped would have had ample motivation to hire other powerful magicians to put curses on him. When Paul described the pain that he experienced as comparable to being buffeted by a thorn—and furthermore attributed it in some way to being an angel of Satan, I suggest that his listeners (and readers) could hardly have kept themselves from thinking about magical power encounters.

THORNS IN MAGIC

Finally, thorns are one of the stabbing instruments used in ancient magic. Practitioners of magic used a variety of stabbing instruments, as illustrated in the texts above, but thorns were one instrument available to them. Here are two texts that make this clear.

---

36. Gager, *Curse Tablets*, 160.

37. *PGM* V. 318–330 (Betz, 106). Lee A. Johnson comments, "The incongruity of the rhetorician's memory loss and the shame that accompanies such a failure were best explained in the ancient world as the intrusion of sorcery" (Lee A. Johnson, "Satan Talk in Corinth: The Rhetoric of Conflict," *BTB* 29 (1999): 148).

Take blood from a nightowl and myrrh ink, and mix the two together, and draw the figure as appended, with a new reed pen on a clean strip of papyrus. At the same time stare at a clean wall and look toward the east. Fasten the figure to an all-linen handkerchief with thorns (*skolopsin phonikos*) / from a male date palm and hide it and stand back from it six cubits ... [38]

In other words, the practitioner is to draw the figure on a piece of papyrus that he or she intends to pierce, and then stick a large palm thorn through both the figure and the handkerchief before hiding both. This action is presumably to be carried out with the intention of binding the recipient of the curse in some way, but the text does not state whether the goal is mundane or sinister.

One text of particular interest for our study is a set of commands to a group of "demons in the dark" to forcibly make the object of the spell-writer's love become sexually interested in him. What particularly interests us in this text is not the aim of the writer, but the means the demon is told to use against the woman. The spell-author tries to coerce the demon to make the woman sleepless until she has sexual relations with him. If she tries to fall asleep, the demon is bidden to: "spread under her knotted leather scourges and thorns upon her temples, so that she may nod agreement to a courtesan's love, because I adjure you who have been stationed over the fire ... " The text then moves from instructing the demon into speaking a spell to the woman: "You, NN, have been bound by the fibers of the sacred palm tree, so that you may love NN forever. And may no barking dog release you, no braying ass, no cock, no priest who removes magic spells, no clash of cymbals, no whining of flute; indeed no protective charm from heaven that works for anything; / rather, let her be possessed by the spirit."[39]

---

38. *PGM* XXXVI. 264–274 (Betz, 275). For Greek text, see *PGM* XXXVI. 264–274 in Karl Preisendanz et al., *Papyri Graecae Magicae: Die Griechischen Zauberpapyri*, vol. 2 (Leipzig: B. G. Teubner, 1931), 171–72.

39. *PGM* XXXVI.134–60 (Betz, 106).

This text is particularly intriguing in the context of our study because the demon has been told to spread "knotted leather scourges" (*sittubas akanthinas*[40]) under her, and "thorns" (*skolapas*) upon her temples (*epi tōn kotraphōn*) (that is, on her face/head).[41] Then, the speaker of the spell claims that the woman will be "bound by the fibers of the sacred palm tree."

Paul wrote about some terrible ongoing pain that he suffered, referring to his ailment as a "thorn in the flesh" and "an angel of Satan." When one attributes appropriate weight to the widespread practice of magic and cursing in Paul's world, including nailing, stabbing, and piercing with thorns, it is difficult to ignore this as a relevant background for understanding Paul's thorn in the flesh.[42]

A PATTERN OF POWER ENCOUNTERS
ASSOCIATED WITH PAUL IN ACTS

The pattern of power encounters associated with Paul in the book of Acts supports my proposal that people would have associated Paul's language of "an angel of Satan" (combined with "thorn" language) with magical attacks against Paul. In the world in which Paul walked, he would undoubtedly have been viewed from the outside as a type of magician himself in light of the many miracles and exorcisms he performed, even though he separated himself from anything that smacked of sorcery (Gal 5:20). Paul engaged in many spirit-world encounters in his ministry. According to the author of Acts, Paul had close

---

40. Note that a common translation for *akanthinos* is simply "thorny" or "of thorns," BDAG, 34; LSJ, 46.

41. For Greek text, see *PGM* XXXVI.134–60 (Preisendanz, 2:167–68).

42. Following is an additional example, the context of which is obscure: "I pierce his impudent eyes with thorns while he is still alive, and, if it be not a sin, eat him raw ... with this omen may I neither myself (set sail), nor a person who has (undertaken a commission?) for me" (Callimachus, *Hecale*, 284, in *Callimachus: Aetia, Iambi, Hecale and Other Fragments; Musaeus: Hero and Leander*, ed. and trans. C. A. Trypanis, T. Gelzer, and Cedric H. Whitman, LCL 421 (Cambridge: Harvard University Press, 1973), 206–7. Note that practice of magicians piercing substitute figures with date thorns can be traced even further back into Old Babylonia. See Daniel Schwemer, *Abwehrzauber und Behexung: Studien zum Schadenzauberglauben im alten Mesopotamien* (Wiesbaden: Harrassowitz Verlag, 2007), 209–14.

encounters with a magician, a girl with a python spirit, Jewish exorcists, and books filled with magical spells, not to mention dramatic
encounters involving pagan gods and goddesses which Paul would
have considered to be animated by demons (1 Cor 10:20–21). Peter
also is recorded as encountering a powerful magician in the book of
Acts (recorded in Acts 8:9–25), but Paul is the primary focus of power
encounters in Acts. The attention to what is often termed spiritual
warfare in Paul's biography raises the plausibility of our suggestion
that magic was an aspect of the accusations of Paul's opponents in
Corinth, including regarding his thorn in the flesh.

A *Magician on the Island of Cyprus (Acts 13:6–12)*. On Paul's first
missionary journey, he traveled with Barnabas (a Cypriot) to the
large island of Cyprus. The narrative rapidly focuses upon a magician named Bar-Jesus or Elymas ("they came upon a certain magician," Acts 13:6). Despite the fact that this magician was with the
proconsul of the island (13:7), and despite the fact that the governor
is said to have become a believer at the end of the story (13:12), the
story emphasizes the challenge Paul faced from the magician along
with Paul's response.[43] When the magician opposed Paul, Paul cast
two labels upon him ("son of the devil," "enemy of all righteousness"),
described his character ("full of all deceit and villainy"), and then
pronounced temporary blindness on him (13: 10-11).[44] As a result,
the proconsul believed, "when he saw what had occurred" (13:12).

Notably, this is not the only time that magic is mentioned in association with the island of Cyprus during the time of Paul. Pliny the Elder

---

43. "In the attempt to define the type of text to which the narrative as a whole belongs,
we should also bear in mind stories of contests between competing magicians. ... We recall
the struggle between Moses and the Egyptian magicians in Exodus (Ex 7–8), between Elijah
and the priests of Baal on Mount Carmel (1 Kgs 18), between Daniel and the priests of Bel
(Dan 14 LXX), or, as mentioned above, the duel between the apostle Peter and Simon Magus
in the apocryphal Acts of Peter. We scarcely need mention who wins in each of these cases"
(Hans-Josef Klauck, *Magic and Paganism in Early Christianity: The World of the Acts of the
Apostles*, trans. Brian McNeil [Edinburgh: T&T Clark, 2000], 47).

44. Luke may have had in mind the curse of blindness ("as the blind grope in darkness")
as he penned this passage. See Susan R. Garrett, *The Demise of the Devil: Magic and the Demonic
in Luke's Writings* (Minneapolis: Fortress, 1989), 82.

testified to the recognition in his day of the existence of Jewish and Cypriot magicians. The historian Josephus mentioned a Jewish magician from Cyprus named Atomus, who served Felix, the Roman governor in Caesarea who would shortly incarcerate Paul for two years.[45] From the perspective of Luke, it was God who empowered Paul to defeat this magician ("the hand of the Lord is upon you," 13:11), but outsiders would have viewed this as one magician (Elymas) opposing another (Paul), with the second magician prevailing over the first.[46]

A Fortune-Teller with a Python Spirit in Philippi (Acts 16:16–18). Another conflict with the spirit-world occurred during Paul's second missionary journey in Philippi. Paul and company were on their way to "a place of prayer" when they came in contact with a slave girl "having a python spirit" (literal translation, 16:18). Readers of Acts would have recognized this as a description of a girl who could work divination, a pathetic copy[47] of the famous *pythia*, the prophetess of the god Apollo who spoke the oracles of Apollo in Delphi.[48] A girl who could divine the will of the gods and predict people's fortunes would have been viewed positively by most hearers, but from the standpoint of Paul's worldview, she was a girl who needed release from a controlling demon.

The girl having the spirit of divination began following Paul and his coworkers and loudly proclaiming, "These men are servants of the Most High God, who proclaim to you the way of salvation." She kept doing this for "many days" (16:18). Finally, Paul "having become greatly annoyed" addressed the spirit in control of the girl, "I command you in the name of Jesus Christ to come out of her" (16:18).

---

45. Matthew W. Dickie, *Magic and Magicians in the Greco-Roman World* (London: Routledge, 2001), 223–24.

46. Benedict H. M. Kent, "Curses in Acts: Hearing the Apostles' Words of Judgment Alongside 'Magical' Spell Texts," *JSNT* 39 (2017): 415–23.

47. Klauck notes that "Luke describes her as a pathetic specimen of humanity. She has been deprived of her freedom and must work as a fairground attraction, practicing her arts for tiny wages" (Klauck, *Magic and Paganism*, 72.)

48. See Craig S. Keener, *Acts: An Exegetical Commentary* (Grand Rapids: Baker, 2014), 3:2424–26, for a short description of the Delphic Pythia.

When the spirit came out and her handlers realized that their source of income had vanished, the masters of the girl dragged Paul and Silas before the magistrates, who ordered the duo beaten with rods and even allowed a mob to attack them before locking them up.

Paul's decision to publicly challenge this girl would have been recognized as a power encounter involving two people who had special access to the spirit world, a girl who had a spirit of divination, and the apostle Paul. Acts portrays Paul as the hero who delivered a girl from the control of a demon, and furthermore portrays him as the victim of an unjust beating. However, it appears that precisely the opposite would have been the perspective of most of the non-Christian participants in this drama in Philippi. The citizens of Philippi would have regarded Paul as a powerful Jewish exorcist who employed foreign magic to destroy an otherwise helpful source of divine knowledge, and thus deserved whatever punishment he received.[49] It is even possible that this young diviner was the only one with the special gift in a town as small as Philippi, in which case Paul's actions would have considerably unsettled the social order.[50]

Exorcisms in Ephesus (Acts 19:11–17). Paul spent the majority of his time on his third missionary journey in Ephesus. While there, astounding miracles and exorcisms took place by his hands—and sometimes even when he was not personally present. "And God was doing extraordinary miracles by the hands of Paul, so that even handkerchiefs or aprons that had touched his skin were carried away to the sick, and their diseases left them and the evil spirits came out of them" (19:11–12). Recognizing Paul as a source of power, some itinerant Jewish exorcists, including seven sons of a Jewish high priest named

---

49. It may even be the case, as argued by Craig S. de Vos, that the charges leveled against Paul and Silas were that they had employed magic to cause property damage and income loss (Craig S. de Vos, "Finding a Charge That Fits: The Accusation against Paul and Silas at Philippi (Acts 16.19–21)," JSNT 21 [1999]: 56–62).

50. Peter Oakes, *From People to Letter*, SNTSMS 110 (New York: Cambridge University Press, 2002), 44–50 estimates that the size of Philippi was ten thousand to fifteen thousand, based on the land mass of the ruins and the size of the theater.

Sceva,[51] tried to tap into Paul's power and perform an exorcism on a man. "I adjure you by the Jesus whom Paul proclaims" (19:13), they uttered. These exorcists appear to have been pragmatic, like many of the writers of the magical texts we observed above, in employing whatever names they thought might accomplish their goals. From the words uttered, it is obvious that they knew that Paul used the name of Jesus when he cast out demons. Therefore, they invoked Jesus's name, but also made sure Paul's name got included as well. Unfortunately, according to Acts, the demon claimed to know about Jesus and Paul, but turned on the would-be exorcists and beat them up, stripping them of their clothes and sending them running (19:16). This was a public power event that "became known to all the residents of Ephesus, both Jews and Greeks" (19:17).

A Public Book-Burning in Ephesus (Acts 19:18–19). One other power encounter occurred in Ephesus, but this one involved a public book burning of magical texts. The flow of the text indicates that Luke considered the defeat of the seven sons of Sceva to have been the impetus for this book burning.[52] We learn in 19:18 that among those who had believed, there were many who had not divulged their continuing involvement in magical practices. The text implies that after the humiliation of the sons of Sceva just described, some of those who had made a profession of belief (of some kind; compare Simon Magus in Acts 8:13, 21–23), began "confessing and divulging their practices" (19:18). In context, this phrase suggests that they decided to bring to light their continued involvement in magical practices and to confess those practices as sin. After this first group, we read about (what may be) a second group, "And a number of those who had practiced magic arts brought their books together and burned them in the sight of all" (Acts 19:19). It appears that the first group (19:18) simply confessed that they had still been involved in using magic like

---

51. There is no known Jewish high priest with this name. Klauck suggests that perhaps it is best to view this as these seven men's "stage name" (Klauck, *Magic and Paganism*, 100)

52. Garrett, *Demise of the Devil*, 95.

most people in the ancient world. In the second case, it appears that those who were more formally involved in magic, that is, the magical practitioners, got together and burned their magical incantations. Presumably, this points to people from among the many magicians in Ephesus who had come to believe. But it is also possible that people who had not believed in Paul's message may also have been afraid to keep their magical books, knowing that they might be targeted by this new much-more-powerful counter-magician in town, and thus decided to stop practicing magic.

This event should not be passed over quickly. The narrative states that the worth of these magical texts was fifty thousand pieces of silver.[53] Magic must have been widespread for such a large sum of money to be associated with magical texts. Relatedly, there existed six magical words (or names) referred to as the "Ephesian Letters" that were considered especially effective in warding off evil spirits.[54] Though associated with Ephesus (per their name), they are attested outside of Ephesus. This gives additional support to the contention that Ephesus was a place where magical activity was widespread and taken seriously.[55] In light of these observations, it is not overly imaginative to suppose that those in the general public who learned about the burning of magical books would have been terrified that the spirits bound by the spells in these books might have somehow been released (before, or as a result, of the burning), and would

---

53. "The combined value of the books was estimated by Luke to be worth as much as 50,000 days' wages" (Arnold, *Powers of Darkness*, 33).

54. Plutarch commented: "The magicians charge those possessed by demons to recite the Ephesian writings by themselves and to pronounce the names" (cited in Klauck, *Magic and Paganism*, 101).

55. Arnold, *Ephesians: Power and Magic*, 15–16. In support of the notion that Ephesus was known as a place of demonic activity and magic, Arnold cites (pp. 30–31) an event from the life of Apollonius of Tyana written in Philostratus 4.10: "A plague-demon who had been wreaking havoc on the city was discovered by Apollonius in the form of a blind beggar. Apollonius instructs the Ephesians to stone the blind beggar, whose appearance immediately changes into the form of a mad dog. The Ephesians later erect a statue of an averting god, Apotropaios, where the mad dog was." For the opinion (contra Arnold) that Ephesus was not any more closely related to magic than anywhere else, see Rick Strelan, *Paul, Artemis, and the Jews in Ephesus*, BZNW 80 (Berlin and New York: Walter de Gruyter, 1996), 83–94.

soon wreak unrestrained havoc upon the city. Moreover, such a fear could have incited anger toward those responsible for the burning (like Paul). It is perhaps worth noting that the next large event narrated in Acts 19 is that of an angry mob associated with the Artemis cult (19:23–41).

Whether outsiders to the event responded in fear and/or anger is not explicitly stated in the text. But what is clear from this text is that Paul was closely associated with powerful challenges to the world of magic while in Ephesus.[56]

Pagan gods and goddesses in Acts: In addition to these explicit power encounters with demons and magic, we find Paul involved in various dramatic events involving various pagan gods and goddesses.

In Lystra, Paul and Barnabas were thought by the local population to be a visitation of the gods Hermes and Zeus.[57] When it was discovered that they were not who the populous thought they were, Paul was stoned and left outside the city for dead (Acts 14:8–20).

In Athens, Paul's "spirit was provoked within him as he saw that the city was full of idols" (Acts 17:16). He ended up addressing a group of philosophers and aspiring philosophers at the Areopagus, building the topic of his address around an altar he had previously observed to "the unknown god" (Acts 17:16–34).

In Ephesus, a full-fledged riot broke out at the instigation of silversmiths who made their living fashioning images of the powerful goddess, Artemis, whose opulent temple was located in Ephesus (Acts 19:23–41).

On the island of Malta, Paul was mistaken for a god once again, but this time when he faced no ill effects after being bitten by a poisonous snake (Acts 28:1–6).[58] The irony is that local residents origi-

---

56. Abernathy, "Paul's Thorn in the Flesh," 75–76.

57. Perhaps a conscious allusion to the tale told by Ovid in his *Metamorphoses* (8:626–724) of a visit by Zeus and Hermes to nearby Phrygia. Cited by Hans-Josef Klauck, "With Paul in Paphos and Lystra: Magic and Paganism in the Acts of the Apostles," *Neot* 28 (1994): 102.

58. M. David Litwa has argued (persuasively, in my opinion) that the well-known story of the snake bite of Philoctetes may lie in the background and as counterpoint for Luke's account of snake bite of Paul on Malta (M. David Litwa, "Paul the 'God' in Acts 28: A Comparison

nally thought that the snake was sent by the goddess Dike ("justice") to bite him.[59]

The point of all this is that Paul lived in a different world than the world in which many who are reading this book live—a world where people really and truly believed in gods and goddesses, enchanters and exorcists, charms and curses. It might be worth pausing at this point to ask yourself whether you have ever noticed how frequently Paul is described as engaging with the spirit-world in the book of Acts. The truth is that Paul not only lived in such a world, he was a full participant in it.

ANGELS AND DEMONS IN THE LETTERS OF PAUL

Not only do we read about the Paul of Acts encountering the evil spiritual world, Paul in his letters liberally includes comments about Satan, demons, and spiritual warfare. This, too, supports the suggestion that we should consider a demonic-world background for Paul's thorn in the flesh, particularly when he uses the description "angel of Satan" as a descriptor for the thorn (2 Cor 12:7).

For example, Paul discusses Satan's relationship to people in the world. Referring to him as "the god of this world," Paul says that Satan "has blinded the minds of the unbelievers, to keep them from seeing the light of the gospel of the glory of Christ" (2 Cor 4:4).[60] He writes that "what pagans sacrifice they offer to demons and not to God," and warns the Corinthians not "to be participants with demons" (1 Cor 10:20–21). Until they believed in Christ, the Ephesian Christians were "following the prince of the power of the air, the spirit that is now at work in the sons of disobedience" (Eph 2:2). He expresses considerable frustration

---

with Philoctetes," *JBL* 136 [2017]: 707–26). I disagree with his conclusion, however, that Luke would have tolerated the idea of some sort of deification of Paul.

59. Klauck, *Magic and Paganism*, 113–15.

60. Paul, like other Jewish authors of his time, divides history into two ages: this present evil age, and an age to come. This suggests that the "God of this age" is not God but Satan, who is the ruler of this present evil age by God's permission. Cf. John 12:31, 14:30, and 16:11, where Satan is referred to as "the ruler of this world." For more, see Brown, *God of This Age*, 130–40.

at the Galatians and tells them that their irrational willingness to listen
to false teachers makes them look like someone had cast an evil eye
on them: "O foolish Galatians! Who has bewitched you?" (Gal 3:1).
(See the longer discussion of this last passage in chapter 10).

Paul writes even more about how believers relate to Satan. He calls
Satan the "tempter" (1 Thess 3:5), tempting people in various ways,
including the committing of sexual immorality (1 Cor 7:5), and mentions that some have even "strayed after Satan" (1 Tim 5:15). Somehow
Satan "hindered" Paul from revisiting the Thessalonians, despite Paul's
deep desire visit them (1 Thess 1:18), and sometimes tries to outwit
Christians, though Paul claims that "we are not ignorant of his designs"
(2 Cor 2:11). A potential church overseer should not be a recent con-
vert, otherwise "he may become puffed up with conceit and fall into
the condemnation of the devil" (1 Tim 3:6), which probably means that
he would incur the condemnation into which the devil himself fell.[61]

Paul writes that in the latter days some will fall away "by devot-
ing themselves to deceitful spirits and teaching of demons" (1 Tim
4:1). Paul envisions a future "lawless one" who will deceive people
through false miracles "by the activity of Satan" (2 Thess 2:8–10).
Paul encourages the Romans with these words, "The God of peace
will soon crush Satan under your feet" (Rom 16:20). He also writes
about the eschaton: "Then comes the end, when he [Jesus] delivers
the kingdom to God the Father after destroying every rule and every
authority and power" (1 Cor 15:24).

Christians are instructed to "give no opportunity to the devil"
(Eph 4:27). Then, in Paul's most famous section on the topic, he
writes, "Put on the whole armor of God that you may be able to stand
against the schemes of the devil. For we do not wrestle against flesh
and blood, but against the rulers, against the authorities, against the
cosmic powers over this present darkness, against the spiritual forces

---

61. George W. Knight takes the genitive to be an objective genitive (George W. Knight, *The Pastoral Epistles: A Commentary on the Greek Text*, NIGTC [Grand Rapids: Eerdmans, 1992], 164). For the subjective genitive view, see Philip H. Towner, *The Letters to Timothy and Titus*, NICNT (Grand Rapids: Eerdmans, 2006), 257–58.

of evil in the heavenly places" (Eph 6:11–12). He goes on to instruct his readers how to do this, that is, by taking up the armor of God. One of the items on Paul's list of armor is the shield of faith, "with which you can extinguish all the flaming darts of the evil one," which contains intriguing similarities to our study, but is difficult to connect with it (see more in chapter 11).

The reader, however, should note that there is a greater density of explicit references to Satan and spiritual warfare in 2 Corinthians 10–13, the discourse which centrally concerns us in this study, than anywhere else in the writings of Paul except, perhaps, in Paul's letter to the Ephesians. When Paul is accused of walking "according to the flesh" (10:2), he counters by claiming that even if he walks in the flesh (that is, living a bodily existence),[62] "we are not waging war according to the flesh. For the weapons of our warfare are not of the flesh but have divine power to destroy strongholds" (10:3–4). In 11:3, Paul writes, "But I am afraid that as the serpent deceived Eve by his cunning, your thoughts will be led astray from a sincere and pure devotion to Christ." Then in 11:13–15 Paul compares the false apostles to Satan himself, who "disguises himself as an angel of light." This concentration of references demonstrates that in the broader discourse (2 Cor 10–13) in which Paul mentions his thorn in the flesh, along with Paul's mention of an "angel of Satan" (12:7), Paul exhibits a heightened focus upon the demonic world that should be taken into account when seeking to identify Paul's thorn in the flesh.

THE THEOLOGICAL ISSUE:
WOULD GOD ALLOW PAUL TO
BE ATTACKED BY A DEMON?

There are two theological questions that need to be addressed in this regard. The first is whether God would allow a servant of God like Paul *to be attacked by a demon*. The second is whether God would allow Paul to be attacked by a demon *at the behest of a magician*.

---

62. Guthrie, *2 Corinthians*, 471.

The first question is readily answered by appeal to other Scriptures and evidence from the teaching of Jesus. Paul had easy access to both (the first in written form, and the second via oral retellings).

In the Old Testament, Satan, as a powerful being who opposes the work of God, appears in three texts: in the first two chapters of the book of Job, in 1 Chronicles 21:1, and in Zechariah 3:1–2.[63] In the following chapter, we will observe the literary and conceptual dependence of Paul in 2 Corinthians 12 upon Job. There we will observe that God allowed Satan to revile Job in the presence of God, obliterate Job's possessions and property, kill his family members, and attack Job's physical flesh with painful sores. Furthermore, in 1 Chronicles 21:1, we learn that Satan incited David to order a census, while the comparison with the earlier-composed 2 Samuel 24:1 suggests that the Chronicler understood that God was ultimately behind what happened. Finally, in Zechariah 3:1–2, we learn that Satan once again accused one of God's servants, and, like Job, that he was ultimately subservient to God's sovereign control.

We also gain some help with this question by observing an event in the life of Jesus (one that Paul would likely have known through oral retelling). Jesus spoke the following words to Simon Peter as recorded in Luke 22:31–32: "Simon, Simon, behold, Satan demanded to have you, that he might sift you like wheat, but I have prayed for you that your faith may not fail. And when you have turned again, strengthen your brothers." Satan, Jesus said, "demanded"[64] to "sift" Simon like wheat, which he apparently did through the events surrounding Peter's denial of Jesus just before the crucifixion. Once again, Satan was the one who carried out the (verbal, in this instance) attack against Simon Peter, but God allowed it for his greater purposes.[65]

---

63. For more on these passages, see Sydney H. T. Page, "Satan: God's Servant," *JETS* 50 (2007): 449–56, and, from a different perspective, Brown, *God of This Age*, 22–25, 50–52. Note also in the following chapter my interaction with and rejection of the new paradigm that places a wedge between *ha satan* of the book of Job and "Satan" of the New Testament authors.

64. BDAG, 344, on ἐξαιτέω: "1) to ask for with emphasis and with implication of having a right to do so, *ask for, demand* … 2) to make an earnest request of someone."

65. For the suggestion that Paul depended on the prologue of Job in 1 Cor 5:5 and 1 Tim 1:20 to show that God uses Satan to fulfill his own purposes, see also Dillon T. Thornton, "Satan

But what about the possibility that God allowed a demon to personally attack Paul *at the behest* of a magician of some kind? I know nothing in the Bible that would directly connect God's permission with the activities of a magician intent on doing evil, but there is one passage in the Old Testament that is still relevant for our discussion: 2 Chronicles 18:18–22.[66] When God invited those surrounding his throne to propose ways to entice the evil king Ahab (who was at that time sitting with the good king Jehoshaphat) to go into battle, and thus to his death at Ramoth-gilead, God gave permission to a being who offered to be a "lying spirit in the mouth of all his prophets" (18:21). God allowed what appears to be a demon to do his deceiving work in conjunction with false prophets, enticing Ahab to go to his death (which seems to have been God's purpose in allowing the demon to perform its deceitful deed). If God gave permission to a demon to use the lying speech of false prophets to accomplish his purposes, by analogy it seems reasonable to assume that he could have allowed a demon working in conjunction with the malevolent curses of a magician to attack Paul, again to accomplish God's greater purposes.[67]

---

as Adversary and Ally in the Process of Ecclesial Discipline: The Use of the Prologue to Job in 1 Corinthians 5:5 and 1 Timothy 1:20," *TynBul* 66 (2015): 137–51. Notice also that Satan's demand or insistent request was to sift Peter and the others (note the plural *hymas* ["you all"]), but that it was especially focused on Peter, as evidenced by the address to "Simon," the singular "I have prayed for you (*sou*)," and all the other singulars in the following verse (v. 32).

66. There are other instances in the Bible where God works with or alongside folk-religious or pagan actions, which he otherwise disapproves of, in order to accomplish his purposes. In Gen 30:14–21, Leah uses the mandrake to increase her fertility, yet God gives Leah her request despite her folk-religious use of the plant. In Gen 30:37–43, Jacob utilizes peeled rods to induce selective breeding; God nevertheless increased his wealth. In 1 Sam 6:7–12, God responds to the test that the pagan Philistines put before him and uses their test to confirm that the plagues did indeed originate from the Lord. In Matt 2:1–2, God even uses the astrology of the magi to lead them to Bethlehem. Many thanks to John Makujina for pointing out all of these examples to me.

67. A counter-example might be the instance of the pagan magician Balaam, whom God did not allow to curse his people in the wilderness (Num 22–24). However, the story of Balaam merely demonstrates that God can and will protect his people when such protection suits his purposes and plans, not that that is the way he always accomplishes it. Even in the case of the terrible sufferings of Job, God limited the actions of Satan along the way ("against him do not stretch out your hand," Job 1:12; "only spare his life," 2:6). It seems that God will not allow Satan to move one inch beyond what falls within God's own purposes. (That the Balaam-donkey-and-angel story lies behind Paul's thorn is unlikely, though the suggestion has been made by Jegher-Bucher, "'The Thorn in the Flesh'/'Der Pfahl im Fleisch,'" 388–89, 396.)

Nevertheless, my contention is not that Paul's jabbing pain was in fact an attack of a magician—how would he know, anyway, since curses were usually done in secret?—but rather that Paul lived in a cultural milieu in which almost everyone around him would have *assumed* that the physical pains described by Paul as a "pointed object in the flesh" and "an angel of Satan" were attacks of black magic.[68] Nor is there a theological problem with the suggestion that a personal demon attacked Paul with God's permission, since analogous situations occurred in biblical history long before Paul faced his own demonic attacks.

In light of the cultural and theological backgrounds regarding magic and Paul's struggle with Satan and his evil angels, it might be appropriate to take this discussion one step further. Perhaps we should consider the possibility that one of the criticisms leveled against Paul in Corinth was that magicians had launched an attack on his physical body, but that Paul was not spiritually strong enough to resist them. Such a suggestion would help us understand Paul's decision to mention his thorn in a letter to a church at all. It also might explain why he would describe it as an attack of an angel of Satan (2 Cor 12:7), even though he himself believed that God was somehow behind it (so, the divine passive in 12:7: "there was given"[69] and God's stated decision to permit it to remain: "my grace is sufficient" in 12:8). It would also fill out the theme of weakness that is prominent in this section of his letter, including the "presence of his body" (literal translation, 10:10).

In summary, if Paul's thorn in the flesh was physical, as other arguments in this book will demonstrate, then the combination of Paul's mention of a thorn together with a comment about an angel of Satan

---

68. Douglas J. Moo, similarly shows how Paul could use such language—in Gal 3:1 in relation to the Galatians, rather than to himself—to refer to actual demonic powers without assuming that it was actually caused by a magician or even efficacious (Douglas J. Moo, *Galatians*, BECNT [Grand Rapids: Baker, 2013], 181). He writes, "While it is unlikely that Paul means to say that the Galatians are under a spell cast by a sorcerer, his choice of this word does suggest that the Galatians' turnaround in their thinking can only be explained by recourse to an evil spiritual influence."

69. See more on the meaning of a "divine passive" in ch. 5.

would have raised suspicions that his ailment was an attack of black magic. This contention is supported by the many events described in the book of Acts in which Paul encountered evil spirits, and via the many comments about Satan's work that pepper Paul's letters. Nor is there any theological problem with this suggestion since analogous situations occurred at other times in biblical history.

CRITERIA SUPPORTED OR ALLUDED TO IN THIS CHAPTER

At the end of each of chapters 3–10, I will include a list of criteria that have been touched upon in some way in the current chapter, drawn from the list of twenty criteria that form the core of this book. The appearance of a given criterion at the end of one of these chapters does not mean that arguments for a particular criterion have been exhausted in the chapter. On the contrary, most criteria will appear at the end of more than one chapter. The presence of a criterion at the end of a chapter simply indicates that a criterion has been touched upon in some way in the chapter. Presenting a cumulative case of *all* the clues together is the direction this book is heading. A summary of that cumulative case appears in chapter 12.

Consequently, here are the criteria that have been supported or alluded to in chapter 3:

1. Viewed by others as black magic attacks

2. Viewed by Paul as attacks by an angel of Satan, though permitted by God

3. Impacting Paul's physical flesh

4. Comparable to the jabbing of a sharp-pointed object

5. Impacting Paul's face (as part of his head)

6. Viewed by others as humiliating and weak

7. Negatively impacting Paul's rhetorical ability

CLUES FROM
THE BOOK OF JOB

There are a number of literary and conceptual connections between 2 Corinthians 12:7 (in context) and the book of Job that help advance the case that Paul's thorn in the flesh was a painful condition of the skin/flesh. A link between 2 Corinthians 12:7 and Job has been suggested by interpreters in the past,[1] but the moment has come for a concerted argument to be advanced that Paul is literarily and conceptually dependent on the book of Job. Job's physical misery, of course, was an agonizing condition of his literal flesh (Job 2:7) that included significant pain (Job 2:13).[2] The exact nature of his skin condition is unknown to us, as it likely was also

---

1. E.g., Cassiodorus, *Explanation of the Psalms* 21.3 (cited in ACCS, 7:305). Barnett, *Second Epistle to the Corinthians*, 570, writes: "The juxtaposition of 'was given [by God]' and 'messenger of Satan' recalls the early chapters of Job."

2. Jeremy Schipper notes that "the Hebrew word translated 'suffering' in this verse refers to physical pain in Gen 34:25; Job 5:18 ['wounds']; 14:22" (Jeremy Schipper, "Healing and Silence in the Epilogue of Job," *Word & World* 30 [2010]: 21–22).

unknown to Paul.[3] But there are various connections that link Job 1–2 (and its broader context) to 2 Corinthians 12 (and its broader context), some of which have not been adequately developed before. Such connections will be detailed below, starting with the more obvious and descending toward the possible but less certain. The presence of an intertextual relationship between what Paul wrote in his thorn-in-the-flesh section and the book of Job heightens the possibility that Paul's suffering, like Job before him, was a painful condition of his literal flesh.

JOB WAS KNOWN AND USED BY PAUL

Before observing possible literary and thematic connections between Paul and Job, we should observe that the book of Job was known and used by Paul in other contexts. This observation bolsters my proposal that Paul is making connections with the book of Job in 2 Corinthians 12:7. In its *Index of Quotations*, the UBS Greek New Testament highlights Paul's apparent quotations of Job 41:11 in Romans 11:35 and of Job 5:13 in 1 Corinthians 3:19. In addition to these clearer quotations, the following possible links between Job and the Pauline corpus are suggested in the UBS Index of Allusions and Verbal Parallels: Job 1:1, 8 with 1 Thessalonians 5:22; Job 1:21 with 1 Timothy 6:7; Job 2:3 with 1 Thessalonians 5:22; Job 4:9 with 2 Thessalonians 2:8; Job 4:19 with 2 Corinthians 5:1; Job 12:7–9 with Romans 1:20; Job 13:16 (LXX) with Philippians 1:19; and Job 15:8 with Romans 11:34. Included also on this list is a suggested allusion to Job 2:6 in 2 Corinthians 12:7, the passage we are studying.[4] Paul's evident familiarity with Job reinforces the argument that follows.

---

3. Identifying Job's specific malady is its own difficult question, apart from it being something painful in his skin/flesh. "Many suggestions have been made for Job's condition, including by professional medics. Here are just a few: chronic eczema, smallpox, malignant or infectious ulcer, ulcerous boil known as the 'Baghdad button', syphilis, pellagra, scurvy, or simply vitamin deficiency. Take your pick!" (Katharine J. Dell, "What was Job's Malady?" *JSOT* 41 [2016]: 63).

4. *The Greek New Testament*, ed. Barbara Aland et al., 5th rev. ed. (Stuttgart: Deutsche Bibelgesellschaft, 2014), 858, 871. Cf. the longer list of *Loci Citati vel Allegati* of Job in the NT in the *Nestle–Aland Novum Testamentum Graeca*, ed. Barbara and Kurt Aland, et al., 27th rev.

Paul's use of Job, though, may go beyond a mere literary relationship. Susan Garrett argues that Paul in 2 Corinthians 12:7–10 was a participant in a shared cultural model, what she has labeled "the Job model of affliction." That is, like other contemporaries, Paul looked to Job as a paradigm of endurance in the face of testing by Satan.[5] Thus, we may need to pay attention not simply to shared linguistic features, but to shared conceptual features as well.

Let us look in more detail at some of the possible dependencies of Paul upon Job in the context of Paul's comments about his thorn in the flesh.

"MESSENGER" OR "ANGEL"

Paul employs the word "angel" or "messenger" (*angelos*, "an angel/ messenger of Satan") in 2 Corinthians 12:7, a word that finds its counterpart in Job 1. If Paul's reference is to an angel (which I think more likely given the cultural background explained in the previous chapter[6]), then the connection is to Job 1:6 where the "sons of God" (com-

---

ed. (Stuttgart: Deutsche Bibelgesellschaft; Peabody, MA: Hendrickson, 1993), 785. Ryan E. Stokes also suggests dependence of 1 Cor 5:5 on Satan's attack of Job in Job 2 (Ryan E. Stokes, *The Satan: How God's Executioner Became the Enemy* [Grand Rapids: Eerdmans, 2019], 206). For three examples of how Paul used Job, see Mario Cimosa and Gillian Bonney, "The Use of the Septuagint Job in the New Testament and Early Christian Exegesis," *Salesianum* 76 (2014): 649–52.

5. Garrett, "Paul's Thorn and Cultural Models of Affliction," 87–91. Garrett compares Jas 5:11; *Testament of Job* 1:5; *Jubilees* 17:16 (Abraham's temptation to sacrifice Isaac modeled after Job's endurance); 1 Pet 5:8–9; and Paul's own words in 1 Thess 3:1–5. Similarly, Abernathy writes, "In a very real way, Paul's experience was the New Testament's equivalent of the story of Job, and the outcome in Paul's case was like that of Job" (Abernathy, "Paul's Thorn in the Flesh," 76). Yong suggests, "The early Christian mind had probably learned the lesson of Job by this time: that any impairment from God may have been mediated through the satan" (Yong, *Bible, Disability, and the Church*, 87). John E. Wood writes more generally about the relationship of 2 Corinthians and Job: "Let it be said at once that 2 Corinthians fills much the same place in the New Testament as does the book of Job in the Old. It is a letter written by one whose heart has been broken by the many intolerable burdens heaped on him: a man struggling with a recalcitrant church and a malignant foe" (John E. Wood, "Death at work in Paul," *EvQ* 54 [1982]: 151). Moss agrees: "It may serve, as many have noted, as an allusion to Job and as such recast his *skolops* as cosmically significant in the way that the suffering of Job is related to cosmic affairs" (Moss, "Christly Possession and Weakened Bodies," 324).

6. Stokes comments, "Some translations, including the NRSV, render *angelos* as 'messenger' rather than 'angel' (of Satan) in 2 Cor 12:7. In light of the numerous texts that speak of the Satan

monly viewed as angels[7]) present themselves before the Lord, Satan being among them. If Paul's reference is to a messenger, as the word is often translated in 2 Corinthians 12:7 in many English translations, the connection is to the messengers (*angeloi* in Greek) who are sent sequentially to deliver the news to Job of Satan's devastating actions after he destroys Job's livestock, servants, and sons and daughters (1:14–15, 16, 17, 18). Thus, whether we read 2 Corinthians 12:7 as "an angel of Satan" (more likely), or as a "messenger of Satan" (less likely), the word *angelos* literarily connects 2 Corinthians 12 with the early section of Job.

"SKIN" AND "FLESH" IN JOB 2:4–5

Observe Satan's words in Job 2:4, "Satan answered the Lord and said, 'Skin for skin! All that people have they will give to save their lives.'" It is true that "skin for skin"[8] appears to be some sort of idiom. Nevertheless, skin is what is called out by the author of Job, and Satan will soon painfully touch Job's literal skin.

In the following verse, Job 2:5, Satan adds bone and flesh to skin: "But stretch out your hand and touch his bone and his flesh, and he will curse you to your face." Then in Job 2:7, the narrator speaks explicitly about the terrible sores inflicted on Job's body. Although it is not clear what ailment the author of Job is describing, Job's ailment is depicted as a painful skin-flesh condition that goes deeper than just the surface skin (thus the mention of bones).[9]

---

as leader of harmful superhuman beings who bring various sorts of physical harm on human beings, 'angel' is the better translation" (Stokes, *Satan*, 207n41).

7. "This term [the sons of God] is used to denote members of the category of gods, i.e., celestial or divine beings, in contrast to human beings. Just as 'the sons of the prophets' (1 K. 20:35) means members of the prophetic guild, and 'the sons of men' (Gen. 11:5, 1 Sam. 26:19) refers to the human race or mankind, 'the sons of God' designates the non-human race, so to say, Godkind. This phrase is not used often (Gen. 6:2, 5; Job 1:6, 2:1, 38:7; cf. Pss. 29:1, 89:6 [H--89:7]), and it is similar to 'sons of the most high' (Ps. 82:6)" (William Brandt Bradshaw, "Demonology in Hebrew and Jewish Tradition: A Study in New Testament Origins" [PhD thesis, University of St. Andrews, 1963], 54).

8. Hebrew: *'or b'd 'or*; Greek: *derma hyper dermatos*.

9. Norman C. Habel, *The Book of Job: A Commentary* (Philadelphia: Westminster, 1985), 95.

"Flesh" (Hebrew: *basar*; Greek: *sarx*) appears elsewhere in Job, and (significant for our study) usually in a literal sense referring to the human body (both *basar* and *sarx*: 4:15; 6:12; 13:14; 14:22; 19:20, 22; 21:6; 33:25; 41:15; *basar* only: 7:5; 10:4, 11; 19:26; *sarx* only: 16:18; 33:21; places it may not mean literal flesh: 12:10 [Hebrew only]; 13:14; 31:31; 34:15). Furthermore, sometimes skin and flesh are connected in the same verse (as in, 10:11; 19:20, 26), a reminder that when the author of Job wrote about "flesh," he was often talking, very literally, about the flesh of Job's body that included his skin; and thus also it was understood by the Greek translator(s).[10]

Accordingly, when Paul wrote that there was given to him a thorn "in the flesh" in 2 Corinthians 12:7, he was using language found extensively in the book of Job in reference to the flesh of a human body, which could suggest that Paul's ailment was, like Job, an ailment of his skin and flesh.

PAUL'S REFERENCE TO "SATAN"

Paul chose to utilize the name or title "Satan" (*satanas*) ("an angel of Satan") in 2 Corinthians 12:7 (elsewhere also in Paul's writings in 1 Cor 5:5; 7:5; 2 Cor 2:11; 11:14; 1 Thess 2:18; 2 Thess 2:9; 1 Tim 1:20; 5:5, as an evil being opposing the work of God). "Satan" or "the satan" (*ha satan*) only appears in the Hebrew Bible nineteen times in reference to a superhuman being (eighteen of those as a title), and fourteen of those occurrences appear in the first two chapters of Job.[11]

---

10. Note Amy Erickson's intriguing thesis that Job, employing a legal metaphor, distances what others would have noticed as his deteriorating skin and flesh from his statement of innocence (Amy Erickson, "'Without My Flesh I Will See God': Job's Rhetoric of the Body," *JBL* 132 [2013]: 295–313).

11. The word often appears as the more generic "adversary." Three of the other four instances where it also seems to appear as a title are found in Zech 3:1–2. The final appearance—that is, the one appearance in 1 Chr 21:1—inasmuch as it is lacking the definite article, could be functioning either as a title or as a proper name. Num 22 (see vv. 22 and 32), is the one other instance where *satan* refers to a superhuman entity. There, the angel of the Lord is described "as an adversary." It does not, however, appear to be a title; rather, it is a description of the opposing work that he is there to do to the pagan prophet Balaam. To this point, it should be noted that in Zech 3:1–2, the angel of the Lord is a *different* entity from *ha satan*.

Although the Greek translators chose to translate *ha satan* as "the devil" (*ho diabolos*),[12] who among us would challenge the assertion that when Paul referred to Satan in his writings, including his use in 2 Corinthians 12:7, he knew that the Hebrew in Job was *ha satan*?[13]

_____

12. If, as has been suggested by John G. Gammie ("The Angelology and Demonology in the Septuagint of the Book of Job," *HUCA* 56 [1985]: 19), the Greek translator of Job "utilize[d] a term still relatively neutral and not yet associated in the public mind with a leader of forces in opposition to the divine intentions," then we perhaps should suggest that Paul intentionally chose the stronger term that would communicate his understanding that the one who dialogued with God was an evil spirit. Paul's other uses of "Satan" would support that contention. Gammie concludes his study of LXX Job angelology and demonology with this overall conclusion: "In sum, the Greek translation of the Book of Job may be seen as a clear, though rather modest and restrained, advance toward a dualistic demonology."

13. Some recent scholars have asserted that the character designated as *ha satan* in Hebrew in the book of Job is not the same Evil One we know as Satan or the devil in the New Testament. Rather, he is a member in good standing of God's council, bearing a title which means something like "the adversary" (functioning as a prosecuting attorney, so Michael S. Heiser, *The Unseen Realm: Recovering the Supernatural Worldview of the Bible* [Bellingham, WA: Lexham, 2015], 56–58; or like a plaintiff in a civil suit, so John H. Walton and J. Harvey Walton, *Demons and Spirits in Biblical Theology: Reading the Biblical Text in Its Cultural and Literary Context* [Eugene, OR: Cascade Books, 2019], 215–17; or as God's executioner, so Stokes, *Satan*, 29–47). I have so far been unconvinced that such approaches are better than the traditional idea that *ha satan* is one and the same as Paul's Satan. The following are four reasons for the traditional view of Satan in Job:

Satan appears to challenge God in Job 1:9–11 and 2:4–5. The tone of the challenge sounds different to me than the questioning of righteous sufferers such as one might find in the lament Psalms (and which usually ends with an assertion of trust). I doubt that a heavenly being in good standing with God could throw around such an accusation without losing his good standing in God's court.

Satan attacks an innocent person in Job 2:3 (cf. 1:8). In the traditional view of Satan, God sometimes permits Satan to do evil deeds even to righteous people because God has greater purposes that he intends (Luke 22:31; 2 Cor 12:7). But in this newer view, God would have to be viewed as more directly complicit in the evil attacks against someone whom the book of Job describes as "blameless" and "upright" (Job 1:8; 2:3).

In Zech 3:1–2, a passage that parallels Job 1–2 in many ways, the Lord calls out Satan with these words: "The LORD rebuke you, O Satan! The LORD who has chosen Jerusalem rebuke you!" These words of rebuke are not the words one would expect to hear God speak toward a valued and upright member of his heavenly staff.

Perhaps most importantly, Satan is viewed throughout the New Testament as the Evil One who opposes the work of God. This is clear in the Gospels (e.g. Matt 4:1–11; Mark 3:22–26; Luke 10:18; John 13:27), in the writings of Paul (e.g., Rom 16:20; 1 Cor 5:5; 7:5; 2 Cor 2:11; 11:14), and in Revelation (e.g., 2:24; 12:9; 20:2, 7). Rev 12:9 equates the dragon of Revelation with the serpent of old who is also known as the devil, who is also known as Satan. Those who support this revised understanding of *ha satan* in Job insert a wedge between the New Testament authors (Jews who were so steeped in the Old Testament that they quote from it hundreds of times, allude to it hundreds more times, and exhibit hundreds more echoes reverberating throughout) and the writings of the Old Testament. This is acutely problematic—as the argument of this

Since fourteen of the eighteen uses of this word as a title are found in the book of Job, and furthermore, since we already know that Paul knew and used the book of Job (far more than either Chronicles or Zechariah, the other two locations where *ha satan* is found as a title), it seems more likely than not that Paul's use of "Satan" in 2 Corinthians 12:7 was particularly influenced by Job.[14]

SATAN "STUNG" OR "STABBED" JOB

A key connection between the two passages is one that is not visible to English-only readers. Paul's mention of a "thorn" in 2 Corinthians 12:7 connects with something appearing only in the Greek text of Job 2:7. (Reminder to non-specialists: Paul was thoroughly acquainted with the Greek translation [Septuagint or LXX] of the Old Testament and drew upon it regularly in his letters. He also knew and drew upon the Hebrew text as well, though not as frequently as the Greek text.[15])

---

chapter supports—if Paul is literarily and conceptually dependent upon the book of Job. Graham A. Cole notes: "The Christian theologian, who works with a *tota scriptura* that includes the NT witness, need not hesitate to identify the figure of Job 1 with that of 1 Chronicles 21 with that of Matthew 4" (Graham A. Cole, *Against the Darkness: The Doctrine of Angels, Satan, and Demons* [Wheaton, IL: Crossway, 2019], 98n85).

But even if someone were to support this newer paradigm (or versions of it), such support does not militate against the main point for which I am arguing—that there is an intertextual relationship between Paul and Job 1–2 that is partially bolstered by Paul's use of the word "Satan," a label that is more prominent in Job 1–2 than anywhere else in the Hebrew Bible. Thanks to my colleague, Charlie Trimm, for interacting with me on this issue, and for several insights that appear in this footnote.

14. Paul, of course, could have been—and even may have been—influenced by other uses of "Satan" in extrabiblical literature (*Jubilees*, the Enochic literature, *Sirach*, *Wisdom of Solomon*, the Qumran community's documents, *Testament of Job*, *The Testaments of the Twelve Patriarchs*, and *Life of Adam and Eve*; see surveys in Brown, *God of This Age*, 21–60, and Stokes, *Satan*, 75–194). Nevertheless, Paul's pattern of dependency upon earlier writings is heavily weighted toward the books that eventually came to comprise the canon of Hebrew Scriptures; consequently, positing dependence upon Job should be considered much more likely than these other writings (a couple of which could actually have postdated Paul's writings).

15. "When Christianity spread outside the borders of Palestine, it was apparently the Greek version of the Jewish Scriptures from which the apostles, especially Paul, preached Christ" (Karen H. Jobes and Moisés Silva, *Invitation to the Septuagint* [Grand Rapids: Baker Academic, 2000], 38). Of course, the sentence I wrote in the main text was intentionally simplistic, ignoring the complicated textual transmission of both the Hebrew and Greek Old Testaments.

The Greek text of Job 2:7 reads, "And the devil departed from the Lord, and stung [*epaisen*] Job with an evil wound/sore from the feet to the head."[16] Notice in this sentence that the Greek translator took a Hebrew verb (*nkh*) that has connotations of "hitting" or "striking," and translated it with a Greek verb that sometimes denotes and commonly includes connotations of "stinging" or "stabbing" (*paiō*). The word the translator employed, as with many other words, can be used in various ways, but the stinging/stabbing connotation still often continues to hang around even when used in other contexts.

To illustrate the idea of associated connotations, think of the English word "assassination." Is "assassination" the same as a "murder"? Very nearly, except that, unlike "murder," the word "assassination" normally includes a political connotation.[17]

The Greek word *paiō* is similar in the sense that it sometimes simply denotes *stinging* (as with the stinger of a scorpion, Rev 9:5), or *piercing* (as with a sword, 2 Sam 20:10).[18] It can be used in other contexts, such as in the case of a king (with his army) striking down enemies (for example, 2 Kgs 25:21), but the connotation of stinging or piercing with a sword still sometimes lingers, especially, it appears, when applied to individuals. This is harder for English-attuned ears to hear because of an unusual convention of English. We English speakers (strangely) use the verb "strike" (a hitting term) to describe what we do with a sword, rather than "stick" or "pierce" or "cut," or some other term that would more naturally associate with the sharpness or pointedness of a sword. We do have a word in English that does such work, the word "stab," but we only use it for very short swords, that is, for a knives or daggers. In other words, we use a hitting term ("strike") in English when we talk about the action of a sword, a

---

16. Unless otherwise stated, I am following for the Greek of Job the text of Joseph Ziegler, *Septuaginta: Vetus Testamentum Graecum Auctoritate Academiae Scientiarum Gottingensis editum XI.4: Iob* (Göttingen: Vandenhoeck & Ruprecht, 1982).

17. Peter James Silzer and Thomas John Finley, *How Biblical Languages Work* (Grand Rapids: Kregel Academic, 2004), 161.

18. BDAG, 751.

convention that keeps us from hearing the stabbing connotation in the Greek word employed in Job 2:7.

Since Paul claimed in 2 Corinthians 12:7 that he was given a "sharp-pointed object" (stake, thorn, or something else sharp, see later discussion) "in the flesh," and since it is also likely that he was aware of the Greek translator's rendering of what Satan did to Job, Paul readily would have been able to connect the Greek translation of this text and the resulting skin/flesh condition of Job with his own stabbing suffering.[19]

Interestingly, if in fact the meaning of *paiō* in Job 2:7 carries connotations of stinging, it may be worth noticing that not only in Job 2:7 and 2 Corinthians 12:7 does the Bible suggest that Satan and his realm can sting or pierce. In the Greek of Hosea 13:14, as well as in its subsequent employment by Paul in 1 Corinthians 15:55–56, "Hades" or "Death" is described as having a sting (*kentron*). In Revelation 9:1–11, locusts from "the angel of the bottomless pit" sent by "Abaddon" or "Apollyon" have stings (*kentra*). Revelation 9:5 uses the same Greek verb as is found in the Greek translation of Job 2:7 (*paiō*) for the stinging that these locusts inflict. Satan, it seems, throughout the Bible has a tendency to sting people.

Support for the stabbing or stinging notion in general is also found in 6:4 where Job complains (in Greek) that "the arrows of the Lord are in my body."[20] The Greek translator took the Hebrew plural "arrows" (*khtsy*), turned it into a singular and located the piercing action "in my body" rather than "in me," as the simpler Hebrew reads. This description is similar to other places in the Old Testament where a lamenter complains that God has shot arrows into his body (Ps 38:3

---

19. In the same sentence of Job 2:7, that same Greek translator also took a Hebrew noun that normally means "a boil" or "a skin eruption" (*shkhyn*) and translated it with a Greek noun that more often is used for "a wound" (*helkos*), even though it can denote other things, including a skin disease or a "sore." The subtle difference may not have been lost on Paul—or at least subconsciously influenced him—since the result of being impacted by a "sharp-pointed object in the flesh" (*skolops tē sarki*, 2 Cor 12:7) could have felt more like an externally caused wound than would most disease-generated skin eruptions.

20. The arrows of 6:4 and archers of 16:13 came to my attention through Dell, "What was Job's Malady?," 67.

[LXX 37:3]; Lam 2:4; 3:12–13).[21] Job 6:4 is similar to the piercing idea of Job 2:7 and also invites parallels to Paul, who claims to have had a sharp-pointed object in his flesh.[22]

Furthermore, the same verb that is used in Job 2:7 (*paiō*) is also used metaphorically in 16:10 when Job complains that people have stung him (or struck him resulting in a stinging sensation?) on the cheek. Though the Hebrew text is about humans opening their mouths in mockery and slapping Job on the cheek, the Greek translator rendered it: "With darts from his eyes he dashed at me; he struck me on the cheek with something sharp."[23] Observe that in 16:10 there are five items that parallel in some way Paul's state of affairs as it will be argued on the pages ahead: (1) The use of the word *paiō* ("sting," "strike") as has already been mentioned, (2) the location of the sharp strike or sting "on the cheek" (*siagona*), (3) "with something sharp" (*oxei*), (4) "with darts" (*akisin*), (5) from the Lord. (That God is being accused of doing the action is clear from the sentences that surround this verse in Greek.) The Greek translator of the book of Job used the language of stinging on the cheek with something sharp from the Lord to describe Job's humiliation (remembering that Satan was the agent, 2:7). Paul said that Paul was given (from the Lord) a messenger of Satan to strike him via a thorn in his flesh to keep him humble (2 Cor 12:7).

OVERLAPPING THEOLOGIES
OF SUFFERING

I have already written in part about Paul's theology of suffering in the previous chapter. A substantial overlapping theology of suffering underlies both Job 1–2 and 2 Corinthians 12:7. In Job 1–2, even though Satan caused the suffering, God permitted it in order to accomplish his

---

21. Scott Jones, "Corporeal Discourse in the Book of Job," *JBL* 132 (2013): 849.

22. Notice also that in the Hebrew of 16:13, God is described as an archer, whereas in the Greek it reads, "they surrounded me, throwing lances into my kidneys" [or possibly, "into my mind"].

23. The English translation is from Claude E. Cox, "Iob," in *A New English Translation of the Septuagint and the Other Greek Translations Traditionally Included under That Title*, ed. Albert Pietersma and Benjamin G. Wright (Oxford: Oxford University Press, 2007), 680.

own inscrutable purposes.[24] Similarly, the main verb of 2 Corinthians 12:7 is almost always viewed by interpreters as a divine passive: "there was given to me [implied: by God] a thorn in the flesh."[25] That is, God permitted the suffering inflicted via the thorn, even though Paul also described it as "an angel of Satan." Activity of Satan that is also allowed by God is alluded to elsewhere in the Bible (Zech 3:1–2; 1 Chr 21:1, cf. 2 Sam 24:1; 1 Kgs 22:19–23; 2 Chr 18:18–22; the temptation of Jesus in Mark 1:12–13, Matt 4:1–11, Luke 4:1–13; and Luke 22:31–32), but in none of these instances is the interplay between the activity of Satan and divine permission as clear as it appears in Job 1–2 and 2 Corinthians 12:7.[26] This shared theological stance is something additional that draws these two passages together.

I will continue to present other possible literary or thematic connections between 2 Corinthians 12:7 in its literary context and Job, but the reader should pause at this moment and consider whether what has already been presented is not adequate on its own to establish an intertextual relationship between the two texts. Job was *stung* in his literal *flesh*, by *Satan*, with *God's permission*, and with other *angels/messengers* playing a role in the narrative—all in the first two chapters of Job. Quite similarly, Paul wrote in 2 Corinthians 12:7 that: "a *thorn* was given me in the *flesh*, an *angel/messenger* of *Satan*." We could stop

---

24. Lee A. Johnson ("Satan Talk in Corinth," 152) posits this kind of theological connection between 2 Cor 12:7 and Job: "Satan appears here as one who enacts the desires of God, much like the Joban Satan who is entirely subject to God (1:12, 2:6–7)." Craig S. Keener comments about 2 Cor 12:7: "As in the Old Testament and most Jewish thought, God is here sovereign even over Satan and his angels" (Craig S. Keener, *The IVP Bible Background Commentary: New Testament* [Downers Grove, IL: InterVarsity Press, 1993], 514). Linda L. Belleville agrees: "Satan intends the stake for Paul's undoing. But God, who has ultimate control over the situation, intends it for Paul's good" (Linda L. Belleville, *2 Corinthians*, IVPNTC (Downers Grove, IL: InterVarsity Press, 1996), 307).

25. Thomas supports the divine passive idea and then comments: "To understate the case, the vast majority of scholars identify the giver as God" (Thomas, "'An Angel from Satan,'" 42n5). Note also Paul's use of the intransitive verb *afistēmi* when he writes in 12:8 that he pleaded three times (in most translations) "that it might leave (*apostē*) me"—translated by NIV simply as asking God to act: "Three times I pleaded with the Lord to take it away from me." For a contrasting view, see Mitzi L. Minor, *2 Corinthians*, SHBC (Macon, GA: Smyth & Helwys, 2009).

26. For more, see Page, "Satan: God's Servant," 449–52, 464–65.

the chapter here, and a likely intertextual connection between Job
(especially chs. 1–2) and Paul on these points alone should be affirmed.

But there exist other possible relevant literary and thematic
connections between the two texts. The connections already presented become mutually reinforcing with the further connections
suggested below. In other words, if in fact a literary and conceptual
connection between 2 Corinthians 12:7 and Job 1–2 has already been
deemed credible from these clues, the value of the suggested allu-
sions/echoes/conceptual similarities detailed below also increases.
Inversely, the sheer number of apparent similarities between things
found more broadly in Job and Paul's 2 Corinthians 10–13 raises the
cumulative likelihood of actual literary and conceptual dependence
of 2 Corinthians 12:7 on Job, even if individual connections on their
own might be disputed.

FOOLISHNESS IN JOB AND
PAUL'S FOOL'S SPEECH

Paul's "fool's speech" in 2 Corinthians 11:21b–12:10[27] displays at least
some surface similarities to Job's words to his wife in Job 2:10: "You
speak as any foolish woman would speak. Shall we receive the good
at the hand of God, and not receive the bad?" (Job 2:10). In Paul's
context, one thinks of 2 Corinthians 11:19, where Paul writes: "For
you gladly put up with fools, being wise yourselves!" and the verse
that immediately follows our central paragraph, "I have been a fool!
You forced me to it ... " (2 Cor 12:11). Paul ironically refers to himself as a fool in order to point out the foolhardiness of one who
rejects the idea that God would ever allow one of his apostles to
experience suffering such as Paul experienced.[28] Job's three friends
are also consistently portrayed in the book of Job as wise men who
speak foolishness.

---

27. Jan Lambrecht, "The Fool's Speech and Its Context: Paul's Particular Way of Arguing in
2 Cor 10–13," *Bib* 83 (2001): 305–24. The starting point and finishing point of the "fool's speech,"
is disputed, but I see it as actually starting at 11:21b and finishing at 12:10.

28. Witherington, *Conflict and Community in Corinth*, 442.

HUMILIATION, BOASTING,
AND WEAKNESS

Paul's thorn not only caused pain but was given for the purpose of humbling Paul (2 Cor 12:7; cf. 12:21). Job similarly employed honor-and-shame language to reflect upon the humiliation that resulted from his own appalling circumstances (Job 19, 29–30). Then, after Job was finally silenced, God spoke the following words: "Look on everyone who is proud and bring him low" (Job 40:12). The social dimension of Job's sufferings is an important theme in the book.[29] Throughout the book, Job "emphasized his weakness and powerlessness, and he chides his friends in chapter 26 for refusing to help one in such a state ... (26:2)."[30]

There exists a contrast between Paul and Job, to be sure. After Job was afflicted with his skin condition, he complained about it—even challenged God about it. Paul, on the other hand, was kept humble by the "thorn" with which he was pierced. There still may be, nevertheless, a relevant comparison in the contrast. Job boasted of things he did not understand, as he confessed in Job 42:3, "I have uttered what I did not understand, things too wonderful for me, which I did not know" (Job 42:3); that is, he owned up to his "words without knowledge," as God labeled Job's folly in 38:2. Paul, in contrast, "heard things that cannot be told, which man may not utter" (2 Cor 12:4), but a few verse later declared, "I will boast all the more gladly of my weaknesses" (2 Cor 12:9). Using language similar to the language of Paul, Elihu chided Job by averring that God does his awesome works, "so that every man might know his own weakness [*astheneia*]" (Job 37:7 Greek only). In light of all the other possible intertextual connections with Job, might we suggest that Paul learned something from Job's initial folly, Elihu's exhortation, and Job's final confession?

---

29. Dell, "What was Job's Malady?" 71–72. More broadly, see Andrew M. Mbuvi, "The Ancient Mediterranean Values of 'Honour and Shame' as a Hermeneutical Lens of Reading the Book of Job," *OTE* 23/3 (2010): 752–68.

30. Jones, "Corporeal Discourse in the Book of Job," 851.

THREE TIMES

Paul writes, "Three times I pleaded with the Lord about this, that it should leave me" (2 Cor 12:8). It is unlikely that Paul would add the detail that he prayed three times about his painful thorn if on a single occasion he had simply prayed, "Lord, take it away, take it away, take it away." Rather, it seems more likely that Paul is referring to three separate periods of prayer during which he presented his heart-wrenching cry for deliverance to the Lord.[31]

It may be worth noting by way of comparison that the largest portion of the book of Job (chs. 3–31) gets structured around three cycles.[32] Those three cycles include the speeches of Job's three friends, followed by Job's rejoinders and expressions of complaint against God. Moreover, at the end of the three cycles, Job stops, as the narrator makes clear: "The words of Job are ended" (Job 31:40). Paul implies, though he does not say it explicitly, that he also stopped seeking release from his suffering because of the message he received from God about the sufficiency of God's grace (2 Cor 12:9–10).

If, in fact, Paul had Job's own sufferings in mind during his own lengthy years of suffering, in addition to his connections with the suffering of Jesus (see ch. 8), he may have been cognizant of Job's own three cycles of complaint and final acquiescence. Too much weight should not be placed upon this possible connection, however, since the number three shows up in disparate contexts throughout the Bible.

---

31. Brown rightly comments: "Like Paul's references to his three beatings ... and three shipwrecks ... in 2 Cor 11:25, it seems most likely that Paul made three separate pleas to the Lord ... for the removal of his thorn. ... Therefore, the number three ... in v. 8 is not ... an allusion to Jesus' three petitions in the Gethsemane (Matt 26:44; Mark 14:41)" (Brown, *God of This Age*, 185n202, following Harris, *2 Corinthians*, 860–61).

32. Francis I. Andersen, *Job: An Introduction and Commentary*, TOTC (Leicester: Inter-Varsity Press, 1976), 22, 75.

SIMILAR RESPONSES BY GOD

After a long wait, Paul received the following response from God: "My grace is sufficient for you, for power is made perfect in weakness" (2 Cor 12:9). Correspondingly, after a long wait, Job received a reply from God (Job 38–41), different from Paul's in some respects, but similar in one key way. In so many words, God tells Job to stop complaining because God is God, and God can allow Job to suffer if and when he deems it appropriate.[33] The similarity of God's response in the two contexts helps pull the passages together.

THE MOVE FROM COMPLAINT
TO ACQUIESCENCE

Toward the end of the book, Job's response moves from complaint about his intense suffering to acquiescence. He says, "Behold, I am of small account;[34] what shall I answer you? I lay my hand on my mouth. I have spoken once, and I will not answer; twice, but I will proceed no further" (Job 40:4–5). Similarly, Paul's response is to move from begging for removal to acquiescence. "Therefore I will boast all the more gladly of my weaknesses, so that the power of Christ may rest upon me. For the sake of Christ, then, I am content with weaknesses … " (2 Cor 12:9–10).

NEITHER RECEIVED HEALING

One arresting literary feature of the book of Job is that Job is never said to have been healed of his skin pain.[35] This strikes the reader as unusual, since the restoration of everything else Job lost is highlighted at the end of the book. What was restored to Job after all his sufferings? (1) His fortune (42:10–12). (2) His social reputation (42:11). (3) His family (42:13–15). (4) His long life (42:16–17). But *not* his

---

33. Tremper Longman III, *Job*, BCOTWP (Grand Rapids: Baker, 2012), 425–26.

34. "He confesses, *I am small* (*qallōtî*). This word for "being small or light" is the opposite of "honor" (*kābôd*, lit. "heavy"). Although Job has been vexed that his misfortune has discredited his prestige (cf. 19:9; 29:20), he defers his personal honor to Yahweh's greater honor" (John E. Hartley, *The Book of Job*, NICOT [Grand Rapids: Eerdmans, 1988], 517).

35. This observation and its possible relevance to Paul's thorn in the flesh was first pointed out to me by my research assistant, Jacob Keeth.

health—at least not explicitly. Jeremy Schipper comments, "One of
the biggest ironies of the book of Job is that, in the end, God explicitly restores everything that Job lost in the prologue, except for his
physical health as the friends had anticipated."[36] Job's friends (18:13;
11:15), Elihu (33:21, 25), and Job himself (7:5; 19:20; 30:30) all alluded
in their speeches to Job's skin-flesh in anticipation of restoration to
healthy skin, but did not allude to the restoration of the other things
lost.[37] The epilogue of Job, by way of contrast, mentions the restoration of the other things in some manner, but not the elimination of
the trouble with Job's skin and flesh (42:12–13).[38]

The text, of course, does not deny that Job was healed. One could
argue that the happily-ever-after ending of the book should cause
the reader to assume that Job did receive healing. But the fact that
Job's afflictions were set up in two distinct stages, the second (loss of
health)—at least from Satan's perspective—worse than the first (loss
of property, family, and reputation), makes me think rather that the
author is not simply offering the sunny ending that many assume
when they read Job. We intuitively know that children lost to death
cannot be replaced by other children; so despite God's blessing, all
was not rosy for Job, even after his restoration. Perhaps the other side
of the ongoing pain of Job's earlier suffering included lingering effects—
including some pain—from Job's skin-flesh affliction, whatever it was.

Similarly, there is no indication that Paul ever received healing for
his affliction. God's response in 2 Corinthians 12:9a indicates, on the
contrary, that Paul should not expect such healing. Furthermore, Paul's
response in 2 Corinthians 12:9b–10 suggests that Paul neither expected
a healing, nor even continued to pray for one. This is one more similarity between Job and Paul, and a connection Paul himself could have
forged with the suffering of Job as Paul endured his own painful suffering.

---

36. Schipper, "Healing and Silence," 21–22. The silence about Job's healing is also supported
by Dell, "What was Job's Malady?," 75–77.

37. Schipper mentions that 8:4 and 19:17 might be possible exceptions (Schipper, "Healing
and Silence," 18).

38. Schipper, "Healing and Silence," 19–20.

A POST-HAYS INTERPRETIVE
ENVIRONMENT

Richard Hays is a modern scholar of the New Testament who has profoundly influenced how recent interpreters think of the relationship between the Old and New Testaments. I find it surprising in this post-Hays era of discussions of intertextuality that so little attention has been given to possible literary influences on 2 Corinthians 12:7. Job is the most obvious influencing text. Hays proposed seven (now widely-used) criteria to employ when judging the likelihood or lack thereof of intertextual connections with Paul. These include: (1) the likelihood that the proposed source was *available* to Paul, (2) the *volume* of the echo, that is, the number and closeness of the echoes in Paul along with the distinctiveness of the employed source, (3) the *recurrence*, or number of times Paul draws upon this same passage, (4) how often the source and receptor passages *thematically cohere*, (5) the *historical plausibility* that Paul could have connected with the source in question in such a way that his readers could have grasped the connection, (6) whether other interpreters have heard the same echoes in the *history of interpretation*, and (7) whether a group of well-trained (critical or pre-critical) readers of Paul are likely to be *satisfied* that such a reading makes good sense.[39] The reading proposed here makes good use of all these tests to some degree, except the sixth, which Hays himself considers the weakest of the seven tests. In light of Hays's tests, one way to underscore the sturdiness of the connection between 2 Corinthians 12:7 and Job (esp. 1–2) is to compare Hays's own application of his tests. Immediately after Hays lays out these tests, he illustrates them by evaluating a proposed echo of Job 13:16 [LXX] in Phil 1:19, an intertextual connection he had earlier defended and used as an example of his methodology in *Echoes of Scripture*.[40] That proposed echo, however, is decidedly weaker than the connections between 2 Corinthians 12 and Job proposed in

---

39. Richard B. Hays, *Echoes of Scripture in the Letters of Paul* (New Haven: Yale University Press, 1989), 29–32.

40. Hays, *Echoes of Scripture*, 32 and 21–24.

this chapter. If interpreters will grant that Hays might have a case with Job 13:16 in Phil 1:19, they have little choice but to acknowledge the far stronger likelihood of literary and conceptual dependency of Paul upon Job in 2 Corinthians 12, particularly in Paul's comments about his thorn in the flesh in 2 Corinthians 12:7.

CONCLUSION

There exists a literary and conceptual relationship between the book of Job and 2 Corinthians 12:7. Since Job's bodily infirmity was a painful affliction of the skin-flesh that was caused by Satan while allowed by God, this increases the likelihood that Paul's affliction also was a Satan-generated, God-permitted painful condition that affected Paul's literal skin and flesh.

CRITERIA SUPPORTED OR ALLUDED TO IN THIS CHAPTER

1. Viewed by Paul as attacks by an angel of Satan, though permitted by God

2. Paralleling Job's sufferings (especially Job 1–2), which included skin/flesh

3. Impacting Paul's physical flesh

4. Comparable to the jabbing of a sharp-pointed object

5. Excruciating, not simply annoying

6. Viewed by others as humiliating and weak

CHAPTER FIVE

CLUES FROM THE LITERARY CONTEXT (PART 1)

THE SENTENCE (2 CORINTHIANS 12:7)

We have now arrived at the heart of the discussion. So far we have observed clues from the historical and cultural context, that is, the piercing of curse tablets, animals, and voodoo dolls, and from the intertextual context, particularly the relationship of 2 Corinthians 12:7 to the book of Job. But the context that typically yields the most clues in a study such as the one in which we are engaged is the literary context. That is indeed the case in the study we have undertaken. The words that lead up to and surround Paul's comment about his thorn in the flesh disclose some suggestive clues that can aid us in narrowing the range of possible maladies for Paul's thorn.

Paul's literary context can be viewed in concentric circles, which is how we will approach what he has written here. The closest context, of course, is the sentence itself in which Paul's thorn comment appears: 2 Corinthians 12:7.[1] The second closest context (which includes the former) is the paragraph: 2 Corinthians 12:1–10. A third and wider contextual circle (which includes the former two) is the main discourse in which the crucial paragraph is found: 2 Corinthians 10–13. Further out, a fourth contextual circle encompasses all of 2 Corinthians. (Although the fourth circle holds some relevance for our discussion, I will largely limit my examination found in the next three chapters to the first three circles, with a few limited forays into the widest circle.) The final and widest literary circle, of course, for ascertaining Paul's mind is all the letters of Paul. Anything relevant that comes from that circle will appear when interacting with other questions in this book. What can we infer about Paul's thorn in the flesh from each of the first three contextual circles surrounding Paul's mention of his thorn, moving from the narrowest to the broadest?

CLUES FROM THE SENTENCE:
2 CORINTHIANS 12:7

"And on account of the extraordinary greatness of the revelations, that I might not become conceited, a thorn in the flesh was given to me, a messenger of Satan, that it/he might punch me, that I might not become conceited" (author's translation). There are six observations we can make about Paul's thorn in the flesh that are germane to our study.

"THORN" OR "STAKE"

Paul labeled his suffering a "thorn" or a "stake." Paul used the Greek word *skolops*, which apart from a specific literary context means nothing more specific than something sharp and pointed.[2] There has been considerable discussion about whether the term signifies a *thorn*

---

1. Wallace (*Snatched into Paradise*, 235) writes: "Second Corinthians 12:10–13 is like a Russian Matryoshka doll, with one theme nested inside of another. Second Corinthians 12:1–10 is the innermost doll."

2. Minn (*Thorn that Remained*, 8) writes: "It signifies literally 'what is pointed,' and is applied in consequence to any object with a sharp point—a sharpened stake, for instance, a pole on which something can be fixed, a sliver, a pike, a spit, a javelin, the barb of a fish hook etc." So also E. A. Sophocles (*Greek Lexicon of the Roman and Byzantine Periods [From B.C. 146 to*

(which might range from a tiny nuisance to a hard pointed three-inch spine of a palm tree), or whether he intended something more like a *stake*, upon which, say, a human body could be impaled in a military context.[3] It would appear from the way it is used outside of Paul that he had the choice of using either sense. But in light of the way Paul actually employed it in 2 Corinthians 12:7, it would seem that Paul was not thinking of a tiny annoyance like a splinter, otherwise the clues regarding the excruciating nature of the thorn and the description of it "punching" him would seem irrelevant (see discussions on each idea below). Neither should it be viewed as a six-foot stake, since such an image makes little sense of a vexation that could repeatedly afflict one's body amidst the daily tasks of life. Thus, we probably should think either of a long (say, three to four inches), hard, and pointed thorn (like a thorn of a date palm[4]), or a shorter stake or sharp-pointed weapon with which someone could be repeatedly stabbed.[5]

"THORN" AND "FLESH"

One of the most important observations in the entire study is that Paul claimed that the "sharp-pointed object" (henceforth "thorn" for convenience) afflicted him "in the flesh" (*tē sarki*). Despite numerous

---

A.D. *1100]*, vol. 2 [New York: Frederick Ungar, 1957], 996), who defines it as "anything pointed, a prick, stake." LSJ, "σκόλοψ," 1613, simply states "anything pointed."

3. Park and Bowens support the idea of a stake or military instrument, whereas Moulton and Milligan, along with Minn, support "thorn" (see David M. Park, "Paul's ΣΚΟΛΟΨ ΤΗ ΣΑΡΚΙ: Thorn or Stake? [2 Cor XII 7]," *NovT* 22 [1980]: 179–83; Bowens, *An Apostle in Battle*, 156–62; J. H. Moulton and G. Milligan, *Vocabulary of the Greek New Testament* [Peabody, MA: Hendrickson, 1997], 578–79; Minn, *Thorn that Remained*, 8–10). Note that English translations have typically rendered *skolops* as "thorn," whereas German translations have used "Pfahl" ("stake"). One wonders how much of the scholarly discussion has been influenced by the respective translational conventions of each language. For ancient Near Eastern examples of impalement, see Charlie Trimm, *Fighting for the King and the Gods: A Survey of Warfare in the Ancient Near East*, RBS 88 (Atlanta: SBL Press, 2017), 348, 355–56, 364.

4. "Date palm thorn injuries are common in Middle Eastern countries, where there are many date palm plantations" (Chandana Chakraborti and Shreya Gayen, "An Unusual Journey of a Periocular Date Palm Thorn," *Saudi Journal of Ophthalmology* 33 [2019]: 165).

5. Moss ("Christly Possession and Weakened Bodies," 323) offers another option: "A "*skolops*" can denote anything pointed, in particular a stake, splinter, or a thorn, but also in some medical texts, a lance or surgical implement."

conjectures as to the nature of Paul's thorn, one common area of
agreement among most Greek grammarians who have looked at this
passage is that the noun in the dative case is a *dative of place* (or a *locative*), identifying the flesh as the *location* of the thorn.[6] The primary
reason for this syntactical category, and not another, is the surface
connection between "flesh" and "thorn." "Thorn" and "flesh" obviously
work together, and promptly bring to mind the image of a thorn, stake,
or other sharp object sticking into the skin and flesh.[7] Despite widespread agreement on this point, in the next breath most interpreters
disconnect this observation from the rest of the discussion. Instead
of observing that such a description is most easily understood as a
condition of the physical flesh that feels like the jabbing of a thorn,[8]
most interpreters move quickly to chronic physical conditions that
are harder to connect with Paul's physical flesh (see my list of previous suggestions found in ch. 2). However, if there exist (and indeed
there do exist) painful skin/flesh conditions that feel like repeated

---

6. Harris, *The Second Epistle to the Corinthians*, 854, is one of many examples. The main
alternatives are a dative of disadvantage or advantage, neither of which are very convincing.
For dative of disadvantage, that is, "for the inconvenience of the flesh," see Abernathy, "Paul's
Thorn in the Flesh," 73; Jegher-Bucher, "'The Thorn in the Flesh'/'Der Pfahl im Fleisch,'" 390;
and McCant, "Paul's Thorn of Rejected Apostleship," 567n6. A. T. Robertson says that it could
be either a dative of advantage or a locative (dative of place) (*A Grammar of the Greek New
Testament in the Light of Historical Research* [Nashville: Broadman, 1934], 538). Pascual, et al.,
writes, "Paul affirms twice that he doesn't know if the heavenly experience was in the body or
out of it. On the contrary, there is no doubt about where the σκόλοψ is hurting. It strikes 'in
the flesh'. Had been the σκόλοψ a spiritual injury, Paul would have not built such a contrasting
parallelism." (Pascual, et al., "Saint Paul's Thorn in the Flesh," 14.)

7. "The primary and literal meaning of *sarx* or flesh is physical and denotes the material
which covers the bones of a human or animal body" (John Wilkinson, *The Bible and Healing:
A Medical and Theological Commentary* [Edinburgh: Handsel; Grand Rapids: Eerdmans, 1998],
211). It is true that the word may also be used in an ethical sense to mean the human carnal
nature but, as Hughes points out in his commentary on this epistle, Paul ordinarily reserves
the ethical usage for a doctrinal-ethical context in which the flesh is opposed to the spirit." His
reference in the quote is to Hughes, *Paul's Second Epistle to the Corinthians*, 315.

8. Technically, the *most literal* way to interpret this would be to view Paul as having a large
painful splinter of some sort literally lodged in his flesh. We can even grant that before the
development of modern antibiotics, a splinter could lead to serious infections or even death.
See a few comments to this end by Moss, "Christly Possession and Weakened Bodies," 321–22.
But this cannot be correct, particularly because of the long-term nature of Paul's ailment and
the fact that he would have gotten someone to dig out such a splinter.

deep and painful jabbings of a sharp thorn, should not such conditions
be preferred—at least as a starting point in our discussions—to other
physical conditions, especially when most interpreters continue to
label the dative here as a dative of place? The suggestion of a condition of the flesh that feels like the stabbing of a pointed object as the
starting point for subsequent discussion receives support from the
intertextual connections to Job that have already been noted—Job,
who was "stung" in his physical flesh by Satan—and by the ubiqui-
tous use of curse tablets in Paul's environment which were fastened
by nails, voodoo dolls which were pierced with sharp objects, and
thorns that were used in various ways in magical texts. Chapter 8
will further bolster this assertion by highlighting Paul's cruciform
connections to the piercings of Jesus, including the crown of thorns.

The suggestion that Paul's thorn in the flesh was a skin/flesh
condition that literally felt like the repeated piercings of a thorn is
the simplest and most straightforward reading of Paul's comment
in 2 Corinthians 12:7. This observation should not be minimized as
other considerations are brought into the discussion.

AN UNUSUAL KIND OF SUFFERING

Tied to this first observation that Paul locates the thorn *in his flesh*, is
the observation that the language Paul chooses to employ is *unusual*,
to say the least. The image of a thorn or stake piercing flesh evokes
something extraordinarily painful. Whatever Paul suffered, he did not
seem to think of it as something commonly experienced by others.
David Alan Black notes, "Paul's language suggests that the thorn he
received was peculiar to him, which would not be the case if the reference were to persecution."[9] Nor would Paul's thorn be peculiar if
his thorn were temptation, or grief, or trials in ministry, or depression,
or general demonic attacks, all of which were common experiences
of first-century believers, and even have been commonly testified to
by believers of all kinds throughout Christian history.

---

9. Black, *Paul, Apostle of Weakness*, 99.

Furthermore, the fourteen-year duration of Paul's terrible suffering combined with the fact that he was still able to carry on strenuous missionary activity despite his sufferings is somewhat unusual (more on this below). Moreover, most sufferings that people experience are not a consequence of God-given visions and revelations. In other words, Paul's suffering was not commonplace suffering; Paul's suffering was special.[10]

"AN ANGEL OF SATAN"

The fourth observation from this central sentence is that Paul refers to the thorn as "an angel of Satan" or "a messenger of Satan."[11] It is possible to translate the word *angelos* either as "angel" or "messenger," depending upon the context. But since Paul was a supernaturalist who believed in the existence of a literal devil (Rom 16:20; 1 Cor 5:5; 7:5; 2 Cor 2:11; 11:14; Eph 4:26; 6:11; 1 Thess 2:18; 2 Thess 2:9; 1 Tim 1:20; 3:6–7; 5:15; 2 Tim 2:26), and since in Paul's worldview, demons are also part of the evil forces at work in the world (1 Cor 10:20–21; 1 Tim 4:1; cf. Gal 4:8; Acts 16:16–18), and furthermore, since Paul almost always uses the term *angelos* in a supernatural way ("angel") rather than in a mundane way ("messenger") (1 Cor 4:9; 6:3; 13:1; 2 Cor 11:14; Gal 1:8; 3:9; Col 2:18; 2 Thess 1:7; 1 Tim 3:16; 5:21; unclear are 1 Cor 11:10; Gal 4:14), it is most natural to translate this expression as "angel of Satan" rather than as "messenger of Satan," and to view Paul's understanding of his malady as inflicted by a living demon who was dispatched by Satan.[12]

Please note that most interpreters take all three of the key expressions in this sentence ("thorn in the flesh," "messenger of Satan," and

---

10. Nor should we simply assume that the expression "thorn in the flesh" was a common idiom for suffering in general in the first century AD. Just because we now use it this way in the twenty-first century (primarily out of dependence upon Paul, of course!) does not constitute an argument that it was thusly employed during the first century.

11. Note Jesus's description of Satan and his demons as "the devil and his angels" in Matt 25:41. Cf. Rev 12:9.

12. Glessner, "Ethnomedical Anthropology," 26; Heckel ("Der Dorn im Fleisch," 74–75); and Bowens (*Apostle in Battle*, 152); point out that Paul never refers to his opponents as *angeloi*.

"to punch me"[13]) as very loose metaphors for suffering.[14] Paul, they say, used the word "thorn" because the condition with which he wrestled was generally painful in some way (physical interpretation), or annoying (relational interpretation), or testing (temptational interpretation), and so on. Paul used the expression "messenger of Satan," it is claimed, for the same general reason: it was truly painful, or annoying, or testing. And they continue to extend the loose metaphorical idea into the "punch" expression as well (see discussion of *kolaphizō* below). However, what I want to suggest here is that an essentially literal reading of all three expressions is the simplest and most plausible way to understand them. Paul struggled with a physical ailment that *literally* felt like he was being stabbed by something sharp and pointed, that he believed was *literally* executed by one of Satan's angels, and that ended up making him feel as though he had *literally* been pummeled in the face. The only thing that is non-literal about this interpretation is that there probably was not a visible sharp object sticking out of his skin (even though Paul might have retorted that it felt like it!).[15]

One might object that there exist no such physical conditions that would fit an essentially literal reading of each of these three expressions. But such an objection merely exposes one's presuppositions (lack of experience or knowledge) rather than arguing against the proposition.[16] In chapter 14, I will present seven physical maladies that fit an essentially literal reading of all three of these expressions.

---

13. Or, more likely, "to punch my face." More on this below.

14. Woods tersely begins her article on Paul's thorn with these words, "Any attempt to understand the meaning and application of Paul's thorn in the flesh must begin with two facts: i) the phrase is a metaphor, and ii) it has a particular context" (Woods, "Opposition to a Man," 44).

15. Paul's request that "it might leave me" (*hina apostē ap' emou*) in v. 8 may also hint at a personal being (such as a demon) rather than something impersonal. The common translation "it might be taken away from me" hides the intransitive nature of this verb. This observation is not decisive, however, since *aphistēmi*, while used for persons leaving, does on occasion refer to something annoying (like an unfortunate purchase) that the person wished would just go away. See a few papyrus examples in Peter Arzt-Grabner (with Ruth E. Kritzer), *2. Korinther*, PKNT 4 (Göttingen: Vandenhoeck & Ruprecht, 2014), 510–12. Also see comments in Abernathy, "Paul's Thorn in the Flesh," 74, and Plummer, *Second Epistle of St. Paul to the Corinthians*, 353.

16. See ch. 14 for a listing of facial neuralgias that fit the piercing flesh pain and hit-in-the-face descriptions. When one remembers that Paul was a supernaturalist who believed in the

"GIVEN" TO PAUL

The fifth observation to glean from our key sentence is that the thorn was "given" to Paul. For those less familiar with theological language, this is a classic example of what biblical scholars commonly refer to as a "divine passive." For a Jewish Christian like Paul, events did not simply happen; God either caused or permitted them to occur. So when Paul wrote that "there was given" him a "thorn in the flesh," this was another way of saying, "God allowed me to get this thorn in the flesh." Barnett comments, "This verse is powerfully intentional; each of these elements is purposive: the *skolops* was given to Paul *lest* he be 'over-uplifted,' *to* beat him, *lest* he be 'over-uplifted.' It was God's will for Paul."[17] That this is a divine passive is one of the few issues in this study generally agreed upon by most interpreters.[18]

"PUNCHED IN THE FACE"

Sixth, Paul asserts that this angel of Satan hit him in the face. This is not the first time that Paul's face/head has been highlighted in this study. We noted in chapter 3 that a common bodily location where magicians stabbed or pierced voodoo dolls was in the face, even though they also pierced their intended subjects in other places as well. Furthermore, one of the most common anatomical locations mentioned in curses by magicians of Paul's day was the face. Facial orientation will show up at later points in this study as well. In Paul's discourse (2 Cor 10–13), allusions to the face get injected at some key

---

possibility of an evil spirit inflicting bodily pain with God's permission, then viewing all three expressions as essentially literal descriptions of his experience of pain is plausible.

17. Barnett, *2 Corinthians*, 567.

18. Harris, *The Second Epistle to the Corinthians*, 855; Glessner, "Ethnomedical Anthropology," 23; Heckel, "Der Dorm im Fleisch," 69. Thomas includes a helpful list of supporters of the divine passive notion ("An Angel from Satan," 42n5). Brown cautions against indiscriminately using the language of "dual agency" to describe God's role and Satan's role in Paul's thorn, suggesting instead the language of "antithetical agency" (*God of this Age*, 186–92). Such language acknowledges that God has purposes that he seeks to accomplish through Paul's thorn, but maintains the oppositional reality of Satan's and God's intentions respectively (so also Neil Gregory Smith, "The Thorn that Stayed: An Exposition of II Corinthians 12:7–9," *Int* 13 (1959): 409–16, and Bowens, *An Apostle in Battle*, 162–165). Though the divine passive is difficult, in light of the connections with Job already drawn out, it would seem the better solution.

points in ways differing from Paul's other writings (see discussion below). Here it is worth noting that in 2 Corinthians 12:7, Paul has selected a word that evokes a face-punch to describe his thorn in the flesh.[19] The common facial orientation of the verb *kolaphizō* has been observed before, but appears not yet to have been sufficiently factored in as a component in the investigation of the nature of Paul's thorn. Most of our translations translate the word with general terms, such as "torment," "trouble," "harass," "buffet," "beat," or "hit." This general usage is possible in certain contexts, but these renderings of *kolaphizō* mask both the word's initial evocation and most common usage.[20] Harris, among others, is correct when he comments that Paul's thorn was "comparable to receiving vicious blows about the face."[21]

Let me expand a bit for the sake of clarity. Some words are more general but can be particularized using additional words if a speaker or author wants to limit the application of the word. In English, words like "hit" or "punch" are such words. But there exist other words that *can* be used generally, but still evoke certain associations even before being employed by a particular author in a particular sentence, because those words commonly have been used in particular ways in the past. That is, for some words, if you could ask people to define a word, even without a sentence, they would normally associate the word with a part of the body, because that is how those words are

---

19. Wallace notes that this word is rare outside of Christian sources and, based upon the sources we have, says: "Taken literally, Paul describes the 'angel of Satan' as striking the head (κολαφίζω)" (*Snatched into Paradise*, 273).

20. Eugene Nida comments on how we need to stay attuned to various nuances of words. He writes, "A serious deficiency in many approaches to referential meaning is the tendency to regard meaning from only one perspective. Those who concentrate upon the denotative significance of lexical units would like to reduce all meaning to a digitally manipulatable series of pluses and minuses; while those who look on meaning in terms of its connotative values see in it the numerous analogical potentialities which give rise to metaphorical extensions and subtle shadings of interrelations between meanings. The truth is that language is both digital and analogic" (*Componential Analysis of Meaning: An Introduction to Semantic Structures*, Approaches to Semiotics 57 [The Hague: Mouton, 1975], 205).

21. Harris, *Second Epistle to the Corinthians*, 857. Witherington (*Conflict and Community in Corinth*, 462) writes: "the verb here means 'batter' or 'beat about the head.'" So also Krenkel, *Beiträge*, 49n3, 64; Karl Ludwig Schmidt, "Κολαφίζω," *TDNT* 3:818; Martin, *2 Corinthians*, 608; and Heckel, "Der Dorn im Fleisch," 88, 92.

most commonly used. For example, in English, when you hear the word "stub," you initially associate it with someone's toe. When you hear the word "spank," you normally think of a person's rump. When you hear the word "slap," you customarily associate it with one's face. Without a qualifier (like "finger" for stub, "leg" for spank, or "arm" for slap), such words are of a category that a listener will initially associate with a particular part of the body unless the author uses additional words to instruct otherwise.[22]

Kolaphizō seems to be such a word. Its most common association appears to be with the face. It occasionally can be used for another part of the body if specified,[23] or more broadly for hitting in general, but its initial evocation based upon its most common usage included the face and would have implied hits on the face unless other words were added to direct a reader in a different direction. This becomes perceptible in contexts where it can actually be inferred what part of the body is being hit. Another way of stating this is that, lacking a particularizing word like "stomach" or "arm," the word *kolaphizō* would have evoked the face for a speaker of Greek. Note that such a qualifier is lacking in Paul's sentence; thus the face should be assumed.

---

22. I know that "stub" is intransitive and "spank" and "slap" are transitive. I am simply giving examples of verbs that evoke an initial connection with a part of a body.

23. One example of a different part of the body that might turn out to be an exception to the normal facial pattern of this word (probably the exception that demonstrates the rule), is the Physiologus version of the allegory of the pelican. The mother pelican strikes (*kolaphizō*) her offspring with "kisses" (on their faces) from her sharp beak (because she loves them so much) and receives back "kisses" and "beatings" (*kolaphizō*) from her young on her face. The mother pelican responds, but ends up boring a hole in their side and killing them. When the father pelican returns after three days, he strikes/pierces himself (*kolaphizō*) with his beak (this is the exception), and raises his young with the sprinkling of his blood. This story gets used by early Christians as an allegory of the piercing of Jesus on the cross. See Physiologus, Thesaurus Linguae Graecae Digital Library, http://stephanus.tlg.uci.edu.ezproxy.biola.edu/Iris/Cite?2654:002:20127, ch. 9, lines 1–20 (note esp. 7–10). Compare the earlier(?) version of Cyranides, book 3, section 39, lines 1–15, which uses the verb *kolaphizō* but does not indicate where the bird is pecking. This story clearly includes the facial orientation of *kolaphizō* but also applies it to the father bird's body. Two more intriguing items relate to this story: (1) notice that it is possible to "beat" with a sharp-pointed object (in this case, a beak of a pelican); (2) this word in this particular context also connects to the piercing and beatings of Jesus, a theme we will pick up later in the book.

There is an infrequently-used English word that may illustrate this idea, though many of us rarely use it: the English word "cuff." The Lexico (Oxford) online dictionary defines the transitive verb "cuff" as: "Strike (someone) with an open hand, especially on the head."[24] In other words, "cuff" can be used to describe hitting someone somewhere besides the face, but is used for hitting "especially on the head." Though the Greek word *kolaphizō* does not seem to be limited to an open-handed slap, it is similar to the English word "cuff" in that it probably should be defined (using the structure of the Oxford definition above) as "strike (someone) with a closed or open hand, especially on the head."[25]

Here is one example that will highlight the facial association of this verb. During the trial of Jesus, Matthew notes, "Then they spit in his face and struck (*kolaphizō*) him. And some slapped him, saying, 'Prophesy to us, you Christ! Who is it that struck you?'" (Matt 26:67–68; cf. Mark 14:65). Because of its connection with the explicit spitting "in his face" and slapping (presumably also on the face), the most natural inference is that *kolaphizō* should also be understood to be blows to the face of Jesus.[26]

Once again, this does not mean that *kolaphizō* could not have been used in settings where someone was punched elsewhere on the body, nor that it could not have been used for hitting in general—it could have been used for either, and was in fact sometimes used in a general sense (see 2 Cor 4:11; 1 Pet 2:20)—but to stress that the meaning that

24. Lexico, "Cuff," definition 2; https://www.lexico.com/en/definition/cuff.

25. Note that there also seems to be some disagreement among lexicographers about whether the hitting associated with this verb was with a closed or open hand. Moulton's note (based upon Lobeck) that *kolaphizō*, which he says was from *kolaphos*, and was vernacular for *konduloi*, which meant "knuckles," may have influenced others to view it only as with a closed fist (James Hope Moulton, *A Grammar of New Testament Greek: Vol. II: Accidence and Word-Formation* [Edinburgh: T&T Clark, 1919], 407). My reading based upon usage is that either open or closed is possible. But it really is not important for this study.

26. Epiphanius (fourth century) interpreted this word as only applying to the head, thus *stratiōtōn kolaphizontōn kephalēn* ("while the soldiers were hitting [*kolaphizō*] the head"; Epiphanius, *Panarion* (= *Adversus haereses*), Thesaurus Linguae Graecae Digital Library, http://stephanus.tlg.uci.edu.ezproxy.biola.edu/Iris/Cite?2021:002:1676304, vol. 3, p. 108, line 9.

is most naturally inferable in contexts such as the one we are studying is "to punch/slap in the face/head/ear."[27] This may prove to be a
helpful clue in seeking to identify Paul's thorn in the flesh because it
may help us with the location of Paul's bodily pain.

Furthermore, the central role of honor and shame in Paul's cultural
context—and particularly in the discourse of 2 Corinthians 10–13, not
to mention in 12:7 "to keep me from becoming conceited"—functions
as a different kind of hint that the "punching" carried out by the angel
of Satan via the thorn involved Paul's face/head. The shame-face
connection is as old as humanity itself, but the face as the primary
anatomical location where shame is primarily exhibited continues to
be studied to this day.[28] People do not hit someone in the face simply
to produce pain; they hit another's face also to disgrace and humili-
ate. The humiliation/boasting/shame theme has already surfaced in
chapter 4 (the chapter about Job) of this volume and will be discussed
further in chapter 7 since it functions as a criterion in its own right
for identifying Paul's thorn in the flesh. At this point, however, the
importance of the face and head for producing shame simply needs
to be unpacked in our discussion about the face and head. In continuing support of the notion that Paul's face and/or head may have
been involved, notice a few Old Testament examples that illustrate
the close conceptual relationship between the face/head and shame
(all italics are mine).[29]

"Then the woman [Hannah] went her way and ate, and her *face* was
no longer sad" (1 Sam 1:18), that is, from the shame of having no child.

"*Shame* is on all *faces*, and baldness on all their *heads*" (Ezek 7:18).

---

27. Some association with the ear even held on for more than a thousand years, as is seen
in the word *kolaphistikos*. Sophocles references *Vita Nili Junioris* 61 (AD 1005) as an example,
defining the adverb *kolaphistikos* as "by boxing the ears" (Sophocles, *Greek Lexicon*, 675).

28. E.g., Lauri Nummenmaa, et al., "Bodily Maps of Emotions," *Proceedings of the National
Academy of Sciences of the United States of America* 111 (2014): 646–51.

29. For more, see "Face, Facial Expressions," in *DBI*, ed. Leland Ryken, James C. Wilhoit,
and Tremper Longman (Downers Grove, IL: IVP Academic, 1998), 259–61.

"We are put to *shame*, for we have heard *reproach*; *dishonor* has covered our *face*, for foreigners have come into the holy places of the LORD's house" (Jer 51:51).

"For it is for your sake that I have borne *reproach*, that *dishonor* has covered my *face* (Psalm 69:7).

"Fill their *faces* with *shame*, that they may seek your name, O LORD (Psalm 83:16).

In a different context, the hitting (*kolaphizō*) of the face of Jesus, according to Jegher-Bucher, "clearly has the connotation of 'irritating somebody in an insulting way, humiliating somebody, making game of somebody.'"[30]

Even modern writers sometimes note the symbolic weight of the face and/or head regarding honor and shame, even in cultural contexts less saturated in notions of honor and shame. "However, you need to remember that the psychological and symbolic significance of the head in the development of self-esteem, body image, and interpersonal relationships confers special meaning on pain in this area."[31] But if this is true in a western cultural setting, surely it is doubly true in a first-century near-eastern cultural setting where honor was a central cultural value.[32]

One will notice that the connection to shame involved either face or head or both. But since Paul wrote that his "thorn" was "in the flesh," we should likely orient our thoughts toward the face rather than the rest of the head, since the face is where the flesh of the head is found.

---

30. Jegher-Bucher, "'The Thorn in the Flesh'/'Der Pfahl im Fleisch,'" 391.

31. Joanna M. Zakrzewska, "Facial Pain: Neurological and Non–Neurological," *J. Neurol.* 72 (2002): ii28.

32. One other possible hint that this word is being used in a more particular way (that is, to refer to the face/head) is that the other words in the sentence also are *particular*, both in their surface sense and in their referents. Per their surface sense, the notion of a thorn sticking in one's skin/flesh is particular, and the idea of an angel being sent by Satan is particular. Moreover, the referent—Paul's special area of suffering—is most likely something particular, as most interpreters acknowledge. Thus, although *kolaphizō* can be used more generally, the particularization of the senses of the two expressions, "thorn in the flesh" and "angel of Satan," as well as the probability that the referent also is particular, may hint that *kolaphizō* should also be used particularly as well, such as in the striking of the face.

The remainder of the head primarily consists of a skullcap covered by a thin layer of skin from which protrudes hair.

In summary, the importance of the facial orientation of *kolaphizō* has not heretofore been adequately incorporated into the discussion of Paul's thorn in the flesh. This clue, among others later to be discussed, suggests that Paul's thorn in the flesh was somehow associated with his head, and his face in particular.[33]

TO KEEP PAUL FROM
BECOMING CONCEITED

This comment leads us directly into our final observation from the central sentence itself. The purpose behind the giving of Paul's thorn was that Paul would not become conceited as a result of the revelations he had received. The comment about avoiding conceit is mentioned twice in the sentence, highlighting its importance to Paul.[34] Whatever Paul's thorn was, it was intricately connected to the issue of conceit and humility, which is another way of saying that it is tied up with honor and shame. More will be said about humiliation, honor, and shame in chapter 7.

---

33. The face/head/ear orientation (see ch. 9 for possible ear connection) was not only a connotation in Greek. The Greek word (and cognates) were borrowed and used by Latin speakers similarly (many of whom also spoke Greek). The only definition appearing for the word *colaphizo* in the Lewis and Short Latin Dictionary is "to box one's ears." See "colaphizo," in Charlton T. Lewis, *A Latin Dictionary: Lewis and Short* (Oxford: Clarendon, 1998), 364. The related noun, *colaphus*, allows for a broader usage, "a blow with the fist, a cuff, a box on the ear." Here is one example of the focus on the head: "He has loosened all my teeth; my head, too, is full of bumps with his cuffs (*colaphis*)" (P. Terentius Afer [Terence], *Adelphi: The Brother*, trans. Edward St. John Parry, Perseus Digital Library, https://www.perseus.tufts.edu). Furthermore, there may be a helpful observation in the cognate *kolazō*, which repeatedly appears in inscriptions of Lydia in connection with one's eyes (see ch. 10 for discussion of a possible eye connection). Examples in Hasan Malay and Georg Petzl, *New Religious Texts from Lydia*, ETAM 28 (Wien: Verlag der Österreichischen Akademie der Wissenschaften, 2017) include: "After being punished on her eyes" (85); "when she because of this reason was punished on her eyes, she made a vow" (142); "Pannychis was punished ... and (the goddess) struck her ... eyes" (159).

34. Most translations include the two mentions of the avoidance of pride in the sentence, though some only include it once (e.g., NIV). Probably because of its repetition, some scribes omitted the second. Nevertheless, the presence of both is the better attested reading. The repetition likely was included by Paul for emphasis, in which case it should not be viewed as redundant. See Bruce M. Metzger, *A Textual Commentary on the Greek New Testament* (London: United Bible Societies, 1971), 585.

Whose purpose was it that Paul not become conceited as a result of the revelations? The presenting answer is that it was the purpose of God, not the purpose of the messenger of Satan. (Why would an angel of Satan want Paul to avoid conceit?) Continuing this thought, if God allowed this suffering to help Paul not become proud, this is another way of saying that God was training, or disciplining, Paul.[35] Paul does not present this as after-the-fact discipline—though we might guess that Paul actually did exhibit at least some internal pride about his visions and revelations at some point after experiencing them—but is, at least in the way Paul describes it, before-the-fact discipline. God was training Paul toward humility by allowing what he suffered. So, whatever Paul's thorn in the flesh was, one criterion should be that it was understood by Paul as training or discipline from God.[36]

Certainly, God could have used various means of disciplining Paul. But the allusions to discipline will cause those familiar with ancient pedagogy to think of the discipline meted out upon young pupils in ancient Greece and Rome. Walter Hazen notes, "Discipline was strict, and inattentive or disruptive students could expect a cuff on the ear."[37] (And such discipline would not have been viewed with the same reprehension many would feel today.) Why did God allow Satan's angel to hit Paul on the face/head through the thorn? Paul says that it was

---

35. This seems to have been the view of Tertullian. Commenting on Tertullian's *De fug.* 2, Moss writes: "It is clear [from what Tertullian has written] that the thorn in the flesh, even as a messenger of Satan, is both permitted by God and serves a correctional and strengthening purpose" (Candida Moss, "The Justification of the Martyrs," in *Tertullian and Paul*, ed. Todd D. Still and David E. Wilhite, Pauline and Patristic Scholars in Debate, vol. 1 [New York: Bloomsbury, 2013], 115).

36. For a development of Paul's thorn in the flesh as education or discipline, see Garrett, "Paul's Thorn and Cultural Models of Affliction," 91–94. Heckel ("Der Dorn im Fleisch," 70) calls it "Erziehung zur Demut." Also see comments in Plummer, *Second Epistle of St. Paul to the Corinthians*, 351. Should we, perhaps, view the thorn as given to puncture Paul's arrogance whenever he started to get inflated (*hyperairōmai*) with himself? Or, to use a different analogy, perhaps his thorn functioned like a lance that would drain the pus out of a boil? For further on this, see Moss, "Christly Possession and Weakened Bodies," 322–23, 329.

37. Walter A. Hazen, *Everyday Life: Ancient Times* (Tucson, AZ: Good Year Books, 2004), 60.

first to train him not to be conceited, and then to help him learn that strength was made perfect in weakness (2 Cor 12:7, 9).

CRITERIA SUPPORTED OR ALLUDED TO IN THIS CHAPTER

1. Viewed by Paul as attacks by an angel of Satan, though permitted by God

2. Impacting Paul's physical flesh

3. Comparable to the jabbing of a sharp-pointed object

4. Impacting Paul's face (as part of his head)

5. Viewed by Paul as educational discipline by God

6. Viewed by others as humiliating and weak

7. Unusual, not like the pains of others

CLUES FROM THE LITERARY CONTEXT (PART 2)

THE PARAGRAPH
(2 CORINTHIANS 12:1–10)

The sentence in which Paul mentions his thorn appears in the middle of a paragraph (12:1–10). It seems that Paul in this paragraph is responding to one of the criticisms leveled against him by the "false apostles" (11:13), whom he sarcastically calls "super-apostles" (11:5; 12:11). It appears that they have been claiming that he, unlike they, had not received any dramatic visions or revelations from the Lord. Paul displays reticence about responding to their criticisms but feels that he must respond (12:1, 11), and thus proceeds to describe his heavenly encounter. [1]

---

1. The criticisms of the "super-apostles" seem to have included various other issues as well, even if visions and revelations are the focus of this particular paragraph. See Harris, *The Second Epistle to the Corinthians*, 69–71, for a list of likely criticisms of Paul by the false apostles, and 71–73 for Paul's criticisms of them. (Note, though, that Harris distinguishes the false-apostles

One evidence of Paul's reticence is his use of the third person ("I know a man ... " 12:2–5) to describe the heavenly ascent.[2] That Paul is talking about himself rather than someone else, though, becomes clear in 12:7, when Paul explains that he was given a thorn in the flesh "because of the surpassing greatness of the revelations" and "to keep me from becoming conceited." It is highly improbable that God would provide a dramatic heavenly experience to someone other than Paul, and, as a consequence of that other person's experience, strike Paul with some sort of suffering to keep Paul humble. Instead, Paul's use of the third person is simply one more reflection of his reticence to talk about his visions and revelations, something he feels compelled at this moment to do.[3]

What clues exist in this paragraph regarding the nature of Paul's thorn?

FOURTEEN YEARS

The first clue is the length of time that Paul suffered with the thorn: fourteen years. When diagnosing an ailment, one of the first diagnostic questions to ask is when the condition started.[4] Granted, Paul

---

designation [11:5; 12:11] from the super-apostles designation [11:13], whereas I tend toward the notion that they are different ways of referring to the same people—that is, those who were opposing Paul in Corinth. Paul simply uses the expression "super-apostles" derogatorily to refer to what they portrayed themselves to be—that is, better than Paul.)

2. "By casting his (autobiographical!) report in the third person, Paul thus distinguishes his present self (= the challenged apostle) from his ecstatic self ('14 years ago')," (Russell P. Spittler, "The Limits of Ecstasy: An Exegesis of 2 Corinthians 12:1–10," in *Current Issues in Biblical and Patristic Interpretation: Studies in Honor of Merrill C. Tenney presented by his Former Students,* ed. Gerald F. Hawthorne [Grand Rapids: Eerdmans, 1975], 264). Similarly, Barrett, *Second Epistle to the Corinthians,* 307.

3. For a contrary view, see Michael D. Goulder, "Visions and Revelations of the Lord (2 Corinthians 12:1–10)," in *Paul and the Corinthians: Studies on a Community in Conflict: Essays in Honour of Margaret Thrall,* ed. Trevor J. Burke and J. Keith Elliott, NovTSup 109 (Leiden: Brill, 2003), 303–12.

4. Modern medical professionals are taught to ask a set of questions during intake of patients. One way to remember the questions is with an acronym: OLD CART. Each letter stands for a word: Onset (When did it start?); Location (Where is the pain located?); Duration (How long does the pain last?); Character (How severe is it?); Aggravating/Alleviating factors (Does anything make it worse or better?); Radiation (Does the pain extend to other places?); Timing (How often?); see Lynn S. Bickley and Peter G. Szilagyi, *Bates' Guide to Physical*

does not explicitly say that he suffered with the thorn in the flesh for fourteen years, but that is a natural inference from what he writes.[5] He states that the heavenly ascent occurred fourteen years prior to his writing (12:2). He also states that the thorn was given to keep him from becoming conceited about the revelations he heard during the ascent (12:7). How soon after seeing what he saw (visions, 12:1) and hearing what he heard (revelations, 12:1, 7) would Paul have been tempted toward arrogance? Since Paul claims that the thorn was given to keep him "from becoming conceited because of the surpassing greatness of the revelations" (12:7), it is probable that the thorn commenced immediately after his heavenly ascent rather than at some other time. Whatever it was that Paul suffered, it was lengthy in duration.[6]

It is common to date the writing of 2 Corinthians somewhere between AD 54 and 56. Fourteen years prior brings us back to a time between AD 40 and 43 (depending upon the use or non-use of inclusive reckoning). This entails that Paul would have suffered on-and-off with his ailment during some of the silent years in Tarsus and Cilicia, during his ministry in Antioch, during the first missionary journey (including his visit to south Galatia[7]), during the second missionary journey (including his ministry in Corinth), and during the third missionary journey up until he wrote 2 Corinthians (including his ministry in Ephesus). More than two-thirds of Paul's Christian life had already been accompanied by the pain of the thorn when he wrote about it in 2 Corinthians 12:7.

Examination and History Taking, 12th ed. (Philadelphia: Wolters Kluwer; Lippincott Williams & Wilkins, 2017), 79. Per our discussion here, the *onset* for Paul was connected with his heavenly vision fourteen years prior to writing; the *duration* seems to have either been for the entire fourteen years, possibly focused on three more intense periods during those fourteen years. (I argue elsewhere in this book that the *location* is Paul's face, the *character* is excruciating, and stress may be an *aggravating factor*. The other questions may be unanswerable.)

5. Glessner, "Ethnomedical Anthropology," 27.

6. Heckel, "Der Dorn im Fleisch," 71. Moss ("Christly Possession and Weakened Bodies," 323) writes: "One can infer from Paul's triple-request for the removal of the thorn that it is a permanent or at least prolonged condition."

7. For the meaning of "Galatia," see Mark Wilson, "Galatia in Text, Geography, and Archaeology," *BAR* (Fall 2020): 54–56.

Still, Paul's thorn had to be of a category that would have permitted extensive travel, including a multitude of hardships that accompanied such travel in the ancient world, and furthermore, had to allow Paul to conduct a vigorous ministry. If the physical pain proposal that I have begun to defend is correct, then Paul's pain could not have been unrelenting pain, but either had to consist of periods of excruciating pain separated by long periods of no pain, or, more likely, had to be a condition in which little or no pain was normally present, but in which Paul would get jabbed with short-term, pain-intense episodes. (Such conditions do exist; see ch. 14.)

The long-term (fourteen-year) duration of Paul's thorn, accordingly, should function as one of the criteria for determining the nature of Paul's thorn in the flesh, but intermittency should be factored in as well.

CONNECTED TO THE HEAVENLY ASCENT

A second clue in the paragraph outside the main sentence itself emerges when we connect Paul's thorn to the heavenly vision he saw and the revelation he heard (whether he was "in the body or out of the body"[8]). Clearly, the second, the thorn, was given to him because of the first, the heavenly ascent.[9] The connection between

---

8. "[A]s the ancient visionaries were said to have traveled sometimes physically (Enoch, Elijah, Baruch), and sometimes astrally (Ezekiel, Moses), Paul also knows both as theoretical possibilities" (Price, "Punished in Paradise," 34). Shantz notes that uncertainty about whether something took place bodily is one common characteristic of testimonies about ecstatic experiences. "The experience of religious ecstasy bears virtually universal characteristics that undergird the culturally determined differences in interpretation. These include disturbance of bodily awareness, often experienced as disembodiment; ineffability; a sense of timelessness; and blurred boundaries of the self—or, to put it positively if somewhat vaguely, a sense of participation in a greater category of being." She adds further, "Like other ecstatic thinkers, Paul genuinely could not know the status of his body by using the sensate signals that would normally inform him. The question of whether he was in the body or outside it is not simply a rhetorical means of dismissing the issue; it is rather an account of one of the phenomena of trance. (Colleen Shantz, *Paul in Ecstasy: The Neurobiology of the Apostle's Life and Thought* [Cambridge: Cambridge University Press, 2009], 71, 98).

9. "There is a clear connection between the heavenly revelation that Paul experienced and the thorn which he was given. Rather than making him immune to infirmities, in this case Paul's visit to the third heaven led to an illness" (Thomas, "'An Angel from Satan,'" 51; see also

the vision and the thorn is confirmed by the twice-repeated purpose statement "in order that" (*hina*) in 12:7 (and a "therefore" [*dio*] in some manuscripts). This is significant because in Paul's world, many people were aware that those who had experienced encounters with God or with angelic representatives of God, or who saw dramatic dreams or visions—think of the examples from the book of Daniel— sometimes ended up anxious or alarmed (Daniel 7:15, 28), discolored (7:28), without strength (10:8, 16), unable to speak (10:15), experiencing pain (10:16), or even falling ill (8:27).[10] This is an additional clue that what we are dealing with could be a physical malady rather than something else.

SEEING AND HEARING

A third clue may lie in the words that immediately precede Paul's mention of his thorn. In 12:6, Paul writes, "but I refrain from it [boasting], so that no one may think more of me than *he sees in me* or *hears from me*" (italics mine). It makes perfect sense for Paul to comment on what someone hears from him, but why comment on what they "see in me" (or "see me," *blepei me*)? Except for the manner in which this comment gets juxtaposed with 12:7, Paul's extra comment about what they see might not be worth mentioning. But since this comment directly leads into Paul's stated reason for why he was given his thorn in the flesh, we need to consider the possibility that Paul might be making a comment about what people *observed* when they encountered Paul,

---

Thomas, *The Devil, Disease and Deliverance: Origins of Illness in New Testament Thought*, 62–63, 73). For more on possible connections between the ascent and the thorn, see Gooder, *Only the Third Heaven?*, 170–72.

10. Schmidt comments: "In the study of ancient religion and medicine there is a connection with 'visions and ecstatic experiences' and physical ailment" (Schmidt, *TDNT* 3:820). Cf. Rev. 1:17, where John "fell at his feet as though dead." Kruse suggests a parallel that slightly postdates Paul where physical ailment accompanied an ecstatic experience: "And in the Babylonian Talmud (*Hagigah* 14b) there is the story of four rabbis who were temporarily taken up into Paradise, but so awesome was the experience that only one, Rabbi Akiba, returned unharmed" (Kruse, *2 Corinthians*, 202). Wallace writes: "This close connection is all the more likely since ascent to heaven was often connected to physical suffering and/or demonic or angelic attack in the ancient world" (Wallace, *Snatched into Paradise*, 269; see also 269–70n113). For more examples, see Bowens, *Apostle in Battle*, 181–89.

which, as we will explain in the following chapter, was someone with
a weak bodily presence (10:10).[11] Another way of stating the issue
is this: Many interpreters interpret the hearing part of this verse as
a reference to something specific, that is, to Paul's speech; whereas
they interpret the seeing part broadly, as the general life Paul lived.[12]
Perhaps in light of the direction everything else is moving in this
study, we should consider taking them both more specifically: Paul
is referring to what they see when they look at Paul (his weak body,
or even possibly visible physical damage) and what they hear from
Paul when he speaks (his weak rhetoric).

EXCRUCIATING

Fourth, there is a set of clues that suggest that Paul's thorn was not
simply annoying; it was excruciating. The starting point, of course, is
that Paul labeled this area of suffering as a "thorn" or a "stake" in his
"flesh." The description on its own sounds excruciating.[13]

Furthermore, Paul pleaded three times that it would leave him
(12:8). It is unlikely that these three requests occurred during a single
prayer time one day in which Paul bowed his head and implored,
"Take it away, take it away, take it away!" Rather, we would do better
to think of three separate periods of prayer in which Paul dedicated
himself to request the removal of the thorn—spaced out over a period
of fourteen years. As an analogy, my wife and I entered into four separate periods of dedicated prayer that were spaced out over ten years
about whether God wanted us to adopt two more children beyond
the two we already had. (We finally did adopt two daughters, ages

---

11. The connection might even be strengthened if the mention of the revelations ("because
of the surpassing greatness of the revelations") is viewed as part of the sentence found in v. 6
(as rendered by the NRSV, NIV, CSB, and NET) rather than as leading off the sentence found
in v. 7 (as in ESV, NASB, KJV).

12. Scott J. Hafemann, 2 *Corinthians*, BECNT (Grand Rapids: Baker, 2015), 460–61; Harris,
2 *Corinthians*, 850–851; Guthrie, 2 *Corinthians*, 587. Akin ("Triumphalism," 137) says that Paul
is simply saying, "Examine my walk and words" (i.e., words are specific, walk is general).

13. "The Apostle speaks of physical pain of a very acute kind; for nothing less can be
implied by his metaphor of a stake driven through his flesh" (Lightfoot, *Galatians*, 189).

nine and eleven, after the final of the four seasons of prayer. Paul, in contrast, appears to have stopped asking for the removal of the thorn after his third period of prayer, 12:9.) In support of the idea that Paul's process of prayer spanned many years, compare the "three times I asked the Lord" of 12:8 with the "three times I was beaten with rods," and "three times I was shipwrecked," of 2 Corinthians 11:25—both of which occurred over a period of years.[14] Simply stated: the many years Paul dealt with the thorn (fourteen years) would have intensified his agony.

Notice, furthermore, that Paul did not simply ask for the thorn to be removed, he "pleaded" (ESV, NIV) or "begged" (NLT) that it might leave him (12:8). The word used here (*parakaleō*) does not require such a vigorous translation as "pleaded" or "begged," but this passage is similar to other passages (such as Acts 16:9) where such a pleading connotation makes more sense than other possibilities, as agreed upon by many translators. In other words, a pleading connotation makes sense in this passage because he is repeatedly turning a prayer in God's direction asking for the removal of something so disturbing that he described it as a thorn in the flesh. And if Paul was pleading rather than simply asking, this also is suggestive of the excruciating nature of Paul's thorn.

That Paul's thorn was excruciating, and not simply annoying, is also supported by other issues already detailed: Paul described his ailment as a thorn or stake in his flesh, like a messenger or angel of Satan, like being punched in the face, and analogous to Job's excruciating pain. These all support the excruciating nature of Paul's thorn. Furthermore, the placement of this particular area of suffering shortly after Paul's most extensive sufferings list (11:23–33) in a letter that

---

14. Brown, *God of This Age*, 185n202, following Harris, *2 Corinthians*, 860–61. Furthermore, in light of Jesus's teaching that people should continue to pray and not give up (Luke 11:5–13; 18:1–8) combined with Paul's own entreaties that we persevere in prayer (Eph 6:18; Col 4:2; 1 Thess 5:17), it seems unlikely that Paul would pray three times about something, say, over the course of a day or a week, and then stop praying after receiving the message about strength-in-weakness from God (2 Cor 12:8–10).

contains other impressive sufferings lists (4:7–11; 6:3–10), suggests that Paul viewed this particular suffering as the pinnacle of his sufferings, not simply as one among others.[15] Moreover, the honor-and-shame connotations in the discourse (mentioned already, and more coming in ch. 7) intensify the discussion in a way that people who do not live in honor-shame cultures might have trouble fully grasping.

WEAKNESSES

A fifth clue concerning the nature of Paul's thorn is the pluralizing of the word "weakness." It appears that Paul took the word "weakness" (*astheneia*, 2 Cor 11:30; first usage of 12:9; cf. 1:21, 29), which he originally employed as a counterpoint to the boasting of the false apostles in Corinth, and turned it into *plural* "weaknesses" (*astheneiai*) in 12:5 as he prepared to mention the thorn. Immediately following the mention of the thorn in 12:7, he pluralized "weaknesses" again in 12:9 (second usage) and again in 12:10 (third usage).

We need to consider the possibility that Paul was nodding toward a bodily sickness, pain, or disability in this (apparently) intentional move on his part. Certainly, "weaknesses" (*astheneiai*) as a plural can apply to weaknesses other than physical ailments; but in the New Testament it normally does not. Outside of this paragraph (2 Cor 12:1–10), "weakness" (*astheneia*) as a singular is used *nine* times for something that is not a physical ailment (Rom 6:19; 8:26; 1 Cor 2:3; 15:43; 2 Cor 11:30; 13:4; Heb 5:2; 7:28; 11:34), *four* times as a singular for a physical ailment (Luke 13:11–12; John 5:5; 11:4; and Paul's own in Gal 4:13), and *five* times as a plural for a physical ailment (Matt 8:17; Luke 5:15; 8:2; Acts 28:9; 1 Tim 5:23). Only once is it used as a plural for a non-physical weakness (Heb 4:15). This pluralizing-for-physical-ailment pattern suggests that Paul had a physical ailment in mind in this passage.

---

15. In addition to being the objective pinnacle of his sufferings (the thing that caused him the most agony), it may also function as a literary pinnacle. Akin ("Triumphalism," 123) notes that the paragraph (12:1–10) under discussion is "often argued to be the climax and primary focus of 2 Corinthians 10–13, keeping in mind of course its vital relationship to 11:16–33."

Even more to the point, Paul's switch to the plural in the verses surrounding the mention of his thorn appears intentional, particularly when contrasted to the general theme of weakness (of various kinds) that pervades 2 Corinthians 10–13, and indeed, all of the Corinthian correspondence.[16] Paul can write generally about weakness in 2 Corinthians 11 in contrast to the boasting of the false apostles in Corinth ("If I must boast, I will boast of the things that show my weakness," 2 Cor 11:30), and he can state a general axiom about weakness ("power is made perfect in weakness," 12:9), but just before and just after his thorn discussion, he writes about "weaknesses" as a plural (2 Cor 12:5, 9–10).

It is important that the reader does not misunderstand. My claim is not that Paul uses a word in the plural that must mean physical ailment, only that Paul's pluralizing looks intentional, and appears to have been done for the purpose of particularization. If we had the opportunity to ask Paul what particular weaknesses he had in mind when he pluralized this word, we should anticipate that he would comment on something that was a physical sickness, disability, or bodily pain, since that is the normal usage of the plural of this word in the New Testament.[17]

Tied to this discussion, but perhaps standing as a clue on its own, is that Paul has failed to clearly mention sickness or physical disability anywhere else in any of his lists of sufferings in 2 Corinthians. This, despite the fact that we know that Paul personally was sick (Gal 4:13), as were close co-workers (Epaphroditus, Phil 2:26–27; Timothy, 1

---

16. For more on Paul's theology of weakness in the Corinthian letters, see Black, *Paul, Apostle of Weakness*, 53–111, 154–58, and Timothy B. Savage, *Power through Weakness: Paul's Understanding of the Christian Ministry in 2 Corinthians* (Cambridge: Cambridge University Press, 1996), 103–90 (particularly 2 Cor 1–9 for Savage).

17. I can see another way to understand Paul's apparent pluralizing "weaknesses" (*astheneiai*) in 2 Cor 12:5, 9–10. That is, in v. 10, Paul intends the plural "weaknesses" (*astheneiai*) to stand as a heading for the other words that follow ("in … insults, hardships, persecutions, and calamities"; *en hybresin, en anankais, en diōgmais kai stenochōriais*). But it seems more likely to me that Paul heads his list with the word that is theologically important in his response to the boasting of the false apostles in Corinth, and he includes the others as additional items on the list rather than as subsumed under a headword.

Tim 5:23; and Trophimus, 2 Tim 4:20).[18] This failure to mention
sickness is significant because in 2 Corinthians Paul has used his sufferings as a badge of his apostleship, as though he were claiming, "I
have suffered in every way possible." But why did he leave sickness
off his multiple mentions of suffering in 2 Corinthians, even though
he was not reticent to mention illness outside of 2 Corinthians? A
look at Paul's lists of sufferings in 2 Corinthians will bring home the
significance of this observation.

How Paul describes the various types of suffering he endured leading up
to his thorn-in-the-flesh comment (2 Corinthians only)

1:4–11

    All our afflictions
    We share abundantly in Christ's sufferings
    Burdened beyond our strength
    Despaired of life itself
    We felt that we had received the sentence of death
    Deadly peril

2:4

    Much affliction
    Anguish of heart
    Many tears

2:13

    My spirit was not at rest

4:8–12

    Jars of clay
    Afflicted in every way
    Perplexed

---

18. Black (*Paul, Apostle of Weakness*, 153) agrees that each of these uses of *astheneia* refers
to bodily illness. Glessner ("Ethnomedical Anthropology," 18–19) reminds us that the illnesses
of Paul's three colleagues were written in a collectivist mindset, where their illnesses impacted
the communities to which they were connected.

Persecuted
Struck down
Always carrying about in our bodies the death of Jesus
Always being given over to death for Jesus's sake
Death at work in us

4:16
Outer self wasting away
Light momentary affliction

5:2–4
In this tent we groan
Being burdened

6:4–10
Afflictions
Hardships
Calamities
Beatings
Imprisonments
Riots
Labors
Sleepless nights
Hunger
Dishonor
Slander
Treated as impostors
Treated as unknown
Treated as dying
Treated as punished
Treated as sorrowful
Treated as poor
Treated as having nothing

7:4
Our affliction

7:5–6

> Our bodies had no rest
> Afflicted at every turn
> Fighting without
> Fears within
> Downcast

11:23–32

> Labors
> Imprisonments
> Countless beatings
> Often near death
> Three times beaten with rods
> Once stoned
> Three times shipwrecked
> A night and a day adrift at sea
> Frequent journeys
> Danger from rivers
> Danger from robbers
> Danger from my own people
> Danger from gentiles
> Danger in the city
> Danger in the wilderness
> Danger at sea
> Danger from false brothers
> Toil
> Hardship
> Many a sleepless night
> Hunger and thirst
> Often without food
> Cold and exposure
> Daily pressure of anxiety for all the churches
> My weakness
> Let down in a basket through a window in a city wall

The natural inference from observing what Paul did and did not include on these lists is that Paul left sickness off these other lists because his thorn, which was an acutely painful and difficult weakness, was itself a sickness or physical ailment. Paul felt compelled by the criticisms he was hearing from Corinth to mention his thorn in the flesh at some point, but chose to wait to include it until much later in his letter. Why did Paul fail to mention sickness or physical ailment anywhere among this extensive compilation of sufferings he amassed in 2 Corinthians? I would suggest that Paul planned to mention a particularly acute suffering as part of his argument, but was waiting until the right moment in his letter to mention it—after he had listed all his other sufferings. The absence of such physical-ailment comments among all these other sufferings is most easily explained as Paul waiting to deal with the physical pain he experienced (and that everyone knew he experienced) until late in his letter.

CONNECTED TO OTHER SUFFERINGS

A final clue in this paragraph concerning the nature of Paul's thorn is that whatever Paul suffered seems to connect in some way with the five general descriptions of suffering at the end of the paragraph. Paul concluded his paragraph with five difficulties about which he had chosen to be content: weaknesses, insults, hardships, persecutions, and calamities (2 Cor 12:10).[19] We have already mentioned his pluralizing of "weaknesses" above, which itself may suggest a physical-illness explanation of some kind, but we should notice that Paul might be flagging for us that his thorn belongs in a list that includes insults, hardships, persecutions, and calamities.[20] This observation does not suggest much positively about Paul's thorn, but does negatively exclude a few suggestions for

---

19. *En astheneiais, en hybresin, en anankais, en diōgmais kai stenochōriais;* "in weaknesses, in insults, hardships, persecutions, and calamities" (2 Cor 12:10).

20. Wilkinson, *The Bible and Healing*, 211. Moss ("Christly Possession and Weakened Bodies," 327) comments on the list in v. 10: "One should be attentive to Paul's taxonomy of hardship. This particular categorization is typical of many authors in the Jesus movement for whom physical impairments fell into a broader category of *thlipsis—suffering* or *affliction*. While not all disabilities were categorized as 'suffering,' this larger category can encompass disability, disease, alienation, and persecution."

the nature of Paul's thorn, such as internal wrestling with lust, despair, grief, anger, or depression.[21] Such internal struggles do not fit well in a list that includes insults, hardships, persecutions, and calamities, despite how many other hardships could potentially fit into such a general list. Paul's thorn, though, cannot simply be equated with external persecutions, for Paul's theology suggests that he would not ask God to take away his persecutions in general the way Paul three times asked for his thorn to be taken away (2 Cor 12:8). Paul's approach to persecutions in his letters and Acts would also argue against the notion that his thorn was simply the persecutions he endured.[22] Nor can his thorn be equated with people who disagreed with him and tried to lead his converts astray, since Paul insinuated that his thorn commenced after the heavenly vision fourteen years prior (2 Cor 12:2), and Paul had encountered antagonists (not to mention physical persecutions) from the earliest days after his conversion (Acts 9:22–30).[23] This criterion, then, is limited in its value as a criterion, but it does hold a certain amount of value for excluding a few of the other suggestions for Paul's thorn in the flesh.

CRITERIA SUPPORTED OR ALLUDED TO IN THIS CHAPTER

1. Excruciating, not simply annoying

2. Viewed by others as humiliating and weak

3. Long-term, but intermittent

4. Analogous to Paul's other sufferings

5. Connected to the heavenly ascent

6. Visible bodily damage

---

21. See list of alternate suggestions for Paul's thorn in the flesh in ch. 2.

22. Yoon, "Paul's Thorn and His Gnosis," 35–39. Yoon is correct in observing that persecutions (like repeated beatings) in and of themselves apparently did not hinder Paul from continuing to pursue his mission, but Yoon's unsupported opinion that the same observation should be applied to any physical ailment is *non sequitur* (39). I can think of a litany of serious physical ailments that could have impacted Paul's ability to travel or preach.

23. Thomas, "'An Angel from Satan,'" 46–47.

CLUES FROM THE LITERARY CONTEXT (PART 3)

THE DISCOURSE (2 CORINTHIANS 10–13)

The next largest concentric circle is the discourse. By "discourse," I refer to a portion of writing that holds together as a unit, shares overlapping themes, and was composed for a central purpose.[1] The central purpose of the discourse surrounding Paul's mention of his thorn in the flesh (2 Cor 10–13) seems to be Paul's reply to verbal attacks by false apostles in Corinth (11:13), whom Paul also refers to sarcastically as "super-apostles" (11:5; 12:11). Paul uses this term of sarcasm twice to call out certain self-proclaimed apostles who had wormed their way into the Corinthian church and started challenging Paul's qualifications as an apostle. Primarily, it appears that

---

1. For helpful discussion about the nature and limits of a discourse, see Dan McCartney and Charles Clayton, *Let the Reader Understand: A Guide to Interpreting and Applying the Bible* (Phillipsburg, NJ: P&R, 2002), 180–86.

these "apostles" claimed that Paul was weak. Paul was purportedly weak in that he experienced sufferings, he was weak in that he didn't speak well enough, he was weak because he hadn't received visions and revelations, he was weak in his physical presentation, and he was weak in regard to this ailment that he referred to as a "thorn in the flesh." The tone of 2 Corinthians markedly changes at chapter 10 from the earlier nine chapters. Previously in the letter, Paul mostly has presented himself as warm and encouraging, but now Paul allows his frustration to boil over, and displays it through derisive and sarcastic prose. Perhaps Paul had received new information about the developing antagonism in Corinth. Perhaps he purposely saved the contentious section of his letter until the end. Some have suggested that chapters 10–13 constitute a different letter altogether, although, as I already note in chapter 1, I am skeptical of that suggestion. Regardless, these four chapters hold tightly together as a single discourse, as almost everyone who has studied these chapters agrees. The casual reader should not be led astray into thinking that a comment by Paul in chapters 10 or 11 is irrelevant for understanding what is going on in chapter 12, since the content and flow of thought in the discourse of chapters 10–13 is closely intertwined. What clues about the nature of Paul's thorn in the flesh lie in this four-chapter discourse?

WEAK BODY

The first clue is on the surface. In 10:10 Paul relates what some people (or possibly one person) in Corinth have been insultingly saying about him. "For they say (lit. "he says"), 'His letters are weighty and strong, but his bodily presence is weak, and his speech of no account.'" It appears that Paul's detractors are criticizing, not just Paul's presence in general, but also the weakness of his body (lit. "the presence of the body [is] weak" *he parousia tou sōmatos asthenēs*). According to their criticisms, Paul struggles with two things: (1) something related to his verbal communication (which they viewed as disdainful, *exouthenēmenos*), and (2) something related to his *weak body*. Their criticism could be viewed as two separate criticisms (poor speech and weak body), or the two could be interconnected in some way (a bodily weakness that affected his speech). Some translators have generalized the expression to "personal presence" (NASB; cf. NIV) or "physical presence" (CSB, NET) instead of employing the more literal "bodily presence" (ESV, NRSV, NKJV). There is no appropriate textual reason, however, to translate it other than "bodily presence"; and even in that way of rendering it into English, the fact that "body" (*soma*) in Greek is a noun rather than an adjective is unrecognized. A more direct translation maintaining *soma* as a noun would be: "the presence of his body is weak." If one were to focus only upon Paul's rhetorical weakness, perhaps the generalization of this expression might be passably acceptable. However, there seems to have existed a long list of accusations leveled against Paul in Corinth (no commendation letters, lording over converts, not accepting payment for ministry, lacking appropriate marks of apostleship, weakness of various kinds, not keeping promises).[2] The false apostles did not merely criticize Paul's speaking ability. As the most straightforward reading of 2 Corinthians 10:10 indicates, one of the criticisms that had been leveled against Paul in Corinth is that when Paul had been with them, his physical body appeared weak.

HUMILIATION, WEAKNESS, AND SHAME

The second clue in the discourse is found in the closely intertwined themes of humiliation, weakness, and shame that permeate the entire section. It appears that at least some in Corinth not only thought of Paul as generally weak, but highlighted his weakness, and sought to use his weakness to discredit him. The accusation that Paul was weak seems to lie behind much of Paul's defense in 2 Corinthians 10–13. Let us observe how chapters 10–13 are saturated with the intertwining themes of humiliation, weakness, and shame. I will spend a bit more time drawing out this theme to emphasize its significance in the discourse.

---

2. Harris, *Second Epistle to the Corinthians*, 69–71.

Paul begins in 10:1 writing ironic words, "by the meekness and gentleness of Christ," commenting that he is "humble" when he is with them, but "bold" when away. In 10:2–6 he warns the Corinthians that he has no desire to show up in "boldness," be forced to wage war against the ideas being promulgated in Corinth, and be compelled to "punish every disobedience."

In 10:7 he alludes to the overconfidence of the Corinthians. In 10:8 he ironically asserts that if he "boasts" about his authority, he will "not be ashamed."[3] In 10:10 he mentions the accusation that his bodily presence is "weak" (as we previously discussed). In 10:12 he comments on "comparing ourselves" with those who are "commending themselves."

In 10:13–18 Paul writes that he will not "boast" beyond the sphere of ministry God assigned to him and not about the assigned ministries of others. He even includes a compressed citation of Jeremiah 9:23–24 in verse 17, "Let the one who boasts, boast in the Lord" (cf. 1 Cor 1:31). He concludes the paragraph with the words: "it is not the one who commends himself who is approved, but the one whom the Lord commends" (10:18).

Paul writes, sarcastically once again, in 11:1, "I wish you would bear with me in a little foolishness." Again, sarcastically, he comments in 11:4 that the Corinthians happily put up with people who preach a different gospel. Then, bitingly, he labels the false apostles as "super-apostles" in 11:5 and claims that he is not at all "inferior" to them.

Sarcastically, once again, Paul asks in 11:7 whether it was somehow a sin "in humbling myself so that you might be exalted" when preaching the gospel without charge to the Corinthians. He says that his "boasting" about not taking money from them will not be silenced because he loves them and is looking out for them (11:10–11). The false apostles, however, are boasting about their work (11:12).

---

3. For more on Paul's understanding of boasting, see Duane F. Watson, "Paul and Boasting," in *Paul in the Greco-Roman World: A Handbook*, ed. J. Paul Sampley, 2nd ed. (London: Bloomsbury, 2016), 90–112, and Kar Young Lim, *The Sufferings of Christ are Abundant in Us: A Narrative Dynamics Investigation of Paul's Sufferings in 2 Corinthians*, TTCLBS 399 (London: T&T Clark, 2009), 162–74.

In 11:16 Paul repeats himself: "let no one think me foolish. But even if you do, accept me as a fool, so that I too may boast a little." Then in 11:18: "Since many boast according to the flesh, I too will boast." In 11:19–20 he accuses the Corinthians of putting up with "fools," but adds sarcastically, "To my shame, I must say, we were too weak for that!" (11:21) and tips off his rhetorical strategy. This is where he starts to employ an unusual rhetorical device that scholars usually refer to as Paul's fool speech. He takes on the guise of a fool to expose the foolishness of the boasting of the false apostles in Corinth.[4] "I am speaking as a fool" and so will "boast" in whatever categories Paul's detractors are boasting of, launching into the longest list of sufferings found in any of Paul's letters (11:23–33). In the midst of this list, he writes, "Who is weak, and I am not weak?" (11:29) and "If I must boast, I will boast of the things that show my weakness" (11:30), concluding the list with an event that would have been viewed as shameful in his cultural context, the escape in a basket through a window in the city wall of Damascus (11:32–33; cf. Acts 9:23–25).[5]

The humiliation, weakness, and shame theme continues in our central paragraph, 2 Corinthians 12:1–10. Paul begins the description of his heavenly ascent by writing "I must go on boasting. Though there is nothing to be gained by it ... " (12:1). When he switches tone, he writes, "On behalf of this man I will boast, but on my own behalf I will not boast, except of my weaknesses" (12:5). He continues in verse 6, "Though if I should wish to boast, I would not be a fool ... " The thorn in the flesh was given "to keep me from being too elated" (stated twice in 12:7). When Paul begged for it to leave him, God's response was: "my power is made perfect in weakness" (12:8). Paul's response was to "boast all the more gladly of my weakness so that the power of

---

4. Lambrecht, "The Fool's Speech," 305–24. The starting point and finishing point of the "fool's speech" is disputed, but I view it as starting at 11:21b and finishing at 12:10.

5. Lim, *The Sufferings of Christ*, 181–82. Barrett comments: "In fact the verses [32–33] are a crowning illustration of the weakness and humiliation of which Paul speaks and boasts. Do you doubt either the depth of the humiliation I have experienced or my willingness to accept it?" (Barrett, *Second Epistle to the Corinthians*, 303).

Christ may rest upon me" (12:9), and adds that he is "content" with weaknesses and suffering "For when I am weak, then I am strong."[6]

The theme of humiliation, weakness, and shame continues after our central paragraph. In 12:11 Paul writes, "I have been a fool! You forced me to it, for I ought to have been commended by you." He goes on to say that he is not "inferior" to the "super-apostles," and then invokes a humility statement "even though I am nothing." Drawing upon sarcasm once again, Paul chides the Corinthians: "Forgive me this wrong!" (12:13)—that is, the wrong of not burdening them (presumably financially; see 11:7–11). Again, sarcastically, he writes, "I was crafty, you say, and got the better of you by deceit" (12:16).

Paul's defensiveness leaks out again in 12:19 when he comments that he is not simply defending himself, but trying to speak for the upbuilding of the Corinthians. He lays out some of his fears: that he won't find them to be what he is hoping and that they won't find Paul to be what they are hoping (12:20). His fears for them are that he will come and find the church overtaken by quarreling, hostility, conceit, and disorder. His fear for himself he states directly: "I fear that when I come again my God may humble me before you," and that he might have to mourn over those who have not repented from immoral lifestyles (12:21).

The humiliation, weakness, and shame theme continues in 13:1–2, when Paul invokes the witness of God and himself (as "in Christ") as the two (or three) witnesses required to challenge the Corinthians, which Paul plans to do on his upcoming third visit to Corinth.[7] The Corinthians were apparently seeking proof that Christ was actually

---

6. Martin Albl writes, "One may perhaps detect a movement in Paul's own thought. He at first stigmatized the disability as a demonic force, a 'messenger of Satan,' and he sought to be free from it. But after his revelation from the Lord, Paul interprets the disability as a condition about which he will be content and even 'boast.' He sees that the disability, even if instrumentally associated with the demonic, is ultimately of divine origin and has a divine purpose" (Martin Albl, "'For Whenever I Am Weak, Then I Am Strong': Disability in Paul's Epistles," in This Abled Body: Rethinking Disabilities in Biblical Studies, ed. Hector Avalos et. al., SemeiaSt 55 [Atlanta: Society of Biblical Literature, 2007], 157).

7. Kenneth Berding, "God and Paul (in Christ) On Three Visits as the 'Two or Three Witnesses' of 2 Corinthians 13:1," JSPL 7 (2017): 5–25.

speaking in Paul (13:3). Paul says that the Christ who is in him "is not weak in dealing with you, but is powerful among you. For he was crucified in weakness, but lives by the power of God. For we also are weak in him, but in dealing with you we will live with him by the power of God" (13:3-4).

Paul challenges them to test themselves to see whether they are in fact in the faith, but confirms that he has not failed the test, "though we may seem to have failed" (13:5-7). Thus, Paul adds, "For we are glad when we are weak and you are strong" (13:9). He says that he wrote these things at a distance so that he does not have to be "severe" in his use of his God-given authority when he comes to them (13:10).

Considering how saturated chapters 10–13 are with the ideas of humiliation, weakness, and shame, and in light of the fact that Paul's comment about his thorn (12:7) is surrounded by these comments and intertwined with them, it seems reasonable to assume that Paul's thorn in the flesh would have been viewed by observers as humiliating and weak. This will function as one of the twenty criteria for narrowing the possibilities for what constituted Paul's thorn in the flesh.

FACIAL ALLUSIONS

The third clue found in the discourse of 2 Corinthians 10–13 that will help us understand Paul's thorn is Paul's concentrated use of facial terminology and allusions to the face especially in, but not limited to, chapters 10–11, the two chapters leading up to Paul's mention of his thorn. This concentration of facial language and allusions may suggest that Paul's face is somehow involved in their criticisms. In this regard, it is, perhaps, noteworthy that of the twenty-two times Paul uses the word commonly translated as "face" (*prosōpon*, with a variety of nuances), twelve of those are in 2 Corinthians. That alone is worth mentioning. But the placement and nature of Paul's used of *prosōpon* and other facial terminology in 2 Corinthians 10:1, 10:7, 11:13-15, 11:20 (and 12:7, *kolaphizō* per our earlier discussion) hints that Paul sarcastically mentions faces because Paul's critics may have been criticizing Paul's face.

In 10:1 Paul comes out swinging with the words, "I, Paul, myself entreat you, by the meekness and gentleness of Christ—I who am humble when face to face with you, but bold toward you when I am away!" These words are biting and ironic, and straightway alter the tone of the letter. Of course, "face to face" has as its primary function in this sentence to indicate that Paul was sometimes "present" (see Acts 25:16; Gal 2:11), as opposed to being absent (*apōn*, same verse). But the placement of "according to face" (lit. trans. of *kata prosōpon*) in the first position just after the relative pronoun (*hos*) and separated from "with/among you" (*en humin*) by the word "humble" (*tapeinos*) in a sentence dripping with irony may hint that Paul was responding to the mocking of his face. Observe that "according to face" (*kata prosōpon*) is not a locked-in expression that always indicates being present as opposed to being absent. Paul's use of it only seven verses later (10:7, see below) demonstrates that such is not the case. Furthermore, "humble" (*tapeinos*) in this sentence, unlike the way it is most commonly used in English, probably does not mean the avoidance of pride, but rather the perception that Paul was weak, feeble, or base. The fact that Paul launches his defense of the criticisms in the first sentence with a comment about a "face" at all is the first thing to observe in this section, especially in light of his further allusions to faces in the upcoming discussion.

The next use of "face" (*prosōpon*) is found in 10:7, even if most of our English translations do not alert us to its presence. This is the identical expression we already encountered in 10:1 (*kata prosōpon*), but is normally taken to mean something different. The usual understanding of this verse is either that Paul is reprimanding them: "You are only judging by appearances" (NIV; cf. NET, NASB), or that he is challenging them: "Look at what is before your eyes" (NRSV; cf. ESV, CSB). Woodenly, the Greek clause (*Ta kata prosōpon blepete*) can be rendered either as an indicative: "You are looking at the things according to face," or as an imperative: "Look at the things according to face." (I have a slight preference for the first.) Once again, we need to be careful not to over-read an idiom (the meaning of which, anyway, is disputed by translators), but we only need to point out that Paul has once again used the word *prosōpon* in a discourse in which he is replying to criticisms (throughout), and where he is about to mention his weak body (10:10, see discussion above). I would submit that by doing this, Paul is helping prepare his readers for the mention of his most difficult suffering, the thorn in the flesh (12:7). Paul may be doing this because he has been criticized for a bodily weakness that somehow manifested on his face.

The next facial allusion regards the "super-apostles" in Corinth (11:5; 12:11) whom Paul considers false apostles. He writes in 11:13–15, "For such men are false apostles, deceitful workmen, disguising themselves as apostles of Christ. And no wonder, for even Satan disguises himself as an angel of light. So it is no surprise if his servants, also, disguise themselves as servants of righteousness."

Paul has no patience whatsoever with those he labels "false apostles" in these verses. Paul draws a direct analogy. Just as Satan disguises himself as an angel of light, so these apostles disguise themselves. A likely facial allusion is contained in the three times that Paul employs the word "disguise" (*metaschēmatizō*). When people attempt to disguise themselves so as not to be recognized, the most important part of their body that they must cover or alter is the face. Paul's invective against these false apostles actually intensifies if he is responding to a criticism about his face.[8]

A truly poignant facial allusion is found in 11:20. Only a few verses prior (11:13), Paul employed a facial allusion to criticize the false apostles; now he uses a painful expression to criticize those who have been taken in, exploited, and hurt by the false apostles. Paul writes in 11:20, "For you bear it if someone makes slaves of you, or devours you, or takes advantage of you, or puts on airs, or strikes you in the face."[9] Paul draws

---

8. For possible Jewish sources that stand behind Paul's use of this word, see Thrall, *2 Corinthians 8–13*, 695–96 . But a single word does not an allusion make, and in this case I find myself skeptical that Paul has an earlier text in mind. So also Hughes, *Paul's Second Epistle to the Corinthians*, 393–94, notes 56–57.

9. *ei tis eis prosōpon hymas derei* (11:20); lit. "if anyone strikes you in the face."

upon various metaphors throughout this verse to scold the Corinthians
for allowing the so-called super apostles to lead them astray (enslav-
ing, devouring, taking advantage, putting on airs). But the final and (at
least for our discussion) the most important metaphor relates to the
striking, hitting, or slapping (as the verb is most often translated in
2 Cor 11:20) of the face. The bodily location of the strike in this verse
is explicitly on the face.

Let us digress, for a moment, and notice something else about
the operative word at the end of this verse that could have some
relevance for our discussion. When we read in translation, we are
sure to fail to notice that a common meaning of the verb employed
by Paul here (*derō*), and one that would have been familiar to his
readers, was "flay" (or for those not familiar with that English word,
"to skin the skin off something.")[10] There were many other verbs
available for Paul to use to describe the striking of someone's face,
as we have already noted in our discussion of 12:7 (*kolaphizō* was
one of those words). But Paul chose a word that was laden with
painful nuances. One of the more disturbing of ancient tortures,
associated sometimes with the conquering and subduing of a people
through war, was that of skinning alive the conquered peoples.[11]
Few tortures are as painful or humiliating. A word toting this connotation is the word Paul chose to finish this sentence. Granted,
the word can be used in a general way to beat, hit, or slap—and
it sometimes was (for example, 1 Cor 9:26). But the skin orientation may still have been purposeful, particularly if Paul's suffering
involved his literal skin and flesh. It may be that Paul chided the
Corinthian Christians for tolerating the false apostles when they
"rip into your face." (Notice that he employed the preposition *eis*,

---

10. *LSJ*, 380.

11. Mark A. Seifrid comments on the military resonance in all five of the verbs Paul
employs in this list (Mark A. Seifrid, *The Second Letter to the Corinthians*, PNTC (Grand Rapids:
Eerdmans; Nottingham: Apollos, 2014), 422–23). Placing this verb in a military list might support the skinning notions so well known in the ancient world and suggested in the text above,
though Seifrid does not pursue this implication.

"into," instead *epi*, the second of which is what one might expect if the verb in this context simply meant "beat."[12])

Paul wrote these comments only twelve verses before he started describing his heavenly ascent and only nineteen before mentioning the thorn in the flesh. That is, in the same sustained rhetorical context, in verses that lead up to his discussion about the thorn, Paul seems to have combined allusions to the *face*, the *skin*, and *beating* in a single sentence, which is what we have already argued that Paul will do in 12:7 where he talks directly about the thorn (see discussion in ch. 5 above).

Take note that these facial allusions are found in a section saturated by the overlapping themes of humiliation, boasting, and shame (see discussion just above). As already mentioned in our previous discussion of *kolaphizō* in 2 Corinthians 12:7, the face is the primary anatomical location of shame. Once again, the face appears to be important for our discussion, and in 2 Corinthians 11:20, gets called out explicitly.

Paul's fourth contextual circle—the whole of 2 Corinthians—is also relevant to the question of facial allusions. Paul has included many other facial allusions in the earlier parts of 2 Corinthians, especially in his repeated use of the word *prosōpon*. The paragraphs found between 3:7–4:6 especially highlight such allusions. In 3:7 Paul mentions that "the Israelites could not gaze at Moses' face because of its glory." In 3:13, he writes that we are bold, "not like Moses, who would put a veil over his face so that the Israelites might not gaze at the outcome of what was being brought to an end." After figuratively applying the veil to his readers, Paul concludes, "And we all, with unveiled face, beholding the glory of the Lord, are being transformed into the same image from one degree of glory to another" (3:18). He continues to use the exposed-face metaphor in chapter 4 when he writes that unbelievers have been blinded from seeing "the light of the gospel

---

12. Suggested by Barrett, who adds, "How far the last verb has to be taken metaphorically is not clear; probably not wholly so" (Barrett, *Second Epistle to the Corinthians*, 291).

of the glory of Christ," who is, Paul writes, "the image of God" (4:4). Said differently, people come to know "the glory of God in the face of Jesus Christ" (4:6).

Interesting for our discussion, after all this face-talk, Paul straightway moves into an extended section of body-talk.[13] He compares his physical body to a jar of clay (4:7), a body in which he carries around the death of Jesus so that the life of Jesus might become manifested in it (4:10–11). He continues writing about earthly and weak bodies in the following paragraph, comparing them to flimsy tents (5:1–4), expressing the longing that "we would rather be away from the body and at home with the Lord" (5:8; cf. 5:6), and warning that everyone should be ready to be judged, "for what he has done in the body" (5:10). All this focus on the body comes immediately after a section that focuses on faces.

Finally, Paul briefly returns to the face, or at least an expression that refers to one's outward appearance when he writes about "those who boast about outward appearance and not about what is in the heart" (5:12). Paul includes the word *prosōpon* here as he counsels his readers about how to reply to those who boast "in the face" (*en prosōpō*). Once again, let us acknowledge that in this context, this expression primarily means something like "outward appearance," but it should not escape our notice that once again Paul is using the word *prosōpon*, a word he doesn't use very often except in 2 Corinthians, and that he is using it after a long discussion in which faces (3:7–4:6) and bodies (4:7–5:10) play an important role.

Other locations in 2 Corinthians where Paul uses the word *prosōpon* include 1:11, 2:10, and 8:24, each with their individual idiomatic nuances. Once again, the point is not that Paul includes these to refer to literal faces, but that Paul (perhaps even unconsciously?)

---

13. On 2 Cor 4:7–12, see Richard I. Deibert, *Second Corinthians and Paul's Gospel of Human Mortality: How Paul's Experience of Death Authorizes His Apostolic Authority in Corinth*, WUNT 2, Reihe 430 (Tübingen: Mohr Siebeck, 2017), 115–76. Observe his note on p. 223 where he expresses his hope to study Paul's thorn in the flesh: "we would like to defend in more detail our working conviction that Paul's affliction in Asia (and thorn in the flesh) is a bodily illness."

has included so many uses of the word *prosōpon* in 2 Corinthians—as many as he uses in all his other letters combined—because he intends to discuss his thorn in the flesh later in the letter, and because the location of his pain was his face. Moreover, as just discussed, in one particular context (described above), he writes extensively about faces (3:7–4:6) and then immediately writes quite a lot about bodies (4:7–5:10). Perhaps this is all coincidental—and these last observations are somewhat contextually distant from 2 Corinthians 12:7—but Paul's repeated use of *prosōpon* and his focus upon physical bodies in 2 Corinthians might make more sense if we knew that Paul was somehow responding (and preparing to respond further in chs. 10–13) to criticisms about a bodily ailment that centered on his face.

KNOWN TO THE CORINTHIANS

Implicit in what has been discussed so far in this chapter is that it is more likely than not that Paul's ailment was known to the Corinthians (and to most everyone else as well). This has not yet been called out in our study, but needs to be highlighted. This observation also helps to somewhat narrow the range of possible sufferings that Paul could have referred to as his thorn in the flesh.

If Paul had a weak body (clue #1 above), and if Paul's opponents in Corinth had been calling out Paul's weaknesses to discredit him (clue #2 above), and if Paul's suffering involved his face in some way (clue #3 above), then the implication is that the nature of Paul's suffering that he referred to as a thorn in the flesh was known to the Corinthians, and probably to everyone else as well.

Four other considerations make it more likely than not that the Corinthians knew what Paul's thorn was. First, Paul's thorn in the flesh appears to be the pinnacle of Paul's suffering in 2 Corinthians. If the Corinthians did not know what the thorn was, this surely would have piqued their curiosity. Had Paul wanted to hide from the Corinthians the nature of his thorn, he certainly should not have written this section in a way that would arouse their curiosity. Second, one of Paul's points appears to be something like: I have suffered in many different ways, and my suffering testifies to the truth of my apostleship. However, if the Corinthians did not know what his thorn was, the force of his argument when we arrive at chapter 12 gets weakened for lack of relevance. Third, Paul has been *very* self-disclosing with the Corinthians throughout his letter, perhaps more so than in any other letter. He emphasizes this over and over (3:18; 4:2; 6:3, 11, 13; 12:6). The notion of being open and vulnerable does not work well with the suggestion that the Corinthians did not know what Paul's thorn was. Fourth, the condition from which Paul suffered was something that would have kept Paul from exalting himself before others.[14]

What is the significance of whether they knew what his thorn was? If the thorn was obvious and known to everyone, it would seem to rule out some inward, hidden suffering that Paul never talked about. For example, it would rule out something current but hidden in Paul's life that Paul never talked about (like temptation, anxiety, or oppression that he kept hidden), something geographically far away from the Corinthians that Paul never talked about (like a problem with a distant church or opponents in another place), or some event that occurred in the distant past that still tormented Paul but that he did not talk about (like past family troubles or past persecutions).

WEAKNESS AGAIN

Returning to clues from the central discourse itself (2 Cor 10–13), we discover a fifth clue in the items Paul tends to connect to the theme of weakness. We have already observed how weakness is intertwined with the theme of humiliation and shame in these chapters in general. But here I want to focus on something more specific than that, a pattern that is suggestive: when Paul mentions weakness, he precedes or follows the word with something that may hint at the *nature* of the weakness.

Mention #1: "To my shame, I must say, we were too weak for that!" (11:21) comes just after Paul writes the bit about ripping into the skin of their face (11:20).

---

14. Wallace, *Snatched into Paradise*, 7.

Mention #2: "Who is weak, and I am not weak?" comes just before and in the same verse as Paul's comment about "burning" when they fall (11:29) and is immediately followed by "If I must boast, I will boast of the things that show my weakness" (11:30).

Mention #3: "But on my own behalf I will not boast, except of my weaknesses" (12:5), comes shortly before Paul's mention of "a thorn in the flesh" that "punched his face," and is followed by the Lord's words that "my power is made perfect in weakness." Paul responds, "I will boast all the more gladly of my weaknesses" (12:9–10).

Mention #4: "He [Christ] is not weak in dealing with you, but is powerful among you" is followed immediately by the mention of Christ's crucifixion which was "in weakness" and the connection with Paul and his band who "also are weak in him" (13:3–4).

There is one more brief mention of weakness as Paul winds down his argument in 13:9, "For we are glad when we are weak and you are strong," but it contains no suggestive connections like the others already noted.

The observation worth highlighting is that Paul's weakness language gets connected to descriptors that might help move us toward a solution for the nature of Paul's thorn in the flesh.

- Like skinning / beating your face (#1)

- Like burning (#2)

- Like a thorn, a messenger of Satan, and hitting your face (#3)

- Like Christ's crucifixion (#4) (See ch. 8 for more on this.)

This pattern of descriptors-connected-to-weakness encompasses much of the thesis I have begun to articulate: Paul experienced face pain that was excruciating, comparable to burning and the stabbing of a sharp object or a face beating, that was a messenger of Satan even though allowed by God, all modeled after Christ's own crucifixion.

All these are connected in some way by weakness—a repeating literary pattern in 2 Corinthians 11–13.

STRESS

A sixth clue in the discourse is the connection with stress. Since stress is an exacerbating issue for many sufferers of face pain, if this solution proves to be tenable, it will surprise no one familiar with face pain to discover that Paul's final set of sufferings that appear at the end of his long list of sufferings in 2 Corinthians 11:28–32 (care for churches; lowered in a basket) are sufferings of psychological stress, rather than mere physical sufferings or labors. In Paul's list of sufferings in 2 Corinthians 11:23–27, Paul includes physical abuse he suffered at the hands of others (imprisonments, floggings, beatings, a stoning) along with physical hardships he faced to accomplish his mission (shipwrecks, journeys, bandits, toil and hardship, hunger and thirst, cold and nakedness). All such sufferings Paul notes with little or no explanation. But when the reader arrives at verses 28–32, the list changes markedly.[15] Paul stops listing and starts explaining in full sentences a primary point of stress, his worry for all the churches. Furthermore, in verse 28, Paul employs two psychological-stress terms ("pressure" [*epistasis*]) and "anxiety" [*merimna*][16]) to describe the emotional burden he carried for the churches he founded.[17] He laments the impact of the churches' weakness and stumblings in verse 29, describing himself as "burning" (*poroumai*) whenever they stumble.[18] He then concludes his list of

---

15. "Conditions such as these would have killed most men; they formed the smaller part of Paul's burden" (Barrett, *Second Epistle to the Corinthians*, 300).

16. "Due to the parallel forms and their relationship as roughly synonymous, ἡ μέριμνα, 'the anxiety' or 'care,' can be read as epexegetical and appositional to ἡ ἐπίστασις: 'the daily weight, that is my anxiety' about all the churches" (Guthrie, *2 Corinthians*, 566).

17. One day, a young man I was mentoring asked me what was the most sorrowful event I had ever experienced. After a few moments of reflection, I came up with three relational conflicts that were harder than anything else I could think of. I bypassed personal physical pain, a near loss to death of one of my daughters, and death threats I received. Relational conflicts touch us at our very core, exacerbated when those conflicts occur with people we count as spiritual children.

18. Sometimes interpreted as burning with anger, but the anger is not stated explicitly.

sufferings by describing an escape from Damascus in a basket low-ered out of a window in the wall of the city (v. 32), which may have been included by Paul both because of the stress and the humiliation involved.[19] This final section (vv. 28–32) of Paul's most extensive list of sufferings (vv. 23–32) is connected literarily to the following chapter (where Paul's vision, thorn, and God's response is listed, 2 Cor 12:1–10) by the themes of boasting (11:30 with 12:1, 5–7), weakness (11:30 with 12:1, 5, 9–10), and I would like to suggest, also by the theme of stress (11:28 "pressure" and "anxiety" with 12:10 "distresses" [*stenochōriai*[20]] and esp. 12:7 Paul's thorn.)

SATAN AND SPIRITUAL WARFARE

A seventh clue in the broader discourse relates to the references to Satan and spiritual warfare in the two chapters leading up to Paul's mention of the thorn in the flesh. This theme in general has already been discussed in chapter 3 in connection with magical attacks in the world of Paul. But keep in mind that in this central discourse, Paul writes about waging a warfare that is not fleshly but has divine power (10:2). He alerts the Christians of his concerns that someone might deceive them in a way analogous to how the serpent tempted Eve (11:3). Then he compares the "super-apostles" to Satan himself who disguises himself as an angel of light (11:13–15). These all help to confirm what we have already sus-pected, that when Paul refers to an "angel of Satan" who hit him in the face (12:7) via the thorn, a personal demonic attack was in view.

PAUL'S RHETORIC: STRONG OR WEAK?

The eighth and final consideration from the discourse of 2 Corinthians 10–13 is the possible connection of Paul's thorn to the disparagement of Paul's speaking ability. The reader at this point will be well aware

---

19. "Whatever the reasons for its inclusion at this point, the episode, narrated here with remarkable economy of language, forms a striking literary backdrop for what follows: first, an embarrassing descent to escape the hands of men, then an exhilarating ascent into the presence of God (12:2–4)" (Harris, *Second Epistle to the Corinthians*, 820–21).

20. "[A] set of stressful circumstances, *distress, difficulty, anguish, trouble*" (BDAG, 943).

that we are already moving in the direction of viewing Paul's thorn
as something physical that has to do with his face. But is there any
connection to the rhetorical issues that are also important in the discourse? In chapters 10–13, the weakness of Paul's rhetorical ability
can be inferred at various points, and is explicitly referenced in a few
spots. For example, in 10:10 Paul's detractors have apparently claimed
that Paul's "speech is of no account." For the sake of argument, Paul
grants the premise that he is a poor speaker when he says, "Even if I
am unskilled in speaking, I am not so in knowledge" (11:6). He may
also allude to their criticisms of his rhetoric when he says, "so that no
one may think more of me than he ... hears from me" (12:6).

But this presents a problem for New Testament scholars. Pauline scholars find themselves in a quandary about how to speak about Paul's rhetorical ability. They struggle to answer the question of how Paul seemed so
familiar with rhetoric that he could persuade multiple listeners to accept
his message, on the one hand, and how he could be criticized for being a
poor speaker, on the other.[21] Ben Witherington is one example of a scholar
who was so impressed by Paul's knowledge of rhetoric that he organized
his commentary on the Corinthian letters around ancient rhetorical categories.[22] But it also appears that detractors in Corinth criticized Paul for his
rhetoric—to such a degree that Paul felt the need to defend himself. How
shall we resolve this dilemma? Was Paul an effective rhetorician or not?[23]

---

21.   Thrall is representative of the struggle, but not alone in it, in her discussion of 10:10.
See Thrall, *2 Corinthians 8–13*, 631–33.

22.   Witherington suggests that Paul used "Attic or Roman plain style, rather than the more
verbose Asiatic style," and "resolved not to declaim the gospel, ... that is, not to use Sophistic
or ornamental rhetoric in his missionary preaching" (Witherington, *Conflict and Community
in Corinth*, 46). For another application of rhetorical categories to 2 Corinthians, see James W.
Thompson, *Apostle of Persuasion: Theology and Rhetoric in the Pauline Letters* (Grand Rapids:
Baker, 2020), 156–67. For an introduction to rhetorical categories for the study of the New
Testament see Ben Witherington III, *New Testament Rhetoric: An Introductory Guide to the Art
of Persuasion in and of the New Testament* (Eugene, OR: Cascade Books, 2009) and Mikeal C.
Parsons and Michael Wade Martin, *Ancient Rhetoric and the New Testament: The Influence of
Elementary Greek Composition* (Waco, TX: Baylor University Press, 2018), the last of which
emphasizes the important role of the *progymnasmata* (elementary lessons in rhetoric) for understanding the influence of rhetoric on New Testament authors.

23.   For a history of the use of rhetorical categories in the interpretation of Paul's letters,
see Ryan S. Schellenberg, *Rethinking Paul's Rhetorical Education: Comparative Rhetoric and*

In anticipation of a solution, what if Paul's speaking was occasionally interrupted by brief, but excruciating, bouts of stabbing craniofacial pain? Paul, then, could be at the same time a powerful and persuasive speaker, but would still have found himself open to criticism about his speaking presentation.[24] This especially would have been the case if his listeners thought that the shooting pain that brought him to his knees for a few seconds, or up to a minute or two, was an attack of black magic. Would not that have engendered criticism of Paul's speaking ability in first-century Corinth, even if Paul was rhetorically adept?

At this point, we need to find a way to reconcile Paul's apparent facility with rhetoric—enough to convince scores of people to follow his message—with the fact that he was being criticized for his poor rhetoric. The suggestion put forth here is that a possible resolution is found in the nature of Paul's thorn in the flesh—sudden jabs of facial pain that sometimes interrupted his speaking (and that would have been viewed as attacks of black magic by many), and thus would have made him less effective as a communicator than he otherwise could have been.[25]

---

2 *Corinthians*, ECL (Atlanta: Society of Biblical Literature, 2013), 17–56. Schellenberg addresses the question of whether Paul was formally trained in rhetoric. Note that Schellenberg himself (focusing on 2 Cor 10–13) argues that Paul was *not* formally trained in rhetoric, though Paul still used informal rhetorical devices effectively.

24. Note Quintilian's comment in his rhetorical instructions (11.3.69–71): "It is the head which occupies the chief place in Delivery (as it does in the body itself)" (cited in Wenhua Shi, *Paul's Message of the Cross as Body Language*, WUNT 2, Reihe 254 [Tübingen: Mohr Siebeck, 2008], 138). Also, "But the face is sovereign. It is this that makes us humble, threatening, flattering, sad, cheerful, proud, or submissive; men hang on this; men fix their gaze on this; this is watched even before we start to speak; this makes us love some people and hate others; this makes us understand many things; this often replaces words altogether" (cited in Beatrice da Vela, "From the Stage to the Court: Rhetorical and Dramatic Performance in Donatus' Commentary on Terence," in *The Theatre of Justice: Aspects of Performance in Greco-Roman Oratory and Rhetoric*, ed. Sophia Papaioannou, et al., MNS 403 [Leiden: Brill, 2017], 164n4).

25. Dale B. Martin comments that Paul's critics in 2 Cor 10–13 would have drawn a connection between his body and his rhetoric and character. "His critics point to his weakness of body (whether due to illness, disfigurement, or simply constitutional infirmity) as irrefutable evidence of weakness of character" (*The Corinthian Body* [New Haven: Yale University Press, 1995]: 54).

CRITERIA SUPPORTED OR
ALLUDED TO IN THIS CHAPTER

1. Viewed by Paul as attacks by an angel of Satan, though permitted by God

2. Impacting Paul's physical flesh

3. Impacting Paul's face (as part of his head)

4. Viewed by others as humiliating and weak

5. Exacerbated by stress

6. Negatively impacting Paul's rhetorical ability

7. Known to the Corinthians

8. Analogous to Paul's other sufferings

CLUES FROM THE
SUFFERING OF JESUS

One helpful way to understand the apostle Paul is to notice how he identified with the suffering and crucifixion of Jesus, what Michael Gorman has termed "cruciformity."[1] According to Gorman, "The term 'cruciformity,' from "cruciform" (cross-shaped) and 'conformity,' may be defined simply as conformity to Jesus the crucified Messiah."[2] Furthermore, "Cruciformity ... is cross-shaped existence in Jesus the Messiah. It is letting the cross of the crucified Messiah be the shape, as well as the source, of life in him. It is participating in and embodying the cross."[3]

Gorman is not the first person to illuminate the degree to which Paul's theology and ethics were formed around the passion and cross of Jesus (though I have benefitted from his insights). Luther

---

1. Michael Gorman, *Cruciformity: Paul's Narrative Spirituality of the Cross* (Grand Rapids: Eerdmans, 2001), 4.

2. Michael Gorman, "Paul and the Crucified Way of God in Christ," *J. Moral Theol.* 2 (2013): 66.

3. Gorman, "Paul and the Crucified Way," 67.

defended a "theology of the cross" against a "theology of glory."[4] Käsemann reinvigorated interest in the centrality of the cross among theologians and New Testament scholars.[5] But even a skim across the surface of Paul's letters readily reveals the impact of the cross in forming Paul's outlook on life. Take, as one well-known example, Galatians 2:20, where Paul asserted, "I have been crucified with Christ. It is no longer I who live, but Christ who lives in me." Paul claimed in this verse that his life had been shaped into conformity with Christ's death to such a degree that he viewed himself as having been "crucified with Christ." Moreover, in Romans 6:3-4, Paul asserted that everyone who has been "baptized into Christ" ought to identify similarly with the death and resurrection of Christ: "Do you not know that all of us who have been baptized into Christ Jesus were baptized into his death? We were buried therefore with him by baptism into death, in order that, just as Christ was raised from the dead by the glory of the Father, we too might walk in newness of life."

Such cruciformity, to continue with Gorman's evocative term, affected many areas of Paul's ethical framework, including self-denial, hospitality to the marginalized, and service to others.[6] Indeed, an argument can be made, and in fact has already been made by Thomas Stegman, that 2 Corinthians, in particular, is permeated by the ethos of Jesus, and that Paul in that letter wanted to make sure his readers

---

4. See, for example, Martin Luther, "Heidelberg Disputation (1518)," in *Martin Luther's Basic Theological Writings*, ed. Timothy F. Lull and William R. Russell (Minneapolis: Fortress Press, 2012), 14-25. For a survey of Luther's theology of the cross, see Alister McGrath, *Luther's Theology of the Cross*, 2nd ed. (Oxford: Wiley-Blackwell, 2011).

5. See, for example, one seminal essay by Ernst Käsemann, "The Saving Significance of the Death of Jesus in Paul," in *Perspectives on Paul*, trans. Margaret Kohl (Philadelphia: Fortress, 1971), 32-59. For a broad treatment of the cross in Paul, see also Charles B. Cousar, *A Theology of the Cross: The Death of Jesus in the Pauline Letters*, OBT 24 (Minneapolis: Fortress, 1990). In the current chapter, we are interested especially in the *physical* connections of Christ's sufferings to Paul's.

6. Michael J. Gorman, "Cruciformity According to Jesus and Paul," in *Unity and Diversity in the Gospel and Paul: Essays in Honor of Frank J. Matera*, ed. Christopher W. Skinner and Kelly R. Iverson (Atlanta: Society of Biblical Literature, 2012), 173-201.

understood that such an ethos figured prominently in his own life.[7] But one of the primary ways that Paul made connections in his writings to the suffering and death of Jesus was via Paul's own suffering.[8] When Paul suffered, he not only suffered *for* Christ, he suffered *with* Christ. He, thus, identified with Christ in his suffering.[9]

Can we further suggest that Paul's own sufferings as an apostle of Christ were not simply analogically or spiritually connected to the sufferings of Jesus, but in his own mind were somehow more tangibly—physically—connected to Jesus?[10] When Paul experienced thorn-like piercing pain, did he, perhaps, find encouragement in knowing that he was suffering *like* Jesus—not just in the fact of his sufferings, but also regarding some particulars as well?[11]

Such a proposition would help to make sense of comments in 2 Corinthians such as "For as we share abundantly in Christ's sufferings … " (2 Cor 1:5), or "always carrying in the body the death of Jesus, so that the life of Jesus may also be manifested in our bodies" (2 Cor 4:10), or in the discourse we are studying, "For he was crucified in weakness, but lives by the power of God. For we also are weak in him, but in dealing with you we will live with him by the power of

7. Thomas Stegman, *The Character of Jesus: The Linchpin to Paul's Argument in 2 Corinthians*, AnBib 158 (Rome: Editrice Pontificio Istituo Biblico, 2005), esp. 213–303.

8. For a study of how Paul grounded his own suffering in the story of Jesus in 2 Corinthians, see Lim, *The Sufferings of Christ are Abundant in Us*. For an application of those insights to 2 Cor 11:23–12:10, see Lim's discussion on 159–90. Note the way Garrett, "Paul's Thorn and Cultural Models of Affliction," 94–96, 98, applies the cross/resurrection model to Paul's thorn.

9. "For him [Paul], Jesus' glory consists in the fact that he makes his earthly disciples willing and able to take up the cross after him; and the glory of the church and of the Christian life is that they are thought worthy to praise the one who was crucified as the power and wisdom of God, to seek salvation in him alone and to turn their existence into the service of God under the token of Golgotha" (Käsemann, "Saving Significance of the Death of Jesus in Paul," 59).

10. As Moss notes, "The connection, of course, is the passion narrative and the crucifixion on the cross. Suffering, in the case of Christ, is not just persecution and social marginalization; it is the painful, immobilizing death on a cross" (Moss, "Christly Possession and Weakened Bodies," 327).

11. As Gorman comments, "For Paul, as for Jesus, participation in the Messiah's suffering and death has two dimensions, literal suffering and self-giving service to God and others" (Gorman, "Cruciformity According to Jesus and Paul," 198).

God" (2 Cor 13:4).[12] Paul, it appears, viewed his physical sufferings as something more than merely a metaphor; he carried on his body suffering akin to the sufferings of Jesus. Deibert avers, "Indeed, the key to reading 2 Corinthians is to read the particulars carefully through the lens of Paul's general thematic concern: to defend his own mortality and endurance and apostolic vocation *as* the actual manifestation of Jesus' death and resurrection."[13]

But what does this have to do with Paul's thorn in the flesh? Since Paul insisted on including the theme of weakness in the context of his thorn, and since Paul's weakness theme is so closely tied up with his theology of the suffering and death of Jesus (for example, 2 Cor 13:3–4), Paul undoubtedly received spiritual encouragement from knowing that Jesus experienced parallels to his own suffering. In particular, anticipating our conclusions, whenever Paul experienced stabbing pain that attacked his face/head with thorn-like jabs, he may have been spiritually strengthened as he remembered the piercings Jesus himself faced. Most pertinent to the direction we are moving, Paul may have meditated on the fact that Jesus was: (1) pierced on his head with a crown of thorns, (2) pierced with nails and a spear, (3) struck on his head and slapped in his face, (4) shamed on his face, (5) all in fulfillment of key messianic Scriptures that mention piercing, beating, and humiliation.[14] Let us look at each of these in turn and observe

---

12. Other good examples outside 2 Cor include Gal 6:17 and Col 1:24.

13. Deibert, *Second Corinthians and Paul's Gospel of Human Mortality*, 9.

14. The scourging of Jesus has not been included in the following analysis for three reasons: (1) the evangelists give no details about the scourging apart from relating that Jesus was "scourged" (Matt 27:26; Mark 15:15) or "flogged" (Matt 20:19; John 19:1); (2) there is no clear pathway that I can identify between 2 Cor 12 and the scourging of Jesus; and (3) there is currently no way to be certain what instrument was used to "scourge" or "flog" Jesus. On this last point, notice the recent comments of Nicolatti, at the conclusion of his investigation into what instrument might have been used to scourge Jesus: "It would be appropriate to go through Bible dictionaries, tools of consultation and studies on the passion of Christ and remove any reference to a specific form of alleged Roman scourge, particularly one with pendants or circular weights at its end, seeing as this is actually the modern product of an overlapping among medieval beliefs, erroneous archaeological identifications and Shroud-related conjectures from the twentieth century" (Andrea Nicolatti, "The Scourge of Jesus and the Roman Scourge," *JSHJ* 15 [2017]: 58).

how closely they relate to Paul's own description of his suffering from
the thorn in the flesh.

PIERCED ON THE HEAD WITH
A CROWN OF THORNS

Matthew, Mark, and John all recall the crown of thorns placed upon
the head of Jesus. The soldiers, Matthew recounts, "twisting together
a crown of thorns, they put it on his head and put a reed in his right
hand" (Matt 27:29). Mark describes it similarly: "and twisting together
a crown of thorns, they put it on him" (Mark 15:17). John's account
is a bit fuller. "And the soldiers twisted together a crown of thorns
and put it on his head and arrayed him in a purple robe" (John 19:2).
John adds that after Pilate spoke to the people again and proclaimed
that he detected no guilt, he displayed the beaten and humiliated
Jesus, presumably to elicit pity from the crowd. But John includes
the crown of thorns in his description, "So Jesus came out, wearing
the crown of thorns and the purple robe. Pilate said to them, 'Behold
the man!'" (John 19:5).

There is, of course, an irony here. From the perspective of the
soldiers, the purpose of the crown was probably twofold: to inflict
sardonic humiliation on Jesus, and to increase Jesus's physical pain
by placing a wreath full of sharp thorns on the head of a man falsely
claiming to be a king. The soldiers certainly did not believe that Jesus
was king. From the perspective of the evangelists, though, the soldiers
placed their crown of mocking upon the head of the rightful ruler.

The crown of thorns intersects with our study in three primary
ways. First, and most directly, it was composed of thorns; and Paul
referred to his suffering as a thorn in the flesh. Even if the underlying
Greek word is different (*akantha*), this connection is worthy of consideration. Second, the crown of thorns was placed on the head and
face of Jesus. These thorns would have literally caused piercing pain
on the back of Jesus's head, but also along his forehead and temples.
Third, the crown of thorns functioned as humiliation upon the head of
Jesus. The theme of humiliation has already been discussed in relation

to 2 Corinthians 10–13 and will be discussed more below in relation
to the sufferings of Jesus. All these connect with 2 Corinthians 12:7–10.

If Paul's special suffering was thorn-like and shame-producing
pain on his face/head, would he not have found spiritual help in
reflecting upon the sufferings of Jesus who endured such stabbing
pain on his head when he was forced to wear a crown of thorns?

PIERCED WITH NAILS AND A SPEAR

If Paul experienced stabbing pain in his skin/flesh, he also may have
found himself thinking about the nails that pinned the hands and
feet of Jesus to the cross and the spear with which Jesus was pierced
in his side after expiring (John 19:34). None of the four evangelists
explicitly mentions the nails at the time they write that Jesus was
crucified; they simply state that he was crucified (Matt 27:35; Mark
15:24; Luke 23:33; John 19:18). Everyone, however, knew that nails
were commonly used in affixing condemned people to crosses.

But after the resurrection, Luke and John refer to the marks of
the nails when they write that Jesus "showed them his hands and
feet" (Luke 24:40) and "showed them his hands and his side" (John
20:20). John gets even more specific. He tells us that Thomas, who
was not present at the first appearance, doubted that the other disciples actually saw Jesus. In Thomas's words, "Unless I see in his hands
the mark of the nails, and place my finger into the mark of the nails,
and place my hand into his side, I will never believe" (John 20:25).
Jesus then appeared to Thomas eight days later and consented to his
request (John 20:26–29).[15]

Thus, in addition to meditating on a crown of thorns piercing
Jesus's head, Paul could have found spiritual aid during his own sufferings by identifying with the other piercings that Jesus experienced in his passion, including the piercings of the nails and the spear.
Assuming for the moment that this is the case, it raises an interesting

---

15. Nails are also implicit in Col 2:14, where Paul tells us how God cancelled our debt of
sin: "This he set aside, nailing (*proselōsas*) it to the cross."

question. Why would Paul call his suffering a thorn or stake instead of, say, a nail? Let me suggest that if the location of Paul's sufferings was his face/head, rather than his hands and feet, Paul might have chosen to align his terminology more closely with the piercing instruments of Jesus's head (thorns) than with the piercing instruments of Jesus's hands and feet (nails) or side (spear). If Paul's sufferings had been in his limbs or trunk instead of his face or head, we might today be trying to determine what Paul meant by his "nails in the flesh" or "spear in the flesh." Nevertheless, if the pain Paul felt was jabbing/stabbing pain, he still could have found encouragement by identifying with all the various ways Jesus was pierced, including the piercings with nails.

STRUCK ON THE HEAD
AND SLAPPED IN THE FACE

Paul not only labeled his suffering as a "thorn in the flesh," he described his experience as akin to being "punched in the face" (*kolaphizō*, 2 Cor 12:7; see discussion in ch. 5). Once again, when Paul suffered cranio-facial pain, he likely would have looked to Jesus and found spiritual help in identifying with his master whose face was pummeled by unfriendly fists along with a reed.

The verb *kolaphizō* outside of 2 Corinthians 12:7 only occurs four other times in the New Testament. Relevant to the current discussion, two of those occurrences are found in the account of Jesus's farcical trial before the priests. Matthew 26:67 is the first, "Then they spit in his face and struck (*kolaphizō*) him. And some slapped him ... " Mark 14:65 is the second, "And some began to spit on him and to cover his face and to strike him (*kolaphizō*), saying to him, 'Prophesy!'" The verb *kolaphizō* is most commonly used for the striking of someone's face, but if there were any doubt that the intended location of the blows and slaps were Jesus's face, both Matthew and Mark specify Jesus's face as the location of the preceding acts of humiliation.

Further abuse to Jesus's face and head occurred after Pilate delivered him to be crucified. The soldiers "took the reed" that was functioning as a mock scepter "and struck him on the head" (Matt 27:30;

cf. Mark 15:19). Might I suggest that the reason they struck his head
with the reed was because they had just placed a crown of sharp
thorns on his head? Could it be that they used a reed instead of their
hands to prevent injury to their own hands (though John 19:3 says
that they continued to slap him—perhaps on the lower parts of his
face)? Whatever the reason, the striking of Jesus's head with the reed
would have driven those long thorns into his skull and forehead—literally sticking thorns in the flesh.

When Paul, who identified so closely with the suffering and death
of Jesus combined "thorn" and "flesh" and "beating" to describe his
own suffering, might he not have been comforted or spiritually
strengthened as he recalled that his Lord had suffered ahead of him
when literal thorns were driven by blows into the flesh of Jesus's
head and face?

SHAMED ON THE FACE

The evangelists in the accounts of Jesus's pre-crucifixion sufferings
underscore the humiliation of Jesus. He was stripped by the Roman
soldiers (Matt 27:28), treated with contempt (Luke 23:11), mocked
before the crucifixion (Matt 27:31; Mark 15:20), and mocked even
more when Jesus was on the cross (Luke 23:36). We have also noted
that the soldiers beat his head, something that was not only painful,
but publicly humiliating.[16]

But nothing communicates the distress of inflicted shame more
intensely than spitting in someone's face. When Jesus was brought
before the priests, Matthew tells us, "Then they spit in his face" (Matt
26:67; cf. Mark 14:65; Matt 27:30 by the Roman soldiers). Luke does
not include the spitting in the passion accounts itself, but does include
it in Jesus's predictions of his future suffering while heading toward
Jerusalem (Luke 18:31–32; cf. Mark 10:32–34). Spitting in this last

---

16. Cf. Jesus's words only days before: "'Again he [the vineyard owner] sent to them another
servant, and they struck him on the head and treated him shamefully'" (Mark 12:4). Note in
particular the connection between hitting on the head and shame.

example is linked by Luke in a triad with "mocked" and "shamefully treated," suggesting its humiliating import.

An interpreter not raised in an honor-and-shame culture might be excused for not apprehending the full symbolic weight of spitting in another's face. Such an interpreter might, for example, assume that spitting was primarily an expression of anger. But this would miss the point. Spitting in someone's face was intended to induce and publicize shame.

An Old Testament example of the symbolic weight of shame from spitting can be observed in the follow-up to Aaron and Miriam's challenge of Moses's leadership after Miriam was struck with leprosy. When Moses pleaded to God for her healing, God replied, "If her father had but spit in her face, should she not be shamed seven days? Let her be shut outside the camp seven days, and after that she may be brought in again" (Num 12:14).

We find another example of the symbolic weight of spitting in the prescriptions for the levirate law in Deuteronomy 25:5–10. If a man will not fulfill his duty to his sister-in-law, we learn, she is to pull off the sandal from the recalcitrant man's foot (a symbol of shame) in the sight of the elders (public humiliation) and spit in his face (25:9), resulting in the man forever carrying a designated label of humiliation. Spitting in one's face both in the Old and New Testaments was all about communicating shame, since the face/head was the primary anatomical location of shame.

When Paul wrote that an angel of Satan was permitted to inflict him with a thorn in the flesh "to keep me from becoming conceited because of the surpassing greatness of the revelations" and again "to keep me from becoming conceited" (12:7), Paul wrote his words into an honor-and-shame culture. If Paul experienced pain on his face/head, it is likely that he would have found spiritual strength in knowing that Jesus also was humiliated on his face, particularly because Paul sought to conform his life to the sufferings and death of Jesus.

IN FULFILLMENT OF SCRIPTURES
ABOUT PIERCING

If indeed Paul drew a conceptual line between his own physical sufferings and those of Jesus, and if indeed the themes of piercing (thorns, nails, spear), abuse of the head, and humiliation played an important role both in the sufferings of Jesus and Paul's own physical sufferings, then the connection would only be strengthened if such themes also appeared in Old Testament messianic passages. The piercing theme does in fact appear in three key Old Testament passages that are treated as messianic by New Testament authors: Psalm 22, Isaiah 52–53, and Zechariah 12. Abuse of the face also appears in Isaiah 52–53, and humiliation plays an important role in both Psalm 22 and Isaiah 52–53.

This is not the place to try to untangle the various ways that the writings of the Old Testament prophets are "fulfilled" in the eyes of various New Testament authors. Nevertheless, let me offer one way to understand how this might have occurred, including in the three passages we will observe. From the perspective of the New Testament authors (evangelists/apostles), God intentionally established patterns in history that would culminate in similar events in the life and death of the Messiah. Jesus, according to these New Testament authors, fulfilled patterns that were historically placed by God to highlight aspects of Jesus's messianic claims. Since the culminating fulfillment was part of a pattern, this meant that an Old Testament author's words could relate to something near to his own historical period, while those same words could be more fully fulfilled in a far-future Messiah.

This pattern-in-history approach (what some interpreters call "typology") is how I understand many (though not all) of the words of the Old Testament prophets find their fulfillment in the life of Messiah Jesus, including the three that relate most closely to this study: Psalm 22, Isaiah 52–53, and Zechariah 12.[17]

For our purposes, what is most significant about these three passages is that each has something to say about piercing. The final verb of

---

17. For more on this, see Berding and Lunde, eds., *Three Views on the New Testament Use of the Old Testament*; for actual examples, see G. K. Beale and D. A. Carson, eds., *Commentary on the New Testament Use of the Old Testament*, xxiii–xxviii.

Psalm 22:16 is translated by most of the major translations as "pierced," rendering the clause, "they have pierced my hands and feet" (ESV; cf. NIV; RSV; NASB; NEB; NLT; CSB; NET; not NRSV).[18] Although Psalm 22 in its historical context is a lament about the psalmist's own sufferings, the New Testament authors later viewed this Psalm as having been divinely placed in order to share a predictive pattern with Jesus who was the "son of David."[19]

Isaiah 53:5 also speaks of piercing in the well-known sentence, "But he was pierced for our transgressions."[20] Although the "servant" of the so-called Servant Songs (42:1–7; 49:1–7; 50:4–9; 52:13–53:12) in its own context appears to be Israel (41:8; 44:1–2, 21; 45:4; 48:20), or in Isaiah 52–53, a faithful remnant of Israel,[21] the New Testament authors understood that Jesus was the suffering servant *par excellence.*[22]

---

18. Kidner writes: "A strong argument in its favour [translating as 'pierced'] is that the LXX, compiled two centuries before the crucifixion, and therefore an unbiased witness understood it so. All the major translations reject the Masoretic vowels (added to the written text in the Christian era) as yielding little sense here (see margin of RV, RSV, NEB), and the majority in fact agree with the LXX. The chief alternatives (*e.g.* 'bound' or 'hacked off') solve no linguistic difficulties which 'pierced' does not solve, but avoid the apprent [sic] prediction of the cross by exchanging a common Hebrew verb (dig, bore, pierce) for hypothetical ones, attested only in Akkadian, Syriac and Arabic, not in biblical Hebrew" (Derek Kidner, *Psalms 1–72: An Introduction & Commentary,* TOTC [Leicester: Inter-Varsity Press, 1973], 107–8). Nor is this reading any longer based only upon the LXX, per Kidner's comment, as a result of the more recent publication of 5/6 HevPsalms from Nahal Hever, which contains a Hebrew text that includes the piercing reading. See Conrad R. Gren, "Piercing the Ambiguities of Psalm 22:16 and the Messiah's Mission," *JETS* 48 (2005), 287–88.

19. Ps 22:1 is cited on the lips of Jesus on the cross (Matt 27:46; Mark 15:34); the division of clothes by casting lots in Ps 22:18 is reenacted by the soldiers who guarded the cross (John 19:23–24); Ps 22:22 gets applied to the glorified Jesus in Heb 2:12; and there exist a number of other allusions that are possible, including the ease with which a first-century Christian might see the connections between Ps 22:14–18 and the sufferings of Jesus on the cross.

20. Hebrew: *mkhll,* here "pierced" or "stabbed." The Greek text of Isa 53:5 uses a more general term for wounding *traumatizō.*

21. See the insightful discussion of Jonathan Lunde, *Following Jesus, the Servant King: A Biblical Theology of Covenantal Discipleship,* BTL (Grand Rapids: Zondervan, 2010), 224–32. Lunde concludes that "the righteous Servant in Isaiah 52–53 is a corporate reference to the righteous remnant in Israel who are caught up in the destructive judgment of the exile, but whose suffering functions in a curse-bearing way to allow God to show mercy once again to his people in bringing them back to the land" (230).

22. "The New Testament authors take for granted that Jesus is the fulfillment of Isaiah's Servant of the Lord. In fact, Isaiah 53 stands as the second-most quoted Old Testament chapter by New Testament authors—second only to Psalm 110. However, if New Testament allusions are included, Isaiah 53 far outdistances every other Old Testament passage. What is remarkable is

The third messianic passage (that is, messianic from a New Testament perspective) is Zechariah 12:10. Zechariah declares the oracle of the Lord, "And I will pour out on the house of David and the inhabitants of Jerusalem a spirit of grace and pleas for mercy, so that, when they look on me, on him whom they have pierced, they shall mourn for him, as one mourns for an only child, and weep bitterly over him, as one weeps over a firstborn" (Zech 12:10). The interpretation of this verse in its original context is widely disputed, though I have some sympathy for Calvin's view that the piercing is metaphorical of the "wounding" that God has felt on account of the sins of his people.[23] But even if we are unable to firmly identify Zechariah's original intention, from the perspective of the author of the Fourth Gospel, Zechariah's words found fulfillment when Jesus was pierced by the spear (John 19:34). John writes, "And again another Scripture says, 'They will look on him whom they have pierced'" (John 19:37).

The piercing theme of these three messianic passages receives further reinforcement when the author of the Revelation looks to a future return of Jesus in the clouds, and declares, "Behold, he is coming with the clouds, and every eye will see him, even those who pierced him, and all tribes of the earth will wail on account of him" (Rev 1:7). This verse combines two citations, one from Daniel 7:13, and the other from Zechariah 12:10, from which the piercing quotation is derived.[24]

Thus, piercing figures prominently in three of the most important Old Testament passages viewed as messianic by early Christians

---

the broad nature of those quotations, including citations by Matthew (Matt. 8:17), Luke (Luke 22:37; Acts 8:32–33), John (John 12:39), Paul (Rom. 10:16), and Peter (1 Peter 2:22)" (Lunde, *Following Jesus, the Servant King,* 70).

23. "Now God speaks ... after the manner of men, declaring that He is wounded by the sins of His people, and especially by their obstinate contempt of His word, in the same manner as a mortal man receives a deadly wound, when his heart is pierced" (John Calvin, *Commentary on the Gospel According to John,* II [Calvin Translation Society, 1847], 242, cited in Joyce G. Baldwin, *Haggai, Zechariah, Malachi: An Introduction & Commentary,* TOTC [Leicester: Inter-Varsity, 1972], 191). Boda summarizes some of the numerous attempts to connect the stabbing with a particular historical character, finally deciding that the one pierced is Yahweh himself (Mark J. Boda, *The Book of Zechariah,* NICOT [Grand Rapids: Eerdmans, 2016] 716–17).

24. G. K. Beale and Sean M. McDonough, "Revelation," in G. K. Beale and D. A. Carson, eds., *Commentary on the New Testament Use of the Old Testament,* 1090–91.

(Psalm 22, Isaiah 52–53, and Zechariah 12). The apostle Paul, who knew and was deeply influenced by the Old Testament, would have been thoroughly conversant with these particular Old Testament passages, and may have found spiritual encouragement when facing his own piercing pain by reflecting on the truth that Jesus himself had encountered piercing pain in fulfillment of Scripture.

The other two themes mentioned in the introduction of this section, facial injury and humiliation, also make appearances in these Old Testament passages. The theme of facial injury appears in Isaiah 50:6 ("my cheeks to those who pull out the beard") and 52:14 ("his appearance was so marred, beyond human semblance"), even though more emphasis is given in context to the general affliction (wounding, crushing, whipping, 53:4–5), oppression (53:7–8), and substitutionary suffering (53:4–6, 8, 11–12) of the servant.[25] The theme of humiliation is prominent in 49:7 ("to one deeply despised, abhorred by the nation, the servant of rulers"), 50:6 ("I hid not my face from disgrace and spitting"), and 53:3 ("as one from whom men hide their faces he was despised, and we esteemed him not").[26] The theme of humiliation is also prominent in Psalm 22 in verses 6–7 ("scorned by mankind and despised by the people ... mock me ... "), 13 ("they open wide their mouths at me"), 17 ("they stare and gloat over me"), and in verse 24 when God's attitude toward his people is exposed

---

25. Matt 8:17 connects Isa 53:4 to Jesus's healing ministry: "This was to fulfill what was spoken by the prophet Isaiah: 'He took our illnesses and bore our diseases.' " Matthew, perhaps representing an early Christian appropriation of Isa 53:4, does not appear to draw upon the Greek translation, but either offers his own literal translation of the Hebrew, or borrows an early Christian rendering which included the word *astheneia* ("weakness" or "sickness"). Paul, who likely composed 2 Cor earlier than Matt was written, could have had access to the same Greek rendering of Isa 53:4 (particularly if mediated through the words of Jesus), and thus in yet another way could have used it as a bridge to identify his own cruciform *astheneia(i)* ("weakness[es]" or "sickness[es]"; 2 Cor 12:5, 9, 10) with the weakness/sickness of the pierced and suffering servant of Isa 53:4–5.

26. Note that in Greek Isa 53:3 reads differently, making it appear that the face belongs to the sufferer rather than the inflictors of suffering: *hoti apestraptai to prosōpon autou ētimasthē kai ouk elogisthē* ("because his face was turned away, he was dishonored and not given his due"). If Paul was familiar with this Greek translation, which he very likely was, it is possible that he could have identified his own facial suffering with face of his Lord, who turned away from the dishonor inflicted upon him.

(" ... he has not despised or abhorred ... and he has not hidden his face from him ... ").

But most remarkable is the presence of the piercing theme in each of these three key messianic passages. Paul certainly knew these passages, and like other New Testament Christians doubtless counted them as fulfilled in Christ. Should we not assume that the apostle, who so closely identified with the sufferings of Jesus, would have found comfort in the fact that his Lord had endured piercing pain along with abuse to and humiliation upon his head, all in fulfillment of messianic Scripture?

CRITERIA SUPPORTED OR
ALLUDED TO IN THIS CHAPTER

1. Impacting Paul's physical flesh

2. Comparable to the jabbing of a sharp-pointed object

3. Excruciating, not simply annoying

4. Impacting Paul's face (as part of his head)

5. Viewed by others as humiliating and weak

6. Paralleling the sufferings of Jesus

CLUES FROM IRENAEUS
AND TERTULLIAN

T he earliest Christian writers to comment about Paul's thorn in
the flesh were Irenaeus and Tertullian. Irenaeus and Tertullian
were the earliest *by far*. It is inadequate in a study such as ours
to draw up a list of early interpretations and leave readers with the
impression that there existed a veritable smorgasbord of opinions
among the church fathers about Paul's thorn in the flesh—implying
that no author's comments should be accorded greater value than the
comments of any other. Contrariwise, in the case of trying to ascer-
tain a historical event, the difference between an author writing one
hundred and fifty years after an event and one writing three hundred
or more years after the same event fall into two distinct categories in
terms of their historical value. In the case of the first, at least in oral
and semi-oral cultures, retellings are alive and often closely connected
to their source, whereas in the case of the second, the chronological
distance raises doubts about whether what is recounted has a legiti-
mate claim of being historically connected to what originally occurred.

Because the value of oral traditions is culturally distant from many reading this book, let me offer an analogy. I recently related to my daughters a conversation I had with an elderly Armenian-American man in Philadelphia in 1998. Our strongest common language was Turkish, so the entire conversation took place in Turkish. This elderly man told me about his escape from Ottoman Turkey in 1915, when he was sixteen years old, just as the Armenian genocide was getting underway. He related many details I can still distinctly remember. One is that his mother bailed three valuable silk rugs together to look like a thin poor-person's mattress that she later sold after reaching Aleppo in Syria for much-needed money. Please observe that the event under discussion, including the detail of the selling of carpets occurred more than one hundred years ago from the time of this writing, and I heard it directly from an eyewitness. One of my daughters to whom I told the story (say, at the age of twenty) could easily write it down at the age of seventy, and she would have no difficulty remembering the particular detail about silk carpets being sold to facilitate the escape. Her writing would occur more than one hundred and fifty years after the original event with only one non-eyewitness separating the event and my daughter's retelling. Furthermore, observe that the conversation I had with this elderly man would probably not arouse nearly the curiosity in a twenty-year-old living in the twenty-first century as a significant part of Paul's suffering would have aroused in Christians living in the late second century and into the first decade of the third century AD. In other words, the nature of Paul's thorn was more likely to be transmitted by early Christians because Paul was extremely important in their community's tradition. Furthermore, note that twenty-first century Southern California is not much of an oral culture, and yet, even in my non-oral culture, the passing on of a story such as the one I just mentioned could readily take place. One hundred fifty years in an oral culture about something as significant from Paul's life as the nature of his thorn in the flesh is simply not a long time.

If we add in the judgment of Markus Bockmuehl that "the early church recognized well into the second century a select group of what we might call sub-apostolic bearers of memory, who were widely regarded as—and in some cases perhaps were in fact—living links between the leaders of the apostolic generation and the churches that followed them,"[1] the case for memory accuracy is strengthened even more. In other words, remembering Paul (or Peter, as Bockmuehl's comment concerns), was not a simple case of oral transmission, as was my analogy, but belongs in the category of a traditional retelling that would have been protected by the community's bearers of the tradition.

That is why the remarks of Irenaeus (ca. 130–202) and Tertullian (ca. 155–240) are in a separate category in terms of their historical value than are the comments of the next earliest writers who comment on the nature of Paul's thorn: Basil of Caesarea (ca. 330–379), Gregory of Nazianzus (329–389), Ambrose (ca. 339–397), John Chrysostom (ca. 347–407), Jerome (ca. 342–420), Severian of Gabala (late fourth to early fifth century), Augustine (354–430), and Theodoret of Cyrus (ca. 393–457).[2] Observe how much time has elapsed between the period of Irenaeus and Tertullian and these later writers. The distance between Irenaeus and Tertullian and the next closest authors who comment on the nature of Paul's thorn in the flesh—one hundred and fifty to two hundred years—is as great or greater than is the chronological distance from Irenaeus and Tertullian back to the time of Paul himself!

So if Irenaeus and Tertullian are uniquely important from the standpoint of oral transmission, what do Irenaeus and Tertullian relate about Paul's thorn in the flesh? Irenaeus indicates that Paul's

---

1. Markus Bockmuehl, *Simon Peter in Scripture and Memory: The New Testament Apostle in the Early Church* (Grand Rapids: Baker, 2012), 16.

2. Note that Origen (ca. 185–254), Novatian (ca. 200–258), and Epiphanius (ca. 315–403) all seem to allude to Paul's thorn in the flesh, but they focus on spiritual lessons connected to the thorn rather than on identifying what it is. It is difficult to tell in the case of Cyprian (ca. 200–258), who may have had in mind a broad combination of difficulties Paul faced—including illness—but perhaps also persecutions and other challenges he might have encountered on his mission. For Cyprian, see *De mort.* 13 (ANF 5:472); *Ad Quirinium* 3.6 (ANF 5:534).

thorn in the flesh was an ailment in his physical body. Tertullian
agrees that Paul's infirmity was in his body, but in one text gets more
specific yet. Tertullian writes that he had heard that Paul's thorn was
pain in the ear or the head. Let us look at what each of these authors
writes in turn.

IRENAEUS ON PAUL'S
THORN IN THE FLESH

Irenaeus anticipates his quotation of 2 Corinthians 12:7 by alluding
to 2 Corinthians 12:9–10. In *Against Heresies* (*Adversus Haeresus*), he
writes that the human body of the believer that has been "nourished"
by the Eucharist during life, after it has been "deposited in the earth,
and suffering decomposition there, shall rise at their appointed time,
the Word of God granting them resurrection to the glory of God, even
the Father, who freely gives to this mortal immortality, and to this
corruptible incorruption, because *the strength of God is made perfect
in weakness, in order that we may never become puffed up.*"[3] Irenaeus
makes this allusion to 2 Corinthians 12:7–10 in the context of writing
about death, decay, and bodily resurrection of the physical body of
believers. He then adds, "And might it not be the case, perhaps, as I
have already observed, that for this purpose God permitted our resolution into the common dust of mortality?"
Irenaeus then moves into a direct citation of 2 Corinthians 12:7–10:

> The Apostle Paul has, moreover, in the most lucid manner,
> pointed out that man has been delivered over to his own infir-
> mity, lest, being uplifted, he might fall away from the truth.
> Thus he says in the second [Epistle] to the Corinthians: "And
> lest I should be lifted up by the sublimity of the revelations,
> there was given unto me a thorn in the flesh, the messenger of
> Satan to buffet me. And upon this I besought the Lord three
> times, that it might depart from me. But he said unto me, My

---

3. *Haer.* 5.2.2 (italics mine). This and the following quotations from Irenaeus are from
ANF 1:528–29.

grace is sufficient for thee; for strength is made perfect in weakness. Gladly therefore shall I rather glory in infirmities, that the power of Christ may dwell in me."[4]

Irenaeus continues in the same paragraph to expand upon the theme of bodily infirmity while still referencing 2 Corinthians 12:7–10.

What, therefore? (as some may exclaim:) did the Lord wish, in that case, that His apostles should thus undergo buffeting, and that he should endure such infirmity? Even so it was; the word says it. For strength is made perfect in weakness, rendering him a better man who by means of his infirmity becomes acquainted with the power of God. For how could a man have learned that he is himself an infirm being, and mortal by nature, but that God is immortal and powerful, unless he had learned by experience what is in both? For there is nothing evil in learning one's infirmities by endurance; yea, rather, it has even the beneficial effect of preventing him from forming an undue opinion of his own nature.[5]

Irenaeus continues his emphasis on the human body in the following paragraph as he writes about the resurrection of the body:

For if He does not vivify what is mortal, and does not bring back the corruptible to incorruption, He is not a God of power. … And surely it is much more difficult and incredible, from non-existent bones, and nerves, and veins, and the rest of man's organization, to bring it about that all this should be, and to make man an animated and rational creature, than to re-integrate again that which had been created and then afterwards decomposed into earth (for the reasons already mentioned), having thus passed into those [elements] from which man, who had no previous existence, was formed. … And

---

4. Irenaeus, *Haer.* 5.3.1.
5. Irenaeus, *Haer.* 5.3.1.

that flesh shall also be found fit for and capable of receiving the power of God, which at the beginning received the skillful touches of God; so that one part became the eye for seeing; another, the ear for hearing; another, the hand for feeling and working; another, the sinews stretched out everywhere, and holding the limbs together; another, arteries and veins, passages for the blood and the air; another the various internal organs; another, the blood, which is the bond of union between soul and body.[6]

Then, in the final relevant paragraph, Irenaeus alludes once more to 2 Corinthians 12:7–10 and connects it to the resurrection-of-the-body theme that he has been expounding:

The flesh, therefore, is not destitute [of participation] in the constructive wisdom and power of God. But if the power of Him who is the bestower of life *is made perfect in weakness*— that is, in the flesh—let them inform us, when they maintain the incapacity of flesh to receive the life granted by God, whether they do say these things as being living men at present, and partakers of life, or acknowledge that, having no part in life whatever, they are at the present moment dead men.[7]

The manner in which Irenaeus weaves together a discussion of the infirmities of the human body and the resurrection of the body with one direct quotation from 2 Corinthians 12:7–10 and two allusions to 12:9–10 compels us to conclude that Irenaeus viewed Paul's thorn in the flesh as a bodily ailment of some sort. Nothing more specific can be inferred from his comments, but it is clear that he considered Paul's thorn to be a bodily ailment.

Irenaeus's observations are the earliest extant commentary from any of the early Christian writers on Paul's thorn in the flesh. The work in which his comments are found, *Against Heresies,* was written

---

6. Irenaeus, *Haer.* 5.3.2.

7. Irenaeus, *Haer.* 5.3.3 (italics mine).

around AD 180. That is roughly one hundred and fifteen years after Paul's death and one hundred and twenty five years after Paul wrote the words about his thorn in the flesh in 2 Corinthians 12:7. Recall that Irenaeus was well-connected in the early church. He grew up in Asia Minor, served as a bishop in Lyon, Gaul (France), seventeen hundred miles away, and made connections with other Christians in Rome on at least a couple occasions. Irenaeus's opinion deserves historical weight (in a way that all others save Tertullian's should not) both because of how early he wrote these words and in light of his breadth of knowledge of Christian history in the latter half of the second century. Irenaeus's opinion was that Paul's thorn in the flesh was a bodily infirmity.

TERTULLIAN ON PAUL'S
THORN IN THE FLESH

Tertullian is the first Christian writer to identify the bodily location of Paul's pain. But before we look at the passage where he locates the pain, let us observe that Tertullian, like Irenaeus, offers clear general evidence that he understood Paul's thorn in the flesh to be a bodily ailment that was inflicted by an angel of Satan with God's permission, and which was comparable to what happened to Job.

In *Against Marcion* (*Adversus Marcionem*) 5.11–12, written sometime in the first decade of the third century, Tertullian clearly alludes to Paul's affliction that came about by an angel of Satan to buffet him.[8] In the passage leading up to his mention of 2 Corinthians 12:7, Tertullian describes at length God's allowance of the sufferings of human bodies over and against Marcion's view that the god of the new covenant is a gentle god (as opposed to the vindictive god of the Old Testament) and that bodily suffering is unspiritual. Tertullian's comments read like a sequential commentary on the physical-suffering aspects of 2 Corinthians. Following a discussion of Paul's veil in 2 Corinthians 3 (in dialogue with Marcion's views of that passage), Tertullian turns toward quotations

---

8. Tertullian, *Marc.* 5.11–12.

from or allusions to 2 Corinthians in order to refute Marcion's understanding of "the god of this world" (2 Cor 4:4) and his supposed nature.
Following is a list of quotations or allusions to 2 Corinthians (with a
few other allusions interspersed) drawn up by Cleveland Coxe.[9] Pay
special attention to the order: 4:6; 4:7; 4:8–12; 4:10 twice; 4:16–18;
4:11; 4:14; 4:16 twice; 5:1; 5:2–3; 5:4 thrice; 5:5; 5:6; 5:8; 5:10 twice;
5:17; 7:1; 11:2; 11:13; 11:14; 12:7–8; 13:1; 13:2; 13:10. Tertullian is working his way through 2 Corinthians in response to Marcion, focusing in
many cases upon the bodily sufferings of the apostle Paul and interacting with comments Paul made about the human body. The quotations
below demonstrate that Tertullian thought of Paul's thorn as bodily
suffering of some kind. (Keep in mind that Tertullian is responding
to Marcion's view that the body is evil.)[10]

For if it is the glory of God that so great a treasure should
be kept in earthen vessels, and the earthen vessels are the
Creator's, then the glory also is the Creator's, and it is his vessels that savour of the excellency of the power of God.

For he sets down the reason, *That the life also of Christ may be
made manifest in our body,* even as, he means, his death too is
borne about in the body.

[E]vidently this is a statement of the resurrection of the flesh:
for he says that our outward man is decaying, yet not as by
everlasting destruction after death, but through the labours
and inconveniences of which he has already observed, *Neither
shall we faint.* For when he says that our inward man is renewed
from day to day, he is here drawing attention to both facts, the
decaying of the body through the harassment of temptations,
and the renewing of the mind by contemplation of the promises.

---

9. See Coxe's footnotes in *ANF* 3, 453–56.

10. These quotations are all from *Marc.* 5.11–12. Throughout this chapter, English quotations of *Marc.* are from Tertullian, *Adversus Marcionem: Books IV–V,* ed. and trans. Ernest Evans
(Oxford: Clarendon, 1972), 584–91 (italics Evans's).

... when he adds that in this tabernacle of an earthly body we groan, desiring to be clothed upon with that which is from heaven, seeing that when unclothed we shall not be found naked; unclothed, the body ...

... for they too will rise again incorruptible, receiving back their body, receiving it entire.

... being not so much divested of the body as clothed upon with that which is heavenly ...

And so it was not without reason that he said, *Not wishing to be divested* of the body *but to be clothed upon.*

... the pledge of that hope of being clothed upon; and that so long as we are in the flesh we are absent from the Lord, and therefore ought to think it better rather to be absent from the body and present with the Lord.

... and has also affirmed the presentment [in court] of the bodies of all men.

Then we come to the paragraph in which Paul's affliction is clearly alluded to:

At present perhaps I have this to marvel at, whether a god with no terrestrial interests can have possessed a paradise of his own—unless perhaps he has by permission made use of the Creator's paradise, as [he has of the Creator's] world. Still, there is the Creator's precedent of lifting a man up to heaven, the case of Elijah. I shall marvel even more if that lord supremely good, so averse from smiting and raging, should have applied not his own but the Creator's messenger of Satan to buffet his own apostle, and though thrice besought by him have refused to yield. So then Marcion's god administers correction after the manner of the Creator who is hostile to those exalted, who in fact puts down the mighty from their throne.

> And is it he also who gave Satan power even over Job's body, that strength might obtain approval in weakness?[11]

That Tertullian understands Paul's affliction to be bodily suffering is supported by: (1) the almost-sequential movement through the bodily suffering sections of 2 Corinthians up to and beyond Paul's thorn-in-the-flesh comment; (2) Tertullian's use of the Latin gloss (*colaphizando*), drawn from the same stem as Paul uses in Greek (*kolaphizō*; 2 Cor 12:7) to describe what Satan did to him; and, perhaps most clearly, (3) the explicit comparison with what Satan did to Job's body: "who gave Satan power even over Job's body, that strength might obtain approval in weakness."[12]

Lest, however, we had any doubt that Tertullian thought of Paul's affliction as being anything other than a bodily condition, in a separate discussion about whether repentance was possible for a believer who had committed egregious sexual immorality, Tertullian off-handedly inserted a comment about Paul's thorn/stake—"But withal himself says that 'a stake was given him, an angel of Satan,' by which he was to be buffeted, lest he should exalt himself"—and stated that potential pride in Paul "was being restrained in the apostle by 'buffets,' if you will, by means (as they say) of *pain in the ear or head?*"[13] In other words, Tertullian off-handedly remarked that he had heard that what people were saying in his day was that Paul's thorn in the flesh was a pain in his ear or head. Notice that this is not what Tertullian *inferred* Paul's thorn must have been, as is the case with all later authors who mention Paul's thorn; it is what people *said* his thorn was.[14]

---

11. Tertullian, *Marc.* 5.12.

12. Keep in mind our defense of Paul's literary and conceptual dependence upon Job (ch. 4). Tertullian's comments would seem to support that connection as well.

13. Tertullian, *De pudicitia* 13.17 (ANF 4:87; italics mine [Latin: *dolorem, ut aiunt, auriculae vel capitis*]).

14. Latin: *ut aiunt*. Note that Tertullian mentions Paul's thorn in the flesh also in *De fuga in persecutione* 2 but does not indicate what he thinks it is. He does comment that he does not believe God would allow a holy man like Paul to be buffeted by Satan "unless it be that at the

An inadvertent comment such as this should be deemed perhaps even more historically valuable than something written in support of a theological or ecclesiastical point. In saying this, I am not claiming that theological or ecclesiastical arguments among early Christian writers lack a historical base. Tertullian, for example, was keenly interested in history; his historical attentiveness is conspicuous in his appeals to history as a counterpoint to "heretics" who focused on myth, as our earlier quotations from *Against Marcion* illustrate.[15] I am simply noting that when an inadvertent comment appears, we should be even less skeptical about the historical value of such a comment than we might be when an author leverages a historical detail to make a theological point. In other words, the way Tertullian wrote this sentence certainly makes it appear that he unassumingly wrote down what he had heard from others about the nature of Paul's thorn in the flesh.

Anticipating one of our later conclusions, notice one detail about Tertullian's comment: Tertullian does not write "ears" (plural); he uses the singular "ear" (*auriculae*). (Of course, "head" [*capitis*] has to be singular!) Granted that this could be a collective singular, it still might be that Paul's pain was on one side of his head rather than on both. Thus, it may not be that Paul experienced general pain in his ears (plural), but that the pain was located on the side of his head where his ear was. If Paul experienced pain on one side of his face/head, one can easily imagine that Paul would put his hand up to the side of his face/head whenever his pain got intense. Observers might have interpreted this as pain of the head or of one ear.

The precise date when Tertullian wrote these comments is difficult to pinpoint, but most scholars place it in the first or second

---

same time strength of endurance may be perfected in weakness"; that is, "unless the design is to humble" (*Fug.* 2 [*ANF* 4:117–18]).

15. "Tertullian would not tolerate an interpretation that disdained the historical, incarnational nature of Christian faith in favor of an ahistorical philosophy. God was the God of nature and history, and his revelation arose in human history. The interpreter had no room to massage the message into a more palatable myth" (R. Kearsley, "Tertullian," in *Historical Handbook of Major Biblical Interpreters*, ed. Donald K. McKim [Downers Grove, IL: InterVarsity Press, 1998], 65).

decade of the third century. This would mean that Tertullian's comment about Paul's thorn in the flesh would have come around twenty to thirty years after Irenaeus commented about Paul's thorn in the flesh, one hundred and forty to fifty years after Paul's death, and one hundred and fifty to one hundred and sixty years after Paul wrote 2 Corinthians 12:7.

We need to take Tertullian's statement more seriously in our quest to identify Paul's thorn than has heretofore been the pattern. Perhaps under the influence of form-critical assumptions, modern interpreters (with the exception of a growing minority of biblical interpreters[16]) have been reticent to acknowledge the value of orally-mediated traditions. This would mean that the comments of Tertullian and Irenaeus would necessarily continue to be treated as most interpreters seem currently to treat them—no more than theological inferences or historical guesses such as we find in the writers of the fourth and fifth centuries and beyond. However, as we asked with Irenaeus, it is reasonable to ask about Tertullian: How likely is it that a well-connected and highly educated Christian jurist, writing around one hundred and fifty to one hundred and sixty years after Paul penned 2 Corinthians would not have had access to this tradition? Which is more likely: that he did or that he did not?

Irenaeus, who grew up in Asia Minor, wrote in Greek while in Gaul (France). Tertullian wrote in Latin in North Africa. Thus, considering only these two authors, a bodily ailment as the explanation for Paul's thorn in the flesh evinces geographical as well as linguistic diversity at the end of the second and beginning of the third century.

---

16. See brief summaries and references in John D. Harvey, "Orality and Its Implications for Biblical Studies: Recapturing an Ancient Paradigm," *JETS* 45 (2002): 99–103, and June F. Dickie, "Communicating Biblical Text to Be Heard Well: Lessons from Orality and Performance Studies," *Neot* 52 (2018): 289–90. A helpful guide is Rafael Rodríguez, *Oral Tradition and the New Testament: A Guide for the Perplexed*, Guides for the Perplexed (London: T&T Clark, 2014), 33–52.

CRITERIA SUPPORTED OR ALLUDED TO
IN THIS CHAPTER

1. Viewed by Paul as attacks by an angel of Satan, though permitted by God

2. Impacting Paul's physical flesh

3. Excruciating, not simply annoying

4. Impacting Paul's face (as part of his head)

5. Involving the ear

CLUES FROM GALATIANS

O ne of the more difficult issues to resolve on our path toward
identifying Paul's thorn in the flesh involves possible connections between 2 Corinthians 12:7 and the book of Galatians,
with Galatians 4:13–15 as the key passage requiring attention. Many
interpreters throughout history have drawn connections between
2 Corinthians 12:7 and Galatians 4:13–15, while a few have rejected
the connection. In this chapter, we will evaluate the strengths (or
lack thereof) of the suggested connection, draw out possible implications, and more briefly evaluate two other verses in Paul's letter
to the Galatians (Gal 3:1 and 6:17) that may hold relevant clues for
identifying Paul's thorn in the flesh.

GENERAL SIMILARITIES BETWEEN
GALATIANS AND 2 CORINTHIANS
(ESPECIALLY CHAPTERS 10–13)

Before examining Galatians 4:13–15 in particular, let us consider
the question of whether there are any notable similarities *in general*
between 2 Corinthians—especially chapters 10–13—and Galatians.

That is, are there any ways in which 2 Corinthians (esp. 10–13) shares similarities with Paul's letter to the Galatians, even in contrast to similarities shared between 2 Corinthians and other letters of Paul? There are, in fact, some surprising ways in which 2 Corinthians and Galatians appear similar to one another in ways (or degrees) that are sometimes dissimilar to what we find in other letters of Paul. Following are five *general* similarities between 2 Corinthians (esp. 10–13) and Galatians that might push us in the direction of greater sympathy toward attempts to use Galatians 4:13–15 as a bridge into understanding what Paul was referencing when he wrote about his thorn in the flesh in 2 Corinthians 12:7.

First, Paul is angry and ironic both in 2 Corinthians 10–13 and Galatians to a degree he is not in any of his other letters. Granted, Paul can exhibit irritation and/or sarcasm elsewhere in his letters (such as in 1 Cor 4:7–13; Phil 3:2), but the sustained exasperation that appears in 2 Corinthians 10–13 and Galatians is unsurpassed in any of Paul's other writings.

Second, Paul calls out his opponents with more specificity in 2 Corinthians 10–13 and Galatians than he does in any of his other letters. Although the characteristics of the two sets of opponents appear to differ in some respects (see 2 Cor 10:12; 11:4, 12–15; Gal 1:6–9; 5:2–12; 6:12–13), what is strikingly similar about the two passages is Paul's insistent calling out of his opponents. Such public challenging of Paul's opponents is more pronounced in these two places than anywhere else in Paul's letters.

Third, 2 Corinthians (12:2–4, 7) and Galatians (chs. 1–2) are the only places that Paul mentions the period between his conversion and the start of the three missionary journeys described in the book of Acts. As Delling observes about 2 Corinthians 12, "v. 7 suggests that the apostle's 'thorn for the flesh' was given in the time of the events mentioned in v. 2, i.e., in that part of his life to which allusion is made in Gl. 1:21."[1]

---

1. Delling, *TDNT* 7:412.

Fourth, Paul refers or alludes to previous visits both in 2 Corinthians 10–13 (see 10:1–2, 10–11, 13–14; 11:2, 7–9, 21; 12:6, 13–16, 21; 13:1–2, 6, 10; cf. 1:19; 2:1–2; 3:2; 7:2) and in Galatians 4 (4:8–11, 12–15, 19; cf. 1:8–9, 11; 3:1–4). Granted, he does the same in some of his other letters (see 1 Thessalonians 1–2; 1 Corinthians 1–4). Nevertheless, Paul's reference to previous visits is prominent in both of these letters.

Fifth, and certainly significant in our study (see ch. 8 above), Paul's theme of identification with the suffering and death of Christ is more pronounced in 2 Corinthians and Galatians than anywhere else in the Pauline corpus except, perhaps, Romans 6 (Gal 2:20; 5:24; 6:14; 2 Cor 1:5; 4:10; 13:3–4).[2]

These general observations should engender a certain degree of sympathy to the suggestion made by many interpreters that the malady of Galatians 4:13–15 overlaps with the thorn of 2 Corinthians 12:7. This, in turn, may help us identify one or two more criteria for identifying Paul's thorn in the flesh to add to our expanding list of criteria.

WHAT GALATIANS 4:13–15 SUGGESTS

Galatians 4:13–15 is the only place in Paul's letters where Paul plainly mentions that he suffered from a bodily illness, pain, or disability of some sort.[3] We learn from other letters that Paul's coworkers suffered physical illnesses (Phil 2:25–30; 1 Tim 5:23; 2 Tim 4:20), but only in Galatians 4:13–15 (apart, I suggest, from 2 Cor 12:7) does Paul openly mention an illness, pain, or disability related to his body. In fact, Paul writes that the physical illness or disability from which he suffered

---

2. See ch. 8 for discussion of cruciformity. For Paul's theology of identification with the suffering of Jesus in Galatians, see John Anthony Dunne, *Persecution and Participation in Galatians*, WUNT 2, Reihe 454 (Tübingen: Mohr Siebeck, 2017).

3. It is highly unusual for an interpreter to argue that Paul's "weakness of the flesh" (4:13) is anything other than a bodily ailment of some sort. But Erhardt Güttgemanns takes this reference to refer to opposition; see Erhardt Güttgemanns, *Der Leidende Apostel und Sein Herr: Studien zur Paulinischen Christologie*, FRLANT 90 (Göttingen: Vandenhoeck & Ruprecht, 1986), 173–77.

while in the region of "Galatia,"[4] became the means by which he was able to declare the good news about Jesus to the Galatians.[5]

> You know it was because of a bodily ailment [lit. "through the weakness/illness of the flesh," *di' astheneian tēs sarkos*] that I preached the gospel to you at first, and though my condition [lit. "in my flesh," *en tē sarki mou*] was a trial to you, you did not scorn or despise me, but received me as an angel of God, as Christ Jesus. What then has become of your blessedness? For I testify to you that, if possible, you would have gouged out your eyes and given them to me. (Gal 4:13–15)

We can infer the following about what Paul endured in Galatia from these verses:

First, Paul suffered from a physical ailment. *Astheneia* can be used either for a general weakness or an illness, but in this passage since it is modified by *sarkos* ("of flesh"), and because "in my flesh" (*en tē sarki mou*) gets added in verse 16 (though sometimes left out of our translations), it is almost certain that Paul is speaking of a physical ailment of some sort, as agreed upon by almost all interpreters.[6]

---

4. I take this to be what is often referred to as "south Galatia," and to be a reference to Paul's visit to such cities as Pisidian Antioch, Iconium, Lystra, and Derbe (and possibly Perga or even Attalia, as well) on his first missionary journey (cf. Acts 13:13–14:26). See Wilson, "Galatia in Text," 54–56. (Note that if Perga and/or Attalia get included in the Galatian designation, then, following Wilson, we might need to start calling Pisidian Antioch, Iconium, Lystra, and Derbe "middle Galatia" and Perga and Attalia the true "south Galatia.") Henceforth, when I write about "Galatia" and "Galatians," I am referring to the region Paul visited on his first missionary journey according to Acts 13–14 and to the people living in that region, acknowledging that most of his readers were not ethnic Galatians.

5. Scott J. Hafemann takes it further. He considers that "Paul's weakness was not merely the circumstance that brought the gospel to Galatia, though it may have been that as well. More importantly, Paul's suffering was the divinely ordained means by which the gospel itself was made clear to the Galatians" (Scott J. Hafemann, "'Because of Weakness' (Galatians 4:13): The Role of Suffering in the Mission of Paul," in *The Gospel to the Nations: Perspectives on Paul's Mission*, ed. Peter Bolt and Mark Thompson [Downers Grove, IL: InterVarsity Press; Leicester: Apollos, 2000], 134).

6. Hafemann, "'Because of Weakness,'" 133; Albl, "'For Whenever I Am Weak, Then I Am Strong,'" 152–53. Although the same expression is used by Paul in Rom 6:19 to refer to the natural limitations of the Roman readers' spiritual insight, the two meanings cannot be inverted since the two contexts are radically different from one another. See comments in Thomas, *Devil*,

Second, the condition from which Paul suffered presented a distressing challenge to the Galatians. It was a trial or a test to them, as Paul says in verse 14 (and implied in the following clause about them not despising him). From these statements, it can be inferred both that the condition from which Paul suffered was an extreme illness or pain and that the Galatians were fully aware of the nature of Paul's ailment.

Third, the condition was something that others might deem contemptible, shameful, or humiliating. This is the implication of the line "you did not scorn or despise me" (4:14).[7]

Fourth, the condition was of a nature that some might have viewed it as a demonic attack. Although not obvious in our English translations, the term translated as "despise" is literally "spit out" (*ekptuō*). Spitting, both in the time of Paul and in our own day, has been a symbolic action that people afraid of evil spirits have used to ward off attacks from such spirits.[8] I personally observed many people making spitting sounds to ward off attacks by evil spirits during the seven years I resided in the Middle East. This folk-religious action is the most obvious cultural background for informing Paul's intended meaning here.[9] Such an interpretation gains some support by Paul's additional and seemingly contrasting comment that his readers had received him like an "angel of God." That is, they were observing a

---

Disease and Deliverance, 56–57. Furthermore, as Moo notes, "Paul does use ἀσθένεια to refer to physical illness in one other text (1 Tim. 5:23), and the Gospels and Acts use the word exclusively in this sense (Matt. 8:17; Luke 5:15; 8:2; 13:11, 12; John 5:5; 11:4; Acts 28:9). And σάρξ often means 'body' in Paul (e.g., Rom. 2:28; 2 Cor. 4:11; Eph. 2:11)," (Moo, *Galatians*, 282–83).

7. Note that Paul also uses the verb *exoutheneō* ("scorn") in 2 Cor 10:10 to describe the Corinthians' criticism of his speech coupled with the weakness of his body (that is, it is "scornable"). Lau notes that the change from the Galatians' former commitment to Paul and their current rejection is a type of betrayal. In referring to this betrayal, Paul uses "retrospective shame" to try to reform his readers. See Te-Li Lau, *Defending Shame: Its Formative Power in Paul's Letters* (Grand Rapids: Baker, 2020), 100–1.

8. Heckel, "Der Dorn im Fleisch," 84–86; Dunne, *Persecution and Participation*, 164–65.

9. J. Louis Martyn rightly notes: "Paul's verb (omitted by p46) is colorful: *ekptuein*, 'to spit out.' Tempted to view the sick apostle as an evil magician momentarily overcome by the malignant powers he normally used to control others, the Galatians could have reacted by spitting, hoping to cleanse their mouths of the unclean odors they inhaled in his presence" (J. Louis Martyn, *Galatians: A New Translation with Introduction and Commentary*, AB 33A [New York: Doubleday, 1997], 421).

physical condition in Paul that they would have been tempted to associate with a demonic attack (note ch. 3 above). Instead, they received Paul like an angel—or even in the manner they would have received Christ himself.

Fifth, Paul's condition might have involved his eyes.[10] Those who have studied the question of Paul's thorn in the flesh will know that this contention is disputed, and I have disputed it myself in the past. But everything else I have come across in this study so far has made me more open to the suggestion that Paul's eyes (or one eye) might have been involved in some way. This is not because we have so-far identified anything related to the eyes, but because we have encountered several clues that Paul's face/head was involved, and maybe also his ear (so, Tertullian)—and because so many craniofacial conditions (see ch. 14) include occasional or regular pain in the eye on the side of the face where other pain is felt.

The reason that Paul's eyes may somehow have been involved emerges from a particular way of interpreting 4:15, "For I testify to you that, if possible, you would have gouged out your eyes and given them to me." It looks like Paul is saying that the Galatians loved him so much that they would have gladly given him their eyes. The inference to be drawn is that Paul experienced difficulties of some kind with his eyes (or one eye) during the period he spent among the Galatians. Now, the reason some interpreters have been skeptical of the involvement of literal eyes is that Paul's mention of eyes appears in the middle of an exasperated exclamation of appreciation, if I may put it that way. I have already been candid that I have been skeptical in the past that Paul's literal eyes were involved. My thinking was: Couldn't the words Paul uttered have been mere hyperbole, akin to the expression: "You would have jumped off a cliff for me," or "You would have given your right arm for me"?

---

10. As Keith Liddell comments about the Roman period, "Blepheritis and other eye infections were widespread" (Keith Liddell, "Skin diseases in antiquity," *Clinical Medicine* 6 [2006]: 83).

I am still willing to grant that Paul's exclamation might simply be hyperbolic. But is hyperbole really the best explanation for this exasperated note of appreciation? Probably not. It should not escape the reader's notice that the exclamation does not stand alone. It functions as an integral piece of Paul's logical flow that moves from (1) the mention of Paul's bodily ailment, (2) into the statement that they did not despise Paul, (3) that contrasts with the Galatians receiving him like an angel of God or Christ himself, (4) that provokes the frustrated question, "What then has become of your blessedness?", (5) and that finally moves into the gouging-out-your-eyes exclamation.[11] In other words, step one (the mention of a bodily ailment) is connected in Paul's argument with step five (the comment about the eyes). In light of the fact that Paul has clearly called out his physical condition in verses 13–14, and linked that condition with an exclamation that includes a specific body part in verse 15, it seems more likely to me that his eyes were involved in his Galatian ailment than that they were not.[12]

Moreover, in a recently published catalogue of new religiously-oriented inscriptions from Lydia (in the first century, part of the Roman province of Asia [Minor]), Malay and Petzl make an intriguing comment that could add plausibility to involvement of Paul's eyes. They write, "The great number of ocular problems recorded in dedications of Lydia is notable. A. Chaniotis observed that fourteen

---

11. For further consideration, might there be some sort of connection between Paul's thorn in his flesh and Jesus's comment about having a beam (*dokos*) in one's own eye? Jegher-Bucher draws a connection between the two, suggesting that both "thorn in the flesh" and "beam in the eye" were in general proverbial usage (Jegher-Bucher, "'The Thorn in the Flesh'/'Der Pfahl im Fleisch,'" 395). At the present, I am skeptical of her suggestion.

12. It is unlikely that Paul's comment in Gal 6:11 about his large handwriting suggests anything about Paul's eyes (contra Nisbet, "Thorn in the Flesh," 126). See the impressive work of Steve Reece, *Paul's Large Letters: Paul's Autographic Subscriptions in the Light of Ancient Epistolary Conventions*, LNTS 561 (London: Bloomsbury T&T Clark, 2017), esp. 198–203. Reece surveys ancient examples of authors taking over for a professional scribe. He concludes that Paul wrote about his large letters because he wanted to add a personal note, to confirm that it was his own letter (against possible forgeries), and that the large letters were simply a reflection of Paul's handwriting ability—functional, but not as adept in writing in small letters as was a scribe. (Reece also suggests that this handwriting at the end would have made Paul's letter more like a legal contract than simply a personal letter. I deem Reece's last suggestion less likely.)

confessions out of thirty record eyes as the afflicted organs."[13] Zucconi
makes a similar observation about the Roman world, "Based solely on
the textual evidence, these were frequent eye diseases for the Romans."[14]
The simple observation that eyes were the most common (almost half)
of all the organs mentioned in the religious texts from Lydia, and that
eye ailments were one of the most common physical challenges in the
ancient world (per the epigraphic evidence) increases somewhat the
plausibility of the proposition that eyes were involved.

SIMILARITIES BETWEEN GALATIANS 4:13–15 AND 2 CORINTHIANS 12:1–10

Nevertheless, even if an interpreter were to grant that Paul's eyes
were involved when he was ill or disabled in Galatia, he or she would
not necessarily have to agree that Paul was writing about the same
condition in 2 Corinthians 12:7. Let us, then, consider some possible reasons for thinking that Paul might have been writing about the
same condition in both passages.[15]

First, there already exist various clues, set forth earlier in this book,
and wholly apart from Galatians 4:13–15, for viewing 2 Corinthians
12:7 as a physical ailment. How easy is it to conceive of Paul under-
going two separate severe bodily trials during the period he ministered in Galatia? No matter how you date the writings of Paul's
letters, Paul's heavenly ascent that occurred fourteen years prior to
his writing 2 Corinthians 12:7—and that was connected to the giving
of the thorn—was already a challenging aspect of his life before vis-
iting Galatia. The difficulty in conceiving of two such severe bodily
conditions wracking the body of an otherwise highly active person

---

13. Malay and Petzl, *New Religious Texts from Lydia*, 159.

14. Zucconi, *Ancient Medicine*, 308.

15. A link between Gal 4:13 and 2 Cor 12:7 is affirmed by Lightfoot, *Galatians*, 186, 190;
Bruce, *Epistle of Paul to the Galatians*, 208; Heckel, "Der Dorn im Fleisch," 65–92; Thrall,
First and Second Letters of Paul to the Corinthians, 178; and Hafemann, "'Because of Weakness'
(Galatians 4:13), 131–46. Ben Witherington is an example of one who answers in the negative
(Ben Witherington III, *Grace in Galatia: A Commentary on Paul's Letter to the Galatians* [Grand
Rapids: Eerdmans, 1998], 309).

at exactly the same time makes it more likely that there was only one physical condition rather than two during Paul's stay in Galatia.

Second, there are conspicuous similarities between the language Paul employed in each of the two passages (Gal 4:13–15 and 2 Cor 12:1–10) that could suggest that he was talking about the same malady in both cases.[16] Here are a few examples:

"Weakness" or "sickness" (*astheneia*) is a key word in both passages (Gal 4:13; 2 Cor 12:5, 9, 10).[17]

"Flesh" (*sarx*) is a key word in both passages (Gal 4:13, 14; 2 Cor 12:7).

Humiliation is a key cultural background in both contexts (Gal 4:14; 2 Cor 12:1, 5–7, 9).

The suggestion of demonic attack is present in both contexts ("spit upon" Gal 4:14; "angel of Satan" 2 Cor 12:7).

The mention of "angel of God" in Galatians 4:14 shares similarities in form to "angel of Satan" in 2 Corinthians 12:7, despite the contrast. At the very least, the presence of the word *angelos* appears in both passages. Paul only uses the word *angelos* thirteen times, including these two, in all his letters (Rom 8:38; 1 Cor 4:9; 6:3; 11:10; 13:1; 2 Cor 11:14; 12:7; Gal 1:8; 3:19; 4:14; Col 2:18; 2 Thess 1:7; 1 Tim 3:16; 5:21).[18]

Finally, Paul finishes his thought in Galatians 4:16 with the words, "Have I then become your enemy by *telling you the truth*?" This comment is similar to 2 Corinthians 12:6, the verse just before Paul's mention of the thorn, " … though if I should wish to boast, I would not be a fool, for I would be *speaking the truth*; but I refrain from it, so that no one may think more of me than he sees in me or hears from me" (italics mine). Paul is defensive in both contexts, and employs the comparable language of truth telling while anticipating opposition to his words.

---

16. "These passages so closely resemble each other that it is not unnatural to suppose the allusion to be the same in both" (Lightfoot, *Galatians*, 186).

17. Wallace, *Snatched into Paradise*, 273.

18. "It is striking that there is such an emphasis on supernatural revelation and angelic mediation in Galatians" (Clinton E. Arnold, "'I Am Astonished That You Are So Quickly Turning Away!' (Gal 1:6): Paul and Anatolian Folk Belief." NTS 51 [2005]: 448).

Such a quantity of overlapping words and ideas between these two brief passages is actually worth noticing. It helps confirm the suggestion that Paul may be talking about the same condition in both passages. My claim is not that there is any intentional literary relationship between Galatians 4:13–15 and 2 Corinthians 12:1–10, merely that Paul employed similar expressions in contexts in which he discussed one particular condition from which he suffered both while in Galatia and in Corinth. When the general similarities listed earlier in this chapter between Galatians and 2 Corinthians (esp. 10–13) also get factored in (frustrated and ironic tone, calling out opponents, mention of Paul's post-conversion/pre-visit period, mention of previous visits, cruciformity as a shared theme), it would seem to make more sense to view these passages as somehow connected than to leave them as two isolated sets of comments describing two separate terrible conditions from which Paul suffered.

Thus, Galatians 4:13–15 helps inform 2 Corinthians 12:7 regarding Paul's thorn in the flesh. More specifically, whatever it was that Paul suffered, it was probably a bodily ailment of some sort.

GALATIANS 3:1

If we allow for a connection between Galatians 4:13–15 and 2 Corinthians 12:7, there are two potentially mutually-supporting verses in Galatians that also need to be brought into the conversation: Galatians 3:1 and 6:17. The problem with appealing to either or both of these verses is that the interpretation of each of these two verses is disputed, even without appeal to the discussion of Paul's thorn in the flesh. But if the pain/illness/disability that Paul endured in Galatia (4:13–15) was in fact one instantiation of his thorn in the flesh, then these other two passages may mutually reinforce what we have already observed in our discussion of Galatians 4:13–15 above, and could perhaps even add something to the discussion.

In Galatians 3:1, Paul writes, "O foolish Galatians! Who has bewitched you? It was before your eyes that Jesus Christ was publicly portrayed as crucified."

There is little here that we can confidently use in our study. Nevertheless, three observations are worth considering regarding this verse.

First, Paul chides the Galatians in 3:1. The reproaching tone is similar to the tone he will take up again in 4:13–15.

Second, Paul appeals to the attack-from-evil-spirits theme implied in his spitting comment in 4:14. But in 3:1, Paul is more explicit than in 4:14. He writes, "Who has bewitched you?" or "Who has cast a spell on you?"[19] It is not necessary to suggest in this particular verse that Paul envisioned an actual magician casting an actual spell on the Galatians, even if he personally had received such attacks before. This expression simply may have been Paul's culturally-relevant way of saying, "What's wrong with you? You're acting in a surprising ('foolish') way. In light of the gospel you received, you should not allow people to lead you astray like this!" In other words, the opponents of the gospel who had convinced some of the gentile converts in Galatia to add circumcision and law-keeping to the gospel had duped them, Paul suggests, so much so that it appears as though the Galatians are under a spell.[20] Regardless of the precise intent of Paul's decision to employ such language, his use of language regarding magic and attacks by evil spirits may connect this passage somehow with Galatians 4:14 and 2 Corinthians 12:7.

Third, the Galatians *saw* something. "It was before your eyes that Jesus Christ was publicly portrayed as crucified." What was it that was displayed before their eyes? Recent commentators have tended

---

19. Note the more specific proposal of John H. Elliott that Paul is specifically referencing the harm that the casting of the evil eye might have had upon the Galatians (John H. Elliot, *Beware the Evil Eye (Volume 3): The Evil Eye in the Bible and the Ancient World: The Bible and Related Sources* [Cambridge: Lutterworth Press, 2016], 216–34).

20. Jerome H. Neyrey views Paul's statement as a formal witchcraft accusation, claiming that the Galatians have become demon-possessed, analogous to his accusation of the false apostles in 2 Cor 11:3, 13–15 (Jerome H. Neyrey, "Bewitched in Galatia: Paul and Cultural Anthropology," *CBQ* 50 [1988]: 72–100).

to think that this is merely a reference to Paul's vivid preaching about the cross.[21]

Let us grant that vivid preaching about the cross might be an interpretive option. Still, there are a couple difficulties to get over if one adopts that view. In this passage Paul is contrasting being under a spell with the impact of something they saw (literally) or "saw" (in their mind's eye). The contrast between being under a spell, on the one hand, with being awake and literally seeing something, on the other, is stronger than a purported contrast between being under a spell and vividly imagining something. Coming out of a spell, after all, is often described as waking up—into physical reality. Imagining the crucifixion because of vivid preaching does not provide the same level of contrast to the spell-boundness comment as seeing something with their literal eyes would. This observation, combined with the more straightforward interpretation of the expression "before your eyes" (*hois kat' ophthalmous*) makes the vivid preaching option less attractive than the option that the Galatians actually saw something.

Consequently, let us consider a different interpretive option in light of this study. Perhaps the Galatians saw Paul suffering from stabbing pain—either with their own eyes or by means of the descriptions Paul relayed when they asked him about the pain he was experiencing. Perhaps in Paul's own sufferings, or in his own descriptions of the stabbing pain he endured before them as he followed in the steps of Christ's own piercing suffering, he was somehow able to introduce the Galatians to the gospel. In other words, Paul used his own suffering, suffering he

---

21. See, for example, Moo, *Galatians*, 181–82; Thomas R. Schreiner, *Galatians*, ZECNT (Grand Rapids: Zondervan, 2010), 181–82; and Keener, *Galatians*, 212–13 (but note Keener's additional comments on p. 214 more in line with my argument: "In Paul's case, the Galatians may have witnessed Christ's crucifixion not only in Paul's preaching but also in Paul's own life. ... Paul may have described Jesus' passion in detail (cf. 1 Cor. 11:23–26) as well as illustrated it in his own experience." Richard B. Hays offers another interesting suggestion: "One other possibility, however, deserves attention. The verb προγράφω (*prographō*, translated as 'clearly portrayed' by the NIV and as 'publicly exhibited' by NRSV) is used elsewhere by Paul to mean 'written beforehand' in Scripture (Rom 15:4). Is it possible that by selecting this verb Paul implies that his story of Christ crucified was told through interpretation of scriptural texts? If so, the reference would be not to the gospel passion narratives—which had not yet been written at this time—but to the lament psalms, interpreted as prefigurations of Christ's crucifixion" (Richard B. Hays, "Galatians," in *The New Interpreter's Bible: Volume XI* [Nashville: Abingdon, 2000], 250–51).

described as analogous to the suffering of Jesus (who wore a crown of thorns, was beaten on his face, and also stabbed in other parts of his body—all in fulfillment of Scripture, per chapter 8), to point people to a crucified Savior and justification by faith in him alone.

Such a reading of Galatians 3:1 might be strengthened if they actually saw something on Paul's skin or could otherwise observe a bodily ailment, but still works if Paul experienced on-and-off agony over a pain that he described as severe and piercing, even if his observers could not see the source on his body. In light of the language Paul actually employs in Galatians 3:1, this interpretation seems slightly preferable to the idea that Paul's description of the death of Christ was so vivid that it was as though they could see it. Nevertheless, the suggestion that Paul may have been able to share his gospel message of a pierced Savior because of his own piercing pain must be held tentatively, since interpretive clues are limited. Other interpretive options are also possible.

GALATIANS 6:17

At the very close of Paul's letter, immediately before he offers his final grace-wish, Paul writes, "From now on let no one cause me trouble, for I bear on my body the marks of Jesus" (Gal 6:17). It appears that Paul writes this comment to motivate the Galatians to stop making his life so difficult, since he has already suffered a lot in his body. There are two items worth pondering in this verse that hold at least the potential of slightly furthering our study.

First, Paul writes that he had suffered from something that was a bodily ailment akin to piercing. The word translated here as "marks" (Greek *stigmata*) has often been interpreted broadly as the scars of Paul's beatings brought about by his testimony for Christ.[22] This may be correct, and I am somewhat sympathetic to that interpretation.

---

22. Slave tattoos and religious tattoos have also been suggested as the conceptual background of Paul's *stigmata*. But most interpreters have opted for scars brought about by persecution. See discussions in Keener, *Galatians*, 582–87, and Anthony Tyrell Hanson, *The Paradox of the Cross in the Thought of St. Paul*, JSNTSup 17 (Sheffield: JSOT Press, 1987), 83–86. Hanson, while finally leaning toward the traditional view, notes that "in fact it [*stigma*] never refers to the marks of a wound *tout simplement*" (83–84).

However, we should at least pause to note that *stigma* was originally formed from and retained semantic connections to *stizō*, a word which normally functions as "'to prick,' 'tattoo,' 'mark' with a sharp instrument (graver)."[23] If Paul's thorn in the flesh was a bodily ailment that felt like the jabbing or stabbing of a thorn or stake (as much of the evidence so far in this study has suggested), it is difficult to ignore the possibility that Galatians 6:17, where Paul claims to bear some sort of piercings or sharp markings of Jesus on his body, is connected somehow to 2 Corinthians 12:7 by the shared idea of piercing with something sharp.

Second, since Paul so closely identified with the sufferings of Jesus, his statement that he bore whatever-he-bore on his body solidly connects us once again to our theme of cruciformity. We observed the importance of this theme already in chapter 8, and suggested in the current chapter that this theme might be relevant also for understanding Galatians 3:1.[24] Marius Victorinus (fourth century) summarized his understanding of Paul's sentiment in Galatians 6:17: "All that Christ experienced on the cross—the imprint of the nails, the spear thrust in his side, the other marks of the crucifixion—I bear in my own body."[25]

Nonetheless, factoring Galatians 6:17 into the discussion of Paul's thorn in the flesh should probably be viewed as even more tentative than other observations that have already been made in this study. The viability of using this verse to further the discussion increases somewhat when the verse is read in tandem with Galatians 3:1 and 4:13–15 rather than in isolation. Nevertheless, we must still admit that there is little that can be drawn upon from 3:1 or 6:17 to argue *for* the nature of Paul's thorn in the flesh. Having acknowledged this, if Paul's thorn was a physical ailment that felt like jabbing somewhere

---

23. Otto Betz, "στίγμα," TDNT 7:657.

24. This passage might also connect with 4:13–15 and 3:1 through the demonic-attack theme already mentioned in each. Dunne writes: "Another line of thought connects these marks to magic and curses, and so in that way the rhetorical significance of v. 17 functions as an authoritative warning. Deissmann and Witherington argued that these marks were seen as a kind of talisman; thus to 'cause me trouble' would lead to bringing down a curse" (Dunne, *Persecution and Participation in Galatians*, 101).

25. Marius Victorinus, *Ep. Gal.* 2.6.17 (Edwards) cited by Keener, *Galatians*, 586.

in his skin/flesh, and if it was caused by an evil spirit (with God's permission), then reading 3:1 and 6:17 as somehow connected to Paul's thorn has some appeal, especially if 4:13–15 is employed alongside those verses.[26] Very tentatively, then, I would like to suggest that one additional criterion that might be inferred from including Galatians 3:1 and 6:17 in this discussion is that Paul's thorn might have included observable bodily damage.[27] Please observe that I would count this criterion as the weakest of my twenty criteria.

It is difficult to argue in general, though, against the notion that Paul would have presented visible bodily damage—most obviously on his face—as a result of his frequent beatings alone. The healing of open wounds, particularly in light of the unavailability of careful stitching of wounds in his time, would have produced noticeable scars.[28] But when we add in Paul's explicit comment about bearing some sort of piercings or sharp marks on his body (6:17), along with his comment about Jesus's crucifixion being openly portrayed (3:1), it might slightly strengthen our initial inclination that visible evidence, presumably on

---

26. Chilton, after quoting Gal 4:13–15 writes: "Paul used his own injuries, most visible in his face, to drive home the message he announced in Derbe. He portrayed Christ Jesus as crucified before the Galatians' very eyes (Galatians 3:1), because—as they could see and he insisted (Galatians 6:17)—he bore the marks of Jesus (the stigmata, he said) on his own body" (Chilton, *Rabbi Paul*, 126). When applied to how the Corinthians could have viewed Paul, it might be worth noting that Corinth was sometimes described as a city of beautiful people who placed high value both on beauty and on eloquence. For more on this, see Savage, *Power through Weakness*, 46–47.

27. One small detail that may need more consideration is that Paul chose to use the preposition *en* (often translated as "in," "among," or "by") rather than *epi* (often translated as "on") to describe the location of what he bore. This is not to deny that *en* could be used to describe marks that would have been visible upon his body; *en* is such a flexible preposition that it must be allowed that Paul could have used it that way. See discussions of these three prepositions in Murray J. Harris, *Prepositions and Theology in the Greek New Testament: An Essential Reference Resource for Exegesis* (Grand Rapids: Zondervan, 2012), 115–36 (*en*) and 137–45 (*epi*). But might it be that Paul is hinting by his choice of *en* over *epi* that it is something felt more internally, since piercings can go deep? That is, might it be that Paul is saying that he experienced jabbing *in* his body rather than marks *on* his body? Nevertheless, the argument above proceeds on the assumption that *on* is the better translation—but only tentatively, since the *in* reading might also be a possibility.

28. This observation was made to me by my colleague, Matthew H. Rouse (author of *Neuroanatomy for Speech-Language Pathologists and Audiologists* [Burlington, MA: Jones & Bartlett Learning, 2016]) in a personal conversation.

the skin—and particularly on the most visible part of the body, the face—could have been an aspect of Paul's (literal) portrait.[29]

As we close this chapter, we should remember that the Galatian connection is one of the more difficult connections to draw upon with confidence. Nevertheless, based upon the various clues we have presented, we should tentatively consider the possibility that Paul's thorn in the flesh involved his eyes in some unspecified way (suggested by Gal 4:15), and that whatever he endured was somehow visible on his body (suggested by Gal 3:1 and 6:17).

CRITERIA SUPPORTED OR ALLUDED TO IN THIS CHAPTER

1. Viewed by others as black magic attacks

2. Impacting Paul's physical flesh

3. Viewed by others as humiliating and weak

4. Long-term, but intermittent

5. Paralleling the sufferings of Jesus

6. Known to the Corinthians, not a secret

7. Excruciating, not simply annoying

8. Involving the eye

9. Visible bodily damage

---

29. Jennifer A. Glancy imagines Paul baring his back during a church meeting to show the marks from beatings and whippings to drive home his point, but she seems to ignore the more-accessible-to-his-audience evidence of a damaged face, which would have always been on display (Jennifer A. Glancy, "Boasting of Beatings (2 Corinthians 11:23–25)," *JBL* 123 [2004]: 103). The late second-century work *Acts of Paul and Thecla* describes Paul as "A man of small stature, with a bald head and crooked legs, in a good state of body, with eyebrows meeting and nose somewhat hooked, full of friendliness; for now he appeared like a man, and now he had the face of an angel." This description probably has no historical bearing on this discussion and may have been concocted by the author of the text to connect Paul's physical appearance with the author's perceived understanding of the personality of Paul. See Heike Omerzu, "The Portrayal of Paul's Outer Appearance in the Acts of Paul and Thecla: Reconsidering the Correspondence between the Body and Personality in Ancient Literature," *R&T* 15 (2008): 252–79.

LAYERED AND LESS-
LIKELY CONNECTIONS

M any connections already have been drawn in this study
between 2 Corinthians 12:7 and other writings and historical
realities. How can there at the same time be so many influences on a single verse? This chapter will begin with an explanation of
the layering of some of the influences that have already been detailed.
The remainder of the chapter will briefly describe other possible literary and historical connections that are worthy of consideration
in the study of Paul's thorn in the flesh, but that will not in the end
be factored into a solution because they lack the requisite density,
proximity, or other supports necessary for inclusion.

LAYERED CONNECTIONS

One key aspect of the argumentative section above is the claim that
various influences have impacted what Paul wrote in 2 Corinthians
12:7. Someone might retort that so many influences upon a single passage are unlikely. But one who would express such a concern likely

also misunderstands what I have claimed and what I have not. This section will clarify how the various proposed influences layer upon and differ from one another.

My claim is that Paul in 2 Corinthians 12:7: (1) drew upon literary connections with Job, (2) lived with a condition that others would have viewed as produced by magical attacks, (3) ethically and spiritually received encouragement from the shared sufferings of Jesus, and (4) shared the same historical referent as the physical ailment of Galatians 4:13–15 (and perhaps 3:1 and 6:17), while not referring to the Galatian letter. In other words, 2 Corinthians 12:7 is not a simple case of intertextuality. The connections with Job are, indeed, literary (as well as conceptual). The connections with perceived attacks of black magic lie in Paul's historical and cultural setting. The connections with Jesus are primarily ethical and spiritual. The connections with the book of Galatians manifest solely because both the readers of Galatians and 2 Corinthians saw Paul struggling with the same physical ailment. In other words, these connections each differ from one another in kind.[1]

Furthermore, all of these connections would have already been part of the discussion before Paul wrote the words about his thorn in the flesh in 2 Corinthians 12:7. Paul would have been making connections between his suffering and the book of Job throughout the previous fourteen years, since Job was the obvious go-to source to help him make sense of his own suffering. Out of necessity, he would have had to offer an explanation to the many who would have attributed his painful stabbing attacks to malevolent magic—and explain those attacks as generated by an angel of Satan but permitted by God. He also likely would have ethically and spiritually connected his sufferings to the sufferings of Jesus as he shared the gospel with unbelievers (cf. perhaps Gal 3:1) and when he spoke about the cruciform life with believers. Finally, since his suffering was not new when he wrote 2 Corinthians, he probably would have commented on past flare-ups, such as he seems to have suffered during his ministry in south Galatia.

---

1. Notice a somewhat similar defense of layered models in connection with Paul's thorn in the flesh by Garrett, "Paul's Thorn and Cultural Models of Affliction," 96–98.

Thus, the sort of intertextuality appealed to in this study contrasts with the majority of instances of intertextuality found in the New Testament in which an author draws upon or alludes to an Old Testament text as support for a theological, polemical, or pastoral point. What allows for the layering of these various connections is the fact that the ailment Paul mentioned in 2 Corinthians 12:7 was a lived reality in Paul's life that would have already been discussed with many Christians before it ever appeared in one of his letters. Paul's thorn-comment, thus, should be viewed as shorthand for a primary pain in his life, perhaps even his most difficult area of suffering.[2] The dependencies and connections run through his personal experience. That is how all four of these connections (Job, perception of magic, suffering of Jesus, and Galatians) are relevant for the study of 2 Corinthians 12:7—at the same time.

LESS-LIKELY CONNECTIONS

More connections and dependencies than the ones already detailed could be suggested by someone studying this topic. What follows are some of those possible connections, each intriguing in its own right. These possible connections have been included because they may prove to be helpful in the study of Paul's thorn in the flesh to someone in the future, but have ultimately been factored out of the present argument because their persuasive potential appears less than other observations already factored in. Still, for those who desire to think more deeply about this topic in the future, awareness of these other possible connections may prove beneficial.

FIERY DARTS?

In Ephesians 6:16, Paul writes, "In all circumstances take up the shield of faith, with which you can extinguish all the flaming darts of the evil one" (Eph. 6:16). This verse is only of interest in our discussion because of the combination of darts (or "arrows"; see NRSV; NIV), the "evil one," and possibly the flaming/burning (cf. the "burning" of 2 Cor 11:29).

---

2. Glessner calls it "his quintessential hardship, the final entry in his catalogues of hardships in the Corinthian correspondence (1 Cor 4:11–13, 2 Cor 4:8–9; 6:4–5; 11:23–28)" (Glessner, "Ethnomedical Anthropology," 28).

Though intriguing, there is probably little interpretive gain in
drawing upon this comparison. For now, it simply needs to be noted
that there could be some sort of connection to the current proposal,
though how to make use of it is yet unclear.

HANDKERCHIEFS AND EVIL SPIRITS?

Acts 19:11–12 relates the following about Paul's ministry in Ephesus:
"And God was doing extraordinary miracles by the hands of Paul, so
that even handkerchiefs or aprons that had touched his skin were carried away to the sick, and their diseases left them and the evil spirits
came out of them" (Acts 19:11).

This is an interesting comment by Luke in the context of the current study only because of the combination of the mention of Paul's
skin with healing and the driving out of evil spirits. Why did Paul's
skin get mentioned—and in a narrative about Ephesus in particular?
Was there something important about Paul's skin? (Contrast Peter's
shadow in Acts 5:15.) Was there something important about Ephesus?
Why were evil spirits mentioned? These questions are interesting, but
I am currently unsure of what to do with this text apart from pointing out the similarities with other things that have already emerged
in this study.

PAUL'S EXPLOSIVE RESPONSE?

In Acts 23:1–5, Paul had just begun his defense before the Sanhedrin
in Jerusalem when the high priest commanded an attendant to strike
Paul on the mouth. Paul retorted explosively to the high priest: "God
is going to strike you, you whitewashed wall!" (23:3). When the other
attendants challenged Paul about reviling the high priest, Paul backed
down, claiming that he did not know that it was the high priest.

This passage has sometimes been used to argue that Paul suffered
from poor eyesight.[3] But this is not necessarily the case, or probably

---

3. In addition, sometimes people argue that Paul had bad eyesight based upon the large size
of his handwriting comment in Gal 6:11. But this is better explained, as it has been argued by
Steve Reece, as the contrast between "a smaller, tidier, more regular and uniform, even elegant,

even the best explanation for what took place. After so many years away from the Sanhedrin, Paul simply may not have known what the high priest looked like.[4] One other possibility to consider, of course, is that if Paul regularly dealt with face pain, he might have lashed out at the high priest as a result of the pain he experienced when getting hit on the mouth (face). Of course, Paul's explosive reaction could just as likely—perhaps more likely—be a response to the injustice of the situation, as his words suggest: "Are you sitting to judge me according to the law, and yet contrary to the law you order me to be struck?" (Acts 23:3).

BEATING WITH THORNS?

An interesting combination of relevant ideas (at least on the surface) cluster in a lesser-known story from the book of Judges. After Gideon routed the army of Midian, his band of 300 men pursued Zebah and Zalmunna, the leaders of the Midianite army across the Jordan River (Judges 7–8). In need of food, Gideon approached the residents of Succoth for bread for his army. When they refused to release the food, Gideon spoke these words: "Well then, when the LORD has given Zebah and Zalmunna into my hand, I will flail your flesh with the thorns of the wilderness and with briers" (Judg 8:7). After routing the retreating Midianite army and capturing Zebah and Zalmunna, the text reads, "And he [Gideon] took the elders of the city, and he took thorns of the wilderness and briers and with them taught the men of Succoth a lesson" (8:16). The intrigue of this possible allusion appears in the combination of *flesh, thorns, beating,* and *teaching a lesson.* Since Paul said that he was *hit* in some way with a *thorn* in the *flesh* resulting in him *learning* a lesson in 2 Corinthians 12:7, it might be worth asking

---

professional hand" of a scribe and "a larger, thicker, more awkward and clumsy, unpracticed, amateurish hand" of a non-professional scribe like Paul. In other words, it is "not a deliberate mark of emphasis but simply an indication of the amateurism of the writer" (Reece, *Paul's Large Letters,* x, 104.)

4. David G. Peterson, *The Acts of the Apostles,* PNTC (Grand Rapids: Eerdmans and Nottingham: Apollos, 2009), 614–15.

whether this passage could in any way have influenced him. Despite these similarities, I am skeptical that Paul had this passage in mind, especially in light of the stronger connections with the book of Job. Moreover, the men of Succoth were taught a lesson after doing something wrong, whereas the point of Paul's lesson was to keep him from becoming proud—before the fact.

THORNS IN YOUR SIDE/EYES?

Another possible allusion is found in the verses where potential non-Israelite enemies are described as "thorns in your side" (Num 33:55 in Hebrew; cf. Judg 2:3) or "thorns in your eyes" (Num 33:55 in Greek; cf. Josh 23:12 in Hebrew) or having "a thorn to hurt" (Ezek 28:24). This connection has sometimes been suggested by people who support the view that Paul's thorn in the flesh was a person or group of persons who opposed Paul.[5] Sometimes the argument is presented as though "thorns in your side" was a common expression that people used in the time of Paul similar to the way we jokingly use "thorn in the flesh" or "thorn in your side" in the twenty-first century to mean anything that annoys us.[6] But, as far as I have yet been able to determine, this is mere speculation. Consequently, the only argument that must be evaluated is whether Paul (and his readers?) consciously had those Old Testament expressions in mind when Paul employed it in 2 Corinthians 12:7.

Although intriguing, as with the other examples presented so far in this chapter, this potential parallel also lacks the requisite density to be treated as an actual allusion. Paul's allusions to Job are strong, as I have already argued. Adding in this allusion would require that Paul employed a double *literary* allusion (at-the-same-moment,

---

5. E.g., Guthrie, who observes that "the 'thorn' in Ezekiel is singular but refers to 'those all around them'" (Guthrie, 2 *Corinthians*, 592).

6. Belleville attributes to Delling the claim that "a stake in the flesh" was a common figure of speech for excruciating physical pain (Belleville, 2 *Corinthians*, 306). But Delling does not appear to claim this. In fact, Delling asks: "Is Paul adopting a current phrase? The 'text' in Fenner, 30: σκόλοψ τῇ σαρκί is obviously not attested anywhere" (Delling, TDNT 7:411n19).

using-the-same-words), which is possible, but happens rarely. Furthermore, the only actual purported connection between 2 Corinthians 12:7 and these passages is found in the similarities between the expressions: "thorn in the flesh" with "thorns in your side/eyes." Contrast this with the Gideon example just discussed that included *thorns, flesh, beating,* and *teaching,* and it appears that the connections with the Gideon story look in many ways to be stronger than the purported connections to these references to Israel's opponents. Since I was skeptical about connecting the Gideon story to Paul, it seems advisable to do the same with this proposed connection. Finally, observe that Paul is an individual (singular) tormented by a thorn (also singular); whereas Numbers 33:55 and Ezekiel 28:24 are references to nations (many individuals) that could potentially torment another nation (also consisting of many people). I consider the presence of an allusion to the expressions less likely, but it is worth keeping in mind in case it somehow intersects with further studies in the future.

BEATING WITH SCORPIONS?

Another curious parallel appears in the young king Rehoboam's response to the people of Israel who requested some reprieve following the austere leadership of his father Solomon. After ignoring the counsel of his older advisers, Rehoboam listened instead to the foolish advice of his young friends. He spoke the following words to the gathering of people, "My father made your yoke heavy, but I will add to your yoke. My father disciplined you with whips, but I will discipline you with scorpions" (1 Kgs 12:14). The "scorpions" mentioned is probably a reference to "a (nail)-barbed scourge as opposed to the common 'whip.'"[7] When Paul wrote about something sharp and pointed *in* his flesh, could he have had Rehoboam's scourge in mind, particularly because of the mention of "disciplining" found in 1 Kings 12:14?

---

7. Donald J. Wiseman, *1 & 2 Kings: An Introduction & Commentary,* TOTC (Leicester: Inter-Varsity, 1993), 141.

The connection with this passage, once again, seems unlikely, largely because of the more prominent dependence upon Job already supported. Somehow connecting this passage via Paul's cruciform theology (Jesus having been scourged) might make the link to this occurrence of the "scorpion" scourge perhaps slightly more likely. Still, the parallel is not strong enough to engender much confidence, and so this possible connection will also be left to the side in our final analysis.

Any of these passages could potentially have some relationship to the discussion, and have been included to alert readers to that possibility. Perhaps some future interpreter might find an appropriate way to factor one or two of these passages into the discussion. But these passages have been left out of my conclusions because they do not appear to be even as strong as the weakest connections that have been presented thus far in this study.

APPLYING THE CRITERIA |

What was Paul's thorn in the flesh? We have now arrived at a moment when a solution can be advanced—or at least a narrower category that includes varying solutions. The way forward is by employing the list of criteria for narrowing the options for Paul's thorn in the flesh that emerged in chapters 3–10. Since this list of twenty criteria is the key to identifying Paul's thorn, our final section of the book will commence with a restatement of the criteria along with a brief summary of supporting reasons each criterion was included. This restatement of arguments will be followed by a chapter of charts in which leading proposals for Paul's thorn in the flesh are weighed and deemed inadequate when judged against the twenty criteria. Seven medical conditions will then be introduced that closely adhere to the twenty criteria, leading to the conclusion that the condition from which Paul suffered was one of the seven. This section will conclude with a list of implications for understanding the person of Paul that flow from the twenty criteria.

CHAPTER
TWELVE

PULLING IT ALL
TOGETHER

T he list of twenty criteria that have already emerged from this
study is the key to identifying Paul's thorn in the flesh. Any
adequate solution, I contend, should appropriately account for
these twenty criteria. Here I will restate these essential criteria and
briefly summarize some of the main observations that have led to each
criterion finding inclusion on the list.[1] Please note that what follows
is nothing more than a list, a list that lacks discussions, details, and
distinctions. Please consult chapters 3–10 for arguments and details,
as well as to glean other less-prominent observations that have not
been included on the summary of observations appearing below.

---

1. Harris lists the following characteristics, which overlap with seven of my proposed criteria: "a direct consequence of the revelations he received in paradise ... caused him acute pain
... he regarded it as simultaneously a gift from God and an instrument of Satan ... a permanent
condition, yet its exacerbations were intermittent ... humbling, for it was designed to curb or
prevent spiritual arrogance ... humiliating, comparable to receiving vicious blows about the
face ... caused Paul to feel weak, yet the weakness it caused was an object of boasting and a
source of pleasure" (Harris, *Second Epistle to the Corinthians*, 857).

A LIST OF THE TWENTY CRITERIA
WITH SUMMARY OF ARGUMENTS

Criterion 1: Viewed by others as black magic attacks

- The practice of magic was a central cultural feature of Paul's world.

- Piercing in (and on) ancient curse tablets, voodoo dolls, and animals was common.

- Such piercing magic included attacks on the head.

- Such piercing magic sometimes sought to hinder speech.

- Thorns were used in magical incantations.

- The combination of piercing language and "messenger of Satan" in 2 Corinthians 12:7 would almost certainly have evoked concern about black magic attacks.

- Ephesus, where Paul had recently spent the previous (almost) three years before writing 2 Corinthians was closely associated with magic.

- Power encounters are prominent in the book of Acts, indicative of their importance in Paul's ministry.

- Spiritual warfare language is common in the letters of Paul and conspicuous in 2 Corinthians 10–13.

- The literary relationship of 2 Corinthians 12:7 and Job 1–2 bolsters the personal satanic-attack motif.

- "You did not spit on me" (Gal 4:14 lit. trans.), an allusion to a folk-religious practice, along with "who has cast a spell on you?" (Gal 3:1) brings Paul's visit to Galatia into conversation with black magic attacks.

Criterion 2: Viewed by Paul as attacks by an angel of Satan, though permitted by God

- Attack by a demon is the most straightforward way of understanding the expression "angel/messenger of Satan" in 2 Corinthians 12:7.

- Paul's two expressions ("thorn in the flesh" and "angel of Satan") both can be interpreted straightforwardly (that is, Paul's pain felt like being stabbed by a thorn in the flesh, and the suffering was inflicted by an angel of Satan), rather than one or both being interpreted as general metaphors for suffering.

- "There was given" (*edothē*) is normally understood to be a divine passive. God permitted, but was not the active agent of the suffering Paul experienced.

- Paul's suffering was simultaneously viewed by Paul as excruciating and spiritually positive.

- A pattern of demonic power encounters is attributed to Paul in the book of Acts.

- Paul writes often about angels, demons, and Satan in his letters, including in 2 Corinthians 10–13.

- 2 Corinthians 12:7 is literarily and conceptually dependent upon Job (esp. 1–2), and God allowed Job to be physically attacked by Satan.

- Tertullian compared Satan's attack of Paul to Satan's attack of Job.

Criterion 3: Paralleling Job's sufferings (especially Job 1–2), which included skin/flesh

- Job was known and used by Paul elsewhere.

- The word *angelos* ("angel" or "messenger") literarily connects 2 Corinthians 12 with the early section of Job.

- Flesh (and skin) is called out explicitly both in Job 2:4–5 (cf. 2:7) and in 2 Corinthians 12:7.

- Paul refers to "Satan," a title appearing fourteen times in the Hebrew text of Job 1–2 (and rarely elsewhere).

- Paul likely would have known that the operative verb in the Greek text of Job 2:7 regarding Job's skin was a verb commonly used for *stinging* or *piercing* (cf. 6:4; 16:10).

- The theologies of suffering underlying Job 1–2 and 2 Corinthians 12:7 overlap substantially.

- Paul's "fool's speech" in 2 Corinthians 11:21b–12:10 displays similarities to Job's words to his wife in Job 2:10.

- The humiliation theme is important both in 2 Corinthians 12:7 (cf. 12:21) and Job (for example, Job 19, 29–30; esp. 40:12).

- Paul's thrice-uttered prayer for release (2 Cor 12:8) and acquiescence (12:10) may parallel the three cycles of Job's complaint (chs. 3–31) and final acquiescence (42:1–6).

- There are overlapping responses by God to Job and Paul.

- Neither Job nor Paul are ever said to have received healing.

Criterion 4: Impacting Paul's physical flesh

- Paul described his thorn as "in the flesh" (*tē sarki*). Most grammarians categorize this as a dative of place because alternatives are weak.

- Literary dependence on Job supports the literal skin-flesh location of Paul's suffering because Job's suffering occurred in his skin-flesh.

- Paul had already developed a special focus on the physical body in 2 Corinthians 4–5 (for example, 4:10; 5:6, 8, 10), preparing the way for his later discussion.

- The reflections of Irenaeus and Tertullian indicate that Paul's physical body was involved.

- Face-head allusions in some cases also support a physical flesh interpretation.

- Paul seems to have intentionally pluralized "weaknesses" (*astheneiai*) around his thorn discussion (2 Cor 12:5, 9 [second appearance], 10), suggesting sickness or physical ailment.

- No physical ailments or disabilities are included among Paul's sufferings in his extensive sufferings-lists of 2 Corinthians, despite the fact that we know that Paul and his co-workers experienced illnesses (Gal 4:13; Phil 2:26–27; 1 Tim 5:23; 2 Tim 4:20). This absence in the other lists makes sense if Paul was waiting in 2 Corinthians to describe a suffering related to his body in 2 Corinthians 12:7, but is otherwise difficult to explain.

- We know that it was because of a "weakness of the flesh" (Gal 4:13) that Paul was able to preach to the Galatians.

Criterion 5: Comparable to the jabbing of a sharp-pointed object

- The most natural way to understand a suffering that Paul referred to as a thorn/stake in the flesh is that Paul felt like he was being stabbed by a sharp-pointed object in his flesh (like a three-to-four-inch date thorn or a small stake). This is a helpful insight that should not be understated.

- Reading "thorn in the flesh" in a more literal way as describing Paul's experience of pain allows Paul's three expressions in 2 Corinthians 12:7 ("thorn in the flesh," "angel of Satan," and "beat me [in the face]") to all be taken as literal descriptions of Paul's feeling/experience of torment (rather than one, two, or three of them being relegated to the category of loose metaphors for suffering).

- Job was "stung" (Greek of Job 2:7) by Satan, and Paul was making connections with Job.

- Ancient voodoo dolls and animals were pierced with various pointed objects, and curse tablets were nailed. Paul's ailment would have been viewed as a black magic attack.

- Jesus was pierced in his hands and side with nails, and on his head with a crown of thorns, all in fulfillment of messianic Scriptures. Paul's cruciform identity connects with the sufferings of Jesus.

Criterion 6: Excruciating, not simply annoying

- Paul described it as a sharp-pointed object (thorn/stake) in the flesh.

- Paul described it as a messenger of Satan.

- Paul described it like being hit, and most probably in the face.

- Paul begged three times (probably three occasions) for it to leave him.

- Paul encountered deep humiliation connected with the thorn in a culture steeped in honor and shame.

- The duration of the suffering was 14 years.

- The placement of Paul's thorn after all his other lists of sufferings in 2 Corinthians suggests that he viewed it as the pinnacle of his sufferings, which were extensive.

- Paul's literary dependence upon Job conjures up the excruciating suffering of Job.

- Paul's identification with the crucifixion of Jesus evokes something more intense than simply an annoyance.

- Paul describes what he suffered in Galatians 4:13–15 as a trial or test, and as a condition for which the Galatians could have scorned or despised him.

Criterion 7: Impacting Paul's face (as part of his head)

- Most commonly, *kolaphizō* (2 Cor 12:7) means to hit in the face, though it can be used more broadly.

- There exists a collocation of facial terminology in 2 Corinthians 10–12 leading up to Paul's mention of the thorn. One example is 11:20, if anyone "strikes you in the face/flays your face."

- There is a strong emphasis first on the face and then on the body in 2 Corinthians 3:7–4:6, preparing the way for Paul's later discussion.

- In total, of the twenty-two times Paul uses the word commonly translated as "face" (*prosōpon*, with a variety of nuances), twelve of those appear in 2 Corinthians.

- Tertullian connects the suffering of Paul's thorn with his ear or head.

- Jesus was struck in the face and forced to wear a crown of thorns on his head and forehead, and Paul identifies with the sufferings of Jesus.

- The face and head is the anatomical location of honor and shame. Honor and shame figures powerfully in the thorn passage and the surrounding context.

- Spells concerning faces and heads are common in the magical papyri and curse tablets.

- If Paul sported a weak body (2 Cor 10:10), and his literal flesh was involved, the only part of his body the Corinthians would have consistently seen was his face.

Criterion 8: Viewed by Paul as educational discipline by God

- Paul twice stated that the purpose of the thorn was "to keep me from becoming conceited."

- The Lord gave instructions to Paul about how his grace is sufficient and how power is made perfect in weakness (2 Cor 12:9).

- Cuffing a person's head or ear was common discipline in educational settings in the first century (and not generally viewed with the same societal disdain as it is today).

Criterion 9: Viewed by others as humiliating and weak

- Paul used the language of "to keep me from exalting myself" (12:7).

- Paul extensively developed the theme of weakness in the immediate context (12:5-6, 9-10), and intertwined it with the related theme of honor and shame in the four contextually nearest chapters (10-13).

- Paul was criticized in Corinth for a variety of things, including having a weak body (10:10).

- The various face and head allusions in the discussion remind one of the anatomical centrality of the face/head in honor-and-shame cultures.

- Paul likely referred to the same ailment in Galatians 4:14 when he wrote "you did not scorn or despise me" (Gal 4:14).

- The humiliation theme is strong in Job, and Paul makes connections to Job.

- The perception of black magic attacks by observers also would have included humiliation.

- The humiliation theme is strong in the four Gospels' accounts of the suffering of Jesus (and in the Old Testament messianic passages upon which they depend, esp. Psalm 22 and the suffering servant passages of Isaiah); Paul identified with the suffering of Jesus.

Criterion 10: Unusual, not like the pains of others

- The descriptive language of "thorn in the flesh" is itself unusual and evokes something unusual.

- It is strange to undergo excruciating suffering that still allows one to continue with extensive and strenuous missionary work such as the work in which Paul engaged.

- Paul's suffering was a consequence of a God-given vision or set of revelations, which is unusual in itself.

Criterion 11: Long-term, but intermittent

- The thorn was given after the heavenly ascent to keep Paul from exalting himself—thus fourteen years before. It was given "in order to" (*hina*, 2x) keep Paul from self-exaltation.

- Paul was still able to engage in vigorous missionary work, suggesting intermittency.

- Three times Paul pleaded for release. It is unlikely that his thrice-repeated request was a reference to a single period of prayer.

- It is more likely than not that Paul's Galatian ailment was the same as what he wrote about to the Corinthians some years later, reminding us that Paul had already encountered this suffering in a previous ministry context.

Criterion 12: Paralleling the sufferings of Jesus

- Paul closely identified with the physical sufferings of Jesus in his letters, including in 2 Corinthians 10–13.

- Jesus was pierced on the head with a crown of thorns.

- Jesus was pierced with nails and a spear.

- Jesus was struck on the head and slapped in the face.

- Jesus was shamed on his face.

- Jesus's sufferings fulfilled three key Old Testament passages about piercing (Ps 22:5; Isa 53:5; Zech 12:10).

- Galatians 6:17 and possibly 3:1 connect Paul's suffering with the suffering of Jesus.

Criterion 13: Exacerbated by stress

- Paul's final set of sufferings before mentioning the thorn— and the ones that seem to have weighed most heavily upon him—were sufferings of stress (11:28–32) rather than sufferings from persecutions or labors (cf. 11:23–27). That final section of Paul's list of sufferings connects literarily to chapter 12 where Paul's vision, thorn, and God's response is recorded (12:1–10).

- There is a relationship in the Old Testament and other Jewish writings between seeing visions and consequent stress tied to those visions.

- The humiliation-weakness theme along with the spiritual-warfare theme are both important in 2 Corinthians 10–13 (including 12:1–10) and are highly stress-related.

Criterion 14: Negatively impacting Paul's rhetorical ability

- Paul's rhetorical effectiveness had been criticized at Corinth (cf. Paul's reaction in 11:6, possibly alluded to in 12:6). Paul connected the criticism of his speech to criticism of his weak body in 10:10.

- How can Paul at the same time be strong in rhetoric while also getting mocked for his lack of rhetorical finesse? This conundrum can be resolved if Paul's preaching and teaching were sometimes interrupted by shooting pains of the type proposed in this study.

- A common purpose of black magic attacks was to hinder someone from speaking in a public forum (as in a court of law), and there are reasons to think that Paul's thorn would have been viewed by others as an attack of black magic.

Criterion 15: Known to the Corinthians, not a secret

- Paul writes that the Corinthians had already criticized him for having a weak body (10:10).

- Paul's suffering seems to have involved his face in some way, as explained above.

- The Corinthians highlighted Paul's weaknesses to discredit him.

- The placement of Paul's thorn after his other lists of sufferings suggests that he viewed it as his most difficult area of suffering. Paul hiding something as important as this from the Corinthians would have piqued their curiosity, mitigated the force of his argument, and worked against his otherwise self-disclosing approach in 2 Corinthians.

- Paul has been very self-disclosing with the Corinthians in this letter (3:18; 4:2; 6:3, 11, 13; 12:6), probably more self-revealing than in any of his other letters.

Criterion 16: Analogous to Paul's other sufferings

- Paul concluded his key paragraph with five broad categories about which he had chosen to be content: "weaknesses, insults, hardships, persecutions, and calamities" in 2 Corinthians 12:10. Paul, thereby, may have been suggesting that his thorn fit within such a list.

- This list of five general descriptions in 12:10 makes one think of the more extensive list Paul had just composed in 11:23–33.

- *Kolaphizō* ("hit [in the face]," 12:7) causes one to think of the sufferings of Jesus just before his crucifixion.

Criterion 17: Connected to the heavenly ascent

- Paul wrote that it was because of the revelations (*dio*, "therefore") that he was given a thorn in the flesh (12:7).

- Paul wrote that the purpose of the thorn was to keep him from exalting himself (*hina*, "in order to," repeated twice) because the revelations were so great.

Criterion 18: Involving the ear

- This criterion is based almost entirely on Tertullian's comment that he had heard that Paul's thorn in the flesh was a pain in the ear or the head. Tertullian was chronologically and geographically positioned to get this right.

- *Kolaphizō* ("hit [in the face]") would presumably sometimes involve the ear.

Criterion 19: Involving the eye

- Paul reminded the Galatians that they would have gouged out their eyes for him (Gal 4:15). There are reasons to connect Galatians 4:13–15 with 2 Corinthians 12:7.

- Eyes are the most common ailment mentioned in religious texts from Lydia.

- Many craniofacial conditions involve the eyes in some way (often one eye on the side of the face where the pain is felt).

- There are other clues that Paul's face was somehow involved.

Criterion 20: Visible bodily damage

- The Galatian connection is key to this argument. See discussion in chapter 10.

- Paul wrote that the Galatians did not scorn or despise him for the "weakness/illness of the flesh" he endured while with them (Gal 4:14). Paul's ailment, thus, was of a kind that could have been viewed as repulsive.

- Paul wrote that he bore on his body the brandmarks of Jesus (Gal 6:17).

- The Galatians saw Jesus somehow crucified before them, which could have involved Paul's own suffering in some way (Gal 3:1).

- The Corinthians were able to observe something related to Paul's body, for which they criticized him (2 Cor 10:10).

- This criterion might be supported by one possible reading of "what they see in me" in 2 Corinthians 12:6.

- Paul described the thorn as "in the flesh." This description would allow, but not require, something visible on his body.

Summary: Paul's thorn in the flesh was some sort of unusual, long-term, intermittent, stabbing, face pain that was viewed by others as shameful and the result of black magic attacks, but by Paul as attacks of a demon permitted by God.

COMPARING POSITIONS |

N ow that we have identified the twenty necessary criteria for determining Paul's thorn in the flesh, we must ask how past proposals succeed in meeting these twenty criteria.

This chapter will use charts to rate the relative strengths of various proposals for Paul's thorn. To keep this chapter from becoming unwieldly, the entire chapter will consist only of these comparative charts. Since the inclusion of explanatory notes to justify each decision would require dozens of pages of text and add little to the plausibility of the argument, such notes have been left out of the discussion. The first chart will focus upon five non-physical proposals, the second on five physical-body proposals, and the third on seven maladies that match up well with the twenty criteria.

Let us acknowledge that there is some subjectivity involved in any attempt to rate the relative strengths of particular criteria as they intersect with various proposed conditions. One person undertaking such a rating might emphasize one aspect of a particular criterion, while another might, say, lack requisite knowledge of a particular condition—and as a consequence, assign a higher or lower rating while connecting criterion to condition. Nevertheless, many of the criteria will quite closely match—or, alternately, will not match at all—many of the proposed conditions. Consequently, this exercise will help readers adjudicate which solutions appear to offer the greatest amount of explanatory power.

The central thing upon which a reader should focus in this chapter, however, is not whether one criterion precisely matches a particular condition, but to observe the overall nearness or distance of various criteria to proposed conditions.

Notes on the charts:

- The numeral 3 (in bold) suggests maximal agreement between a criterion and a proposed malady. In other words, the malady works extremely well with the criterion.

- The numeral 2 suggests moderate agreement between a criterion and a proposed malady. The criterion works reasonably well with the malady.

- The numeral 1 suggests minimal agreement between a criterion and a proposed malady. It is possible to conceive of a way that the criterion and the malady could work together, but the match is of minimal possibility.

- A dash (-) communicates that there is no reasonable agreement between a criterion and a proposed malady.

Our first chart includes five proposals that do not involve a bodily ailment or disability. Notice how inadequately overall these proposed "thorns" match up with our list of criteria.

	Verbal opposition from inside the Christian movement (false apostles, Judaizers, etc.)	Persecutions from the outside (insults, beatings, etc.)	Inner psycho-logical pressure (temptations, grief, etc.)	Demonic attack during Paul's past heavenly ascent (non-physical)	Ongoing demonic oppression (without physical manifestation)
C1 Viewed by others as black magic attacks	-	-	2	-	3
C2 Viewed by Paul as attacks by an angel of Satan, though permitted by God	3	3	3	3	3
C3 Paralleling Job's sufferings (especially Job 1–2), which included skin/flesh	2	2	2	2	2
C4 Impacting Paul's physical flesh	-	3	-	-	-
C5 Comparable to the jabbing of a sharp-pointed object	2	2	2	2	2
C6 Excruciating, not simply annoying	3	3	3	2	3
C7 Impacting Paul's face (as part of his head)	-	3	2	-	2
C8 Viewed by Paul as educational discipline by God	2	2	-	2	-
C9 Viewed by others as humiliating and weak	3	2	3	-	2
C10 Unusual, not like the pains of others	-	-	2	3	2
C11 Long-term, but intermittent	3	3	3	-	3
C12 Paralleling the sufferings of Jesus	2	3	2	1	2
C13 Exacerbated by stress	-	-	3	-	2
C14 Negatively impacting Paul's rhetor-ical ability	2	-	2	-	2
C15 Known to the Corinthians, not a secret	3	3	-	-	-
C16 Analogous to Paul's other sufferings	3	3	2	-	-
C17 Connected to the heavenly ascent	-	-	2	3	3
C18 Involving the ear	-	2	-	-	-
C19 Involving the eye	-	2	-	-	-
C20 Visible bodily damage	-	-	-	-	-

Our second chart includes five of the leading suggestions for "thorns" that connect with Paul's physical body in some way. Notice that the following proposals fare better in relation to our list of criteria than did the items on the list above, but not nearly as well as those appearing on our final chart.

	Migraine (common)	Recurrent Malarial or Maltese Fever	Epilepsy	Speech Impediment	Poor Eyesight
C1 Viewed by others as black magic attacks	2	2	3	2	2
C2 Viewed by Paul as attacks by an angel of Satan, though permitted by God	2	2	3	2	2
C3 Paralleling Job's sufferings (especially Job 1–2), which included skin/flesh	2	2	1	-	2
C4 Impacting Paul's physical flesh	3	2	2	2	2
C5 Comparable to the jabbing of a sharp-pointed object	1	2	2	2	2
C6 Excruciating, not simply annoying	3	3	3	3	2
C7 Impacting Paul's face (as part of his head)	3	2	1	2	3
C8 Viewed by Paul as educational discipline by God	2	2	2	2	1
C9 Viewed by others as humiliating and weak	2	2	3	3	2
C10 Unusual, not like the pains of others	1	2	2	2	2
C11 Long-term, but intermittent	3	3	3	2	-
C12 Paralleling the sufferings of Jesus	2	2	1	-	-
C13 Exacerbated by stress	3	3	3	3	-
C14 Negatively impacting Paul's rhetorical ability	3	2	3	3	2
C15 Known to the Corinthians, not a secret	3	3	3	3	3
C16 Analogous to Paul's other sufferings	2	2	2	-	2
C17 Connected to the heavenly ascent	2	2	3	2	2
C18 Involving the ear	2	-	-	-	-
C19 Involving the eye	3	2	-	-	3
C20 Visible bodily damage[1]	(2)	-	-	-	-

---

1. An observer might have connected Paul's facial scars with his description of head pain, even if they were not medically connected (thus the parentheses). See page 212, footnote 2.

Our final chart highlights seven maladies that line up closely with the twenty criteria. Notice that all the items on this list fare better than did the strongest of the proposed ailments appearing on the chart just above. In fact, all of the maladies on this final chart perform extremely well.

	Trigeminal Neuralgia Type 1	Posttraumatic Trigeminal Neuropathic Pain	Shingles + Postherpetic Trigeminal Neuropathic Pain	Short-lasting Unilateral Neuralgiform Heachache Attacks	Episodic Paroxysmal Hemicrania	Episodic Cluster Headaches	Primary Stabbing Headaches (or Migraines with Primary Stabbing Headaches)
C1 Viewed by others as black magic attacks	3	3	3	3	3	3	3
C2 Viewed by Paul as attacks by an angel of Satan, though permitted by God	3	3	3	3	3	3	3
C3 Paralleling Job's sufferings (especially Job 1–2), which included skin/flesh	2	2	3	2	2	2	2
C4 Impacting Paul's physical flesh	3	3	3	3	3	3	3
C5 Comparable to the jabbing of a sharp-pointed object	3	3	3	3	3	3	3
C6 Excruciating, not simply annoying	3	3	3	3	3	3	2
C7 Impacting Paul's face (as part of his head)	3	3	3	3	3	3	3
C8 Viewed by Paul as educational discipline by God	3	3	3	3	3	3	3
C9 Viewed by others as humiliating and weak	3	3	3	3	3	3	3
C10 Unusual, not like the pains of others	3	3	3	3	3	2	3
C11 Long-term, but intermittent	3	3	3	3	3	3	3
C12 Paralleling the sufferings of Jesus	2	2	2	2	2	2	2
C13 Exacerbated by stress	3	3	3	3	3	3	3

C14 Negatively impacting Paul's rhetorical ability	3	3	3	3	3	2	3
C15 Known to the Corinthians, not a secret	3	3	3	3	3	3	3
C16 Analogous to Paul's other sufferings	2	2	2	2	2	2	2
C17 Connected to the heavenly ascent	2	2	2	2	2	2	2
C18 Involving the ear	3	3	2	2	2	2	2
C19 Involving the eye	3	3	3	3	3	3	2
C20 Visible bodily damage[2]	(2)	3	3	(3)	(3)	(3)	(2)

CONCLUSION

The seven maladies appearing on this final chart present a high degree of agreement with the criteria. Consequently, I conclude that the most likely diagnosis for Paul's thorn is one of the conditions appearing on this final chart. But what are these ailments? This question is addressed in the following chapter.

---

2. The reader will notice that a few of the ratings for the final criterion are listed in parentheses. This is because the medical condition from which Paul suffered may not have been *directly* connected with the scars people observed on his face. But it is quite likely that an observer in Paul's day would have connected Paul's descriptions of pain with the visible bodily damage that was undoubtedly evident on Paul's face from his many beatings. Since all the conditions on this final chart involve Paul's (likely) scarred face, they all receive either a 3 or 2 rating, though the numbers in parentheses represent those conditions that are medically disconnected from the observable facial damage (that is, from the perspective of modern medicine). In addition, since a few of the conditions in parentheses also add eye-redness, tearing, stuffy nose, or sweating to the manifestations, there is more that an observer might have seen on Paul's face, and thus conditions in that category received a higher rating.

CHAPTER
FOURTEEN

FACE-TO-FACE WITH A PARTIAL SOLUTION

Following are descriptions of medical conditions that closely fit the criteria detailed in chapters 3–10, summarized according to criteria in chapter 12, and appearing on the final chart at the end of chapter 13. I have selected an order of these maladies that, at least to my mind, ranges from most likely to least likely; but given the criteria listed, all of the following should be viewed as serious contenders for what Paul's thorn in the flesh actually was. A simple description of each disorder has been included. For the sake of readers of this book who may be less familiar with medical terminology, I have made the descriptions intentionally simple—employing limited medical jargon—though the curious student can follow the footnotes to learn more about each condition. Since the focus of this book is on what Paul experienced, the descriptions focus on what sufferers of a particular condition feel, not on how modern medical practitioners treat these conditions.

Following, then, is a brief description of seven maladies that closely cohere with the list of criteria.

TRIGEMINAL NEURALGIA TYPE 1

Trigeminal Neuralgia Type 1 (TN1)[1] is a condition in which sudden stabs of pain are felt in the sections of the face into which the branches of the trigeminal nerve extend, including the temple, forehead, eyes, nose, lips, teeth, and jaw.[2] In many cases, TN1 is caused by a blood vessel or artery pressing against an exposed nerve that has lost some of its protective coating (myelin sheath) at the location where the trigeminal nerve leaves the brain stem. The unprotected nerve then sends shock-like pain signals throughout one side of the face whenever the nerve gets irritated by the offending vessel. In some cases, the cause of TN1 pain is unknown.

The pain episodes of TN1 are sudden and intense, regularly described as: "Jabbing. Shock-like. Searing. Spearing. Shooting."[3] The pain is frequently classified among the worst of human pains (see discussion of intensity below). The pain of TN1 (contrast TN2 in the next paragraph) is brief and intense, raging for only seconds to as much as two minutes at a time, but sometimes repeatedly occurring again after a short rest, and creating clusters of attacks that range from minutes to a couple of hours. A pain episode can sometimes be set off by triggers as mundane as a cool wind on the face, chewing food, or smiling. A TN1 sufferer will often experience remissions for months

---

1. Stine Maarbjerg et al., "Trigeminal Neuralgia—Diagnosis and Treatment," *Cephalalgia* 37 (2017): 648–57; Smruti K. Patel and James K. Liu, "Overview and History of Trigeminal Neuralgia," *Neurosurg. Clin. N. Am.* 27 (2016): 265–76; Headache Classification Committee of the International Headache Society, "The International Classification of Headache Disorders, 3rd edition (beta version)," *Cephalalgia* 33 (2013): 774–76; Joanna M. Zakrzewska and Mark E. Linskey, "Trigeminal Neuralgia," in *Orofacial Pain*, ed. Joanna M. Zakrzewska (Oxford: Oxford University Press, 2009), 119–33; *Taber's Cyclopedic Medical Dictionary: Edition 23* (Philadelphia: F. A. Davis Company, 2013), 1621. Trigeminal Neuralgia is suggested as a possibility for Paul's condition by Heckel, "Der Dorn im Fleisch," 90–92.

2. Wilkinson notes that if we take Tertullian's comment about Paul having an earache or headache (*dolor auricular vel capitis*) seriously, it is "a description which might suggest that Paul suffered from the condition of trigeminal neuralgia" (Wilkinson, *The Bible and Healing*, 215). Wilkinson does not, however, seem to take Tertullian's comment seriously.

3. "Historically, TN has been characterized by sharp, stabbing, usually brief paroxysms of pain" (Kenneth Casey and George Weigel, *Striking Back: A Layman's Guide to Facial Pain*, 3rd ed. (Las Vegas: NV: Kenneth Casey, 2020), n.p.). Also see Steven Graff-Radford and Bahareh Safaie, "Diagnosing and Managing Trigeminal Nerve Pain," in *Facial Pain: A 21st Century Guide: For People with Trigeminal Neuropathic Pain*, ed. Jeffrey A. Brown and Anne Brazer Ciemnecki (Facial Pain Association, 2020), 29.

or even years at a time when life is normal, only to start experiencing pain episodes all over again.[4] TN (both types) normally worsens over time, though not always. Sufferers of Multiple Sclerosis (MS) have a higher risk than the normal population of developing TN, though a majority of TN sufferers have never been diagnosed with MS.[5]

Trigeminal Neuralgia Type 2 (TN2) has been left off our list since it is normally characterized by strong pain that is felt more than 50% of the time. It is difficult to see how Paul could have maintained his active missionary work if he experienced 50% constant pain at the levels often described by sufferers of TN2.[6]

TN1 has been listed first among the seven conditions described here because the sudden and intense jabbing pains associated with TN1 fit the description of "thorn in the flesh" more closely than perhaps any of the other conditions, even though with TN1 there is no visible evidence on the skin that is caused by the condition (criterion #20).[7] Still, the remaining six conditions should all be viewed as serious contenders as well.

POSTTRAUMATIC TRIGEMINAL NEUROPATHIC PAIN

Posttraumatic Trigeminal Neuropathic Pain (PTNP)[8] is pain on one side of the face caused by unintentional damage to the trigeminal nerve, that is, the largest nerve of the face. The damage

---

4. "TN with purely paroxysmal pain is also marked by periods of complete pain-free remissions" (Graff-Radford and Safaie, "Diagnosing and Managing," 29).

5. Seth Love and Hugh B. Coakham, "Trigeminal Neuralgia: Pathology and Pathogenesis," *Brain* 124 (2001): 2347–60.

6. The reader should note that there are other very rare craniofacial neuralgias that are characterized by intense lancinating pain, including geniculate neuralgia (in the ear), glossopharyngeal neuralgia (throat/tongue), and occipital neuralgia (upper neck/back of the head), but trigeminal neuralgia is the most common.

7. In actual fact, Paul very likely had visible scars or disfigurement of some sort on his face from his multiple beatings. So even though such marks would not have caused TN1—if, in fact, this is the condition from which Paul suffered—he still would have had visible marks that witnesses, and even Paul himself, could have connected to his pain. This would be true of all the conditions listed, since they all involve the face.

8. R. Benoliel and his coauthors propose a different terminology: "peripheral painful traumatic trigeminal neuropathy" (R. Benoliel et al., "Peripheral Painful Traumatic Trigeminal

can result from impact to the face (like the kind Paul received when he was beaten), from another medical condition (like stroke), or, in modern times, from surgeries that unintentionally damage the nerve. As with Trigeminal Neuralgia Type 1, the pain is often described as intensely jabbing, stabbing, or like being jolted with an electric shock, though in some cases more generally as burning.[9] PTNP can be viewed as a subcategory of TN (since, technically, the term "trigeminal neuralgia" simply means nerve pain of the trigeminal nerve), but is sometimes separated into a category of its own the way I have separated it here. Since no one can doubt that Paul received many blows to his face over the years from his persecutors, it makes sense in the context of this study to treat this condition as separate from classic TN and as a possible option for Paul's pain in its own right.

HERPES ZOSTER (SHINGLES) IN THE TRIGEMINAL NERVE + POST-HERPETIC TRIGEMINAL NEUROPATHIC PAIN

Herpes Zoster,[10] or shingles, as this disease is more commonly known, is a reactivation of the virus that causes chickenpox. The latent chickenpox virus hides out in one's nerve roots until the virus works its way up to the skin, especially in people with a weaker immune system or older patients. The virus manifests as painful, blistering rashes on the

---

Neuropathies," *Oral Diseases* 18 (2012): 317–32). See also Lene Baad-Hansen and Rafael Benoliel, "Neuropathic Orofacial Pain: Facts and Fiction," *Cephalalgia* 37 (2017): 670–79; G. K. Essick, "Psychophysical Assessment of Patients with Posttraumatic Neuropathic Trigeminal Pain," *J. Oral Facial Pain Headache* 18 (2004): 345–54; Headache Classification Committee of the International Headache Society, " International Classification of Headache Disorders," 776–78; Suthipun Jitpimolmard and Steven Graff-Radford, "Neuropathic Pain," in *Orofacial Pain,* ed. Joanna M. Zakrzewska (Oxford: Oxford University Press, 2009), 135–40.

9.   Olga Khazen and Julie G. Pilitsis, "Motor Cortex Stimulation," in *Facial Pain: A 21st Century Guide: For People with Trigeminal Neuropathic Pain,* ed. Jeffrey A. Brown and Anne Brazer Ciemnecki (Facial Pain Association, 2020), 93; Jitpimolmard and Graff-Radford, "Neuropathic Pain," 137.

10.   Roy Rafael Dayan and Roni Peleg, "Herpes Zoster—Typical and Atypical Presentations," *Postgrad. Med.* 129 (2017): 567–71; Kenneth Schmader, "Herpes Zoster," *Clin. Geriatr.* 32 (2016): 539–53.

area of skin ("dermatome") supplied by the infected nerve root, and conducts painful, shock-like jolts through the branches of that nerve root. Shingles most commonly exhibits in one of two places: either as a half-belt on one side of one's trunk or on one side of one's face. Subsequent outbreaks typically manifest in a different quadrant of the body from the first outbreak, that is, on the other side of the trunk or the other side of the face (but are not limited to those areas).[11] Per our criteria, we are interested only in the facial version of the disease.

Following an outbreak of shingles, some people experience continuing stabbing nerve pain in the places where shingles lesions originally broke out on the skin. This nerve pain often is exacerbated by stress. In modern times, ongoing post-shingles pain (known as postherpetic neuralgia or PHN[12]) can be somewhat mitigated if anti-viral drugs have been administered during the first three days after the onset of the shingles rash. Modern medicine has also provided some pain-blocking medications that sometimes help with ongoing pain, but such medicines were unknown in the world of Paul. Even today, painful PHN is a common side effect of shingles.

Shingles is a disease known to us from ancient records. Since shingles often manifests either on the face or on a half-belt of one's trunk, ancient observers were able to recognize the belt pattern, and occasionally mentioned it.[13] Ancient medical recorders probably did

---

11. Contrary to popular belief, one study suggests that people who get shingles have about the same chance of contracting it again as do people who have never had it before. See Barbara P. Yawn et al., "Herpes Zoster Recurrences More Frequent Than Previously Reported," *Mayo Clin. Proc.* 86:2 (2011): 88–93.

12. Graham R. Hadley et al., "Post-herpetic Neuralgia: a Review," *Curr Pain Headache Rep* 20 (2016): 17; Headache Classification Committee of the International Headache Society, "International Classification of Headache Disorders," 776–77; C. B. Archer and D. J. Eedy, "The Skin and the Nervous System," in *Rook's Textbook of Dermatology*, ed. Tony Burns and Arthur Rook, 8th ed., vol. 4 (Chichester: Wiley–Blackwell, 2010): 63.6; Jitpimolmard and Graff-Radford, "Neuropathic Pain," 140–42.

13. This is where the word "zoster" comes from in "herpes zoster," the medical term for shingles. *Zoster* is the Greek word for belt. T. S. L. Beswick writes: "There is definite evidence, however, that after Hippocrates the Greeks did call shingles 'herpes,'" citing passages from Scribonius Largues and Pliny the Elder as examples (T. S. L. Beswick, "The Origin and Use of the Word 'Herpes,'" *MH* 6 [1962]: 216).

not recognize that facial shingles was the same disease as the belt manifestation, but this does not alter the fact that the disease was active and known during the time of Paul.

In his biography of Paul, Bruce Chilton suggests shingles as Paul's thorn. He does not present any argumentation for his assertion, however, and actually appears to misunderstand the nature of the disease, thinking of it primarily as an eye affliction.[14]

The following three conditions all belong to a diagnostic group known as Trigeminal Autonomic Cephalalgias (TACs).[15]

SHORT-LASTING UNILATERAL NEURALGIFORM HEADACHE ATTACKS

Short-lasting Unilateral Neuralgiform Headache Attacks (SUNHA)[16] are stabbing headaches that, as their name implies, are: (1) short lasting: seconds to minutes, (2) unilateral: occurring on only one side of the head, (3) neuralgiform: related to nerve pain, (4) headache: affecting the head, (5) attacks: the feeling of being pierced once or repeatedly, usually in the region near the eye. Unlike trigeminal neuralgia, the condition is accompanied by other symptoms, such as a bloodshot eye and/or excessive tears and/or swelling or drooping around the eye, nasal congestion or runny nose on one side, and sweating on the affected side of the face.

---

14. See Chilton, *Rabbi Paul*, 60–61, 125–27, 279–80.

15. Mark J. Burish and Todd D. Rozen, "Trigeminal Autonomic Cephalalgias," *Neurologic Clinics* 37 (2019): 847–69. Hemicrania Continua, which is discussed in this article, has not been included here because of the continuousness of the pain associated with it, even though the jabbing nature of the pain fits the other criteria. See also Rafael Benoliel, "Trigeminal Autonomic Cephalalgias," *BJP* 6 (2012): 106–23; Steven Graff-Radford and Suthipun Jitpimolmard, "Trigeminal Autonomic Cephalalgias," in *Orofacial Pain*, ed. Joanna M. Zakrzewska (Oxford: Oxford University Press, 2009), 157–69.

16. Karissa N. Arca and Rashmi B. Halker Singh, "SUNCT and SUNA: an Update and Review," *Curr Pain Headach Rep* 22 (2018): 56; Andrew Levy and Manjit S Matharu, "Short-lasting Unilateral Neuralgiform Headache Attacks," *Ann. Indian Acad. Neurol.* 21 (2018): 31–38. SUNHA can be subdivided into SUNCT (Short-lasting Unilateral Neuralgiform Headache Attacks with Conjunctival Injection and Tearing) and SUNA (Short-lasting Unilateral Neuralgiform Headache Attacks with Cranial Autonomic Symptoms). See Headache Classification Committee of the International Headache Society, "International Classification of Headache Disorders," 667–68.

EPISODIC PAROXYSMAL HEMICRANIA

Episodic Paroxysmal Hemicrania[17] are stabbing headaches around the eye that, as their name implies, are: (1) episodic: occurring at least a couple times a year, lasting at least a week and no more than a year in duration, with lengthy periods without pain in between (at least months), (2) paroxysmal: occurring suddenly and without warning, (3) hemicrania: pain occurring only on one side of the head. Pain events occur anywhere from five to forty times a day and last two to thirty minutes. Eye redness or excessive tears, runny or stuffy nose on one side, and sweating on the affected side of the face commonly accompany paroxysmal hemicrania and aid medical professionals in diagnosing the condition.

Some who suffer paroxysmal hemicrania have chronic pain, that is, they rarely experience remissions. Chronic suffering of this condition has been left out of consideration, like other chronic conditions already mentioned, because it is difficult to see how Paul could have maintained his active ministry, especially of teaching and preaching, without experiencing lengthy periods of remission. But episodic (on-and-off) paroxysmal hemicrania matches up well with the criteria already established.

EPISODIC CLUSTER HEADACHES

Episodic cluster headaches also seem to fit our criteria. Cluster headaches[18] manifest as severe pain in the face/head that occurs far more commonly in men than in women. The pain often jolts a sufferer awake one or two hours after the sufferer has fallen asleep. The pain episodes last, on average, about forty-five minutes

17. Sanjay Prakash and Rushad Patell, "Paroxysmal Hemicrania: An Update," *Current Pain and Headache Reports* 18 (2014): 407; Headache Classification Committee of the International Headache Society, "International Classification of Headache Disorders," 666–67.

18. S. A. Kandel and P. Mandiga, *Cluster Headache* (Treasure Island, FL: StatPearls Publishing, 2019); Jan Hoffmann, "Diagnosis, Pathophysiology, and Management of Cluster Headache," *Lancet Neurol.* 17 (2018): 75–83; Jacqueline Weaver-Agostoni, "Cluster Headache," *AFP* 88 (2013): 122–28; Headache Classification Committee of the International Headache Society, "International Classification of Headache Disorders," 665–66.

(anywhere from fifteen minutes to three hours). The experience of burning or piercing pain often concentrates in or around one eye on one side of the head, though the pain can radiate to other parts of the face or head. The explosive pain is often accompanied by other indicators on the affected side: eye redness and/or excessive tears from the eye, stuffy or runny nose, and sweating on the affected side. After a pain episode, the pain suddenly stops, after which the sufferer is pain-free, but exhausted. Periods of cluster attacks can last for weeks or months and are normally followed by periods of remission during which the afflicted person experiences no headaches for months or even years before another cycle starts. Cluster headaches often occur in patterns, such as at the start of each spring or fall.

Chronic cluster headaches are also a reality for some, although most people with cluster headaches experience the episodic variety. Chronic cluster headaches, which is face/head pain of the sort described above that continues without remission for at least a year or includes periods of remission lasting less than three months, have been left off our list. As with some other conditions that have been excluded, it is difficult to see how Paul could have maintained his active missionary activity if cluster headaches were an unremitting aspect of his life, unless his pain levels were lower than are normally described by people who struggle with the pain of cluster headaches.

PRIMARY STABBING HEADACHES, OR MIGRAINES WITH PRIMARY STABBING HEADACHES

Primary Stabbing Headaches[19] are unexpected stabs of pain ("jabs and jolts") in the face or head. The sudden pains occur at most a few times a day and can range from moderate to severe. Unlike all the

---

19. Danielle Murray and Esma Dilli, "Primary Stabbing Headache," *Curr Neurol Neurosci Rep* 19 (2019): 47; S. Hagler et al., "Primary Stabbing Headache in Adults and Pediatrics: a Review," *Curr Pain Headache Rep* 18 (2014): 450; Xiping Liang et al., "Characteristics of

other conditions listed, subsequent pain episodes are not necessarily limited to one side of the sufferer's head; subsequent occurrences of pain can move around, even to the other side of one's face/head. These headaches also frequently do not involve the trigeminal nerve. There are no accompanying symptoms apart from the sudden, unexpected, few-seconds-in-duration stabbing pains.

What about migraines? The reader will notice that migraines in general have not made the list, primarily because people normally describe migraines as *throbbing, pounding,* or *pulsing,* rather than as *jabbing, piercing,* or *stabbing.*[20] Sufferers of migraines, however, face a higher risk of also experiencing primary stabbing headache pains than do those who do not suffer from migraines.[21] Stated differently, because some migraine sufferers experience piercing pain in addition to the normal throbbing pain, the combination of migraine plus primary stabbing headaches should also be considered a possible explanation for what Paul called the "thorn in the flesh," though migraines by themselves perhaps should not. It also may be helpful to keep in mind that people who have suffered traumatic brain injuries (concussions that have impacted some part of the brain) have higher incidences of migraines and headaches of various kinds than do others.[22] Since Paul undoubtedly received many blows to his head and face on various occasions, he certainly had an increased risk of suffering migraines or other headaches.

Primary Stabbing Headache in a Tertiary Neurological Clinic in China," *Pain Medicine* 15 (May 2014): 871–75; Headache Classification Committee of the International Headache Society, "International Classification of Headache Disorders," 677.

20. Furthermore, migraines tend to start earlier (say, in puberty) and typically become less severe as one ages. Paul, in contrast, was middle-aged at the outset of the suffering of his thorn. See comments in Wilkinson, *Bible and Healing,* 215–16, and Heckel, "Der Dorn im Fleisch," 90.

21. Elcio Juliato Piovesan et al., "Prevalence and Semiologic Aspects of the Idiopathic Stabbing Headache in a Migraine Population." *Arquivos de Neuro-Psiquiatria* 59 (2001): 201–5.

22. Ruth Defrin, "Chronic Post-traumatic Headache: Clinical Findings and Possible Mechanisms," *J. Man. Manip. Ther.* 22 (2014): 36–44; Sophia Lahz and Richard A. Bryant, "Incidence of Chronic Pain following Traumatic Brain Injury," *Arch. Phys. Med. Rehabil.* 77 (1996): 889–91; Dawn A. Marcus, "Disability and Chronic Posttraumatic Headache," *Headache* 43 (2003): 117–21.

LOCATION AND NATURE OF THE PAIN

The Trigeminal Nerve[23]

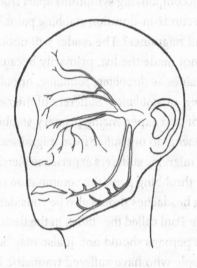

The primary carrier of the pain associated with most of the conditions described above is the trigeminal nerve (the fifth cranial nerve, the largest of the twelve cranial nerves), although connected nerves are also often involved.[24] The primary branches of the trigeminal nerve fan out onto one side of the face from a mass of nerve tissue (known as a ganglion) just in front of the place where the upper edge of the ear connects with the skin. There are three primary branches of the trigeminal nerve: (1) one that runs just above the eye (ophthalmic nerve), (2) one that runs across the cheek toward

---

23. The trigeminal nerve. Illustration by Ana Berding. Used with permission.

24. See H. H. Taurig and B. E. Maley, "The Trigeminal System," in *Neuroscience in Medicine*, ed. P. M. Conn (Philadelphia: J. B. Lippincott, 1995), 239–48. Unlike the other conditions listed here, people with primary stabbing headaches experience the pain outside the trigeminal regions in 70 percent of the cases.

the nose (maxillary nerve), and (3) one that runs down the side of the face toward the teeth and along the jaw line (mandibular nerve). In other words, the three branches of the trigeminal nerve impact almost the entire side of the face. (All but the last of the conditions listed above are normally felt only on one side of the face.) Nerve pain in the face can be excruciating, as the home page of the Facial Pain Association notes about TN: "Trigeminal neuralgia (TN) is considered to be one of the most painful afflictions known to medical practice."[25]

But since most people have no experience with severe nerve pain in the face (and many others have no experience with serious nerve pain at all), and since all but one of the above conditions focus on pain associated with the trigeminal nerve, I have chosen to include some descriptions of pain from people who experience attacks of trigeminal nerve pain. I have deemed this necessary for the persuasiveness of the argument, as has already been stated in chapter 1 where I discuss presuppositions, because a common reason people reject new proposals is that they have trouble personally relating to what has been proposed. In other words, people often do not accept arguments for which they can find no personal analogy. To help alleviate this problem, I have drawn upon comments from various support groups populated by people who suffer from nerve-related face pain. These comments will help to illustrate why Paul might have described his own face/head pain as *a sharp-pointed object in his flesh* and as being *beaten on the face* (not to mention, viewing it as an attack by an angel of Satan!). I have kept the names of the support groups and the names of the commenters anonymous to protect their privacy.[26] Warning: many of these descriptions are difficult to read.

---

25. Facial Pain Association, "What is Trigeminal Neuralgia?," https://fpa-support.org/learn.

26. I have names and dates for each comment stored in my own files. Note that the comments have been slightly edited for punctuation and grammar, but no wording has been impacted.

NATURE AND SEVERITY PAIN

"It's as if someone is trying to pull my teeth out, super sensitivity in my teeth, being stabbed in the temple area with an ice pick, staples piercing my eyebrow, fire ants biting my lips, electric shock that feels exactly like what a lightning bolt looks like running along my jawline and cheek area under my eye, needles stabbing me in the eye, and being punched. Who would say that's an accurate description for their pain?"

Someone at the forum responded to the questioner: "Add red hot poker in the ear, and yep, pretty accurate."

"My husband ... describes the pain like someone is hammering a hot spike into his face, and on bad pain days they are twisting it as well."

"Didn't sleep at all last night. My teeth feel like little needles are stabbing up into my nose, my eye feels like it's being pulled out of the socket, my entire nose on the left side feels like it's being ripped away from my head. I can't even close my eyes because it hurts so bad. My left temple feels like it's being pounded by a hammer. I just want it to go away. I don't wish this on anyone."

In a different forum for people struggling with facial nerve pain, a questioner asked co-sufferers how they described their pain to others who struggle to understand and empathize. This particular question received more than one hundred follow-up responses in the space of a month. I have included the original question and seven representative responses.

"So I have an odd question for all of my fellow TN sufferers ... what do you say when people keep asking you: 'How does it feel? What is the pain like? What does it actually feel like?' I've tried to say it's like a shock, as that's what I kept reading when I was first learning about my illness, but it's more than that. I am struggling to describe it. Everyone has different symptoms, and maybe I just can't find the words to really express it. All I can say is that it is extremely sharp, hot, stop-you-in-your-tracks, one long throb of pain. I broke my back and now consider my back seizing a 6 compared to the actual 10 pain

I feel during an attack. Sorry I am going on and on. But how do you try to get people to really understand the pain ... ?"

Here are some representative responses to the question:

"Stabbing an ice pick in my temple."

"For me it is like biting on an electric fence while being smashed in the face with a shovel."

"Like when the dentist hits a nerve in your tooth."

"The only thing they can relate to is the dentist metaphor ... plus getting electrically charged needles plonked into your face in a totally random way, plus sinusitis, plus an ear infection, plus a sore throat, plus .... By then, they usually say: 'you have got to be kidding me.'"

"Electric shock or a relentless stinging (depending on the type)."

"I say it has many different pain variations for different people, but common ones are 'electric shock' pain, 'dagger stab' pain, 'bee sting' pain, 'boiling water burn' pain, 'ice pick' pins and needles pain at levels up to 10/10."

"I've asked them the question: 'When you were young did you ever put a nine-volt battery on the tip of your tongue?' Most will say yes, and if they say yes I tell them that instead of a nine-volt battery it's the battery for a semi-truck that's hooked up to your face. The electrical shocks don't stop; they just keep coming until your skin and muscles inside your face explode into a raging fire. Basically that's what mine feels like, and then after the shocking stops you are left with a face that feels like you have gone ten rounds with Mohammed Ali, beaten to a pulp."

Once again, I apologize for the graphic nature of the descriptions you have just read (though there are dozens of other similar comments in my files), but as I previously noted, it seemed necessary to include a few descriptions to reinforce the plausibility of the argument. Students of 2 Corinthians 12:7 need to understand that face pain connected with the trigeminal nerve fits well the descriptions of *thorn in the flesh* and being *punched in the face*, and in the first-century Greco-Roman world, *an angel of Satan*.

A FULLER PORTRAIT
OF PAUL

What implications can be drawn from this study beyond the singular quest to identify Paul's thorn in the flesh? This study helps to fill out our understanding of the person of Paul, which in turn may help us read the letters of Paul more sentsitively in the future. Since the means of arriving at the partial solution supported in this book focused on twenty criteria used to draw a descriptive dragnet around Paul's thorn, I will organize my list of implications around these twenty criteria. In other words, even though to this point in our discussion, these criteria have been employed solely for the purpose of identifying Paul's thorn in the flesh, they also suggest other implications beyond simple identification. These implications for the most part relate to our understanding of the person of Paul. I will limit myself to one implication that can be drawn from each criterion beyond simply using them to identify Paul's thorn.

An Implication of Criterion 1: Viewed by others as black magic attacks

If those around Paul thought that Paul was experiencing black magic
attacks, it can be surmised that differing reactions toward Paul
would have been forthcoming from various groups. Those outside
the early Christian movement most likely would have viewed Paul
as a magician (on account of reports that he did miracles) but might
also have supposed he was not quite so strong a magician as people
claimed since he seemingly was not able to protect himself from
the magical attacks of others.[1] Newer Christians whose theology
of spiritual warfare was in its infancy might have thought the same
thing. But those who had deeper roots in the now twenty-year-old
Christian movement—including those who had seen the miracles
and heard the teaching of Christ himself, or others who had witnessed the miracles and teaching of other apostles, and especially
those who had served with Paul on mission—would have known
that Christians sometimes encountered demonic opposition of
various kinds, including sometimes via opposing magicians. But
most of Paul's recipients were still young in the faith and inexperi-
enced in Christian spiritual warfare. Paul could have been partially
motivated in his writing of 2 Corinthians 12 to help nudge these
believers toward a fuller understanding of spiritual warfare and the
Christian's response to it. This helps to fill out our portrait of Paul.

*An Implication of Criterion 2: Viewed by Paul as attacks by an angel of
Satan, though permitted by God*

Though there can be no way for a human to fully comprehend the
mystery of divine providence that allows suffering at the hands of
Satan or one of his demons, this study draws back the curtain for a
moment on one of the great inscrutabilities of the Bible. The apostle

---

1. The reader should keep in mind that I have not attempted to argue that Paul's pain *in
fact* was caused by a magician, but only that people around Paul likely would have thought
that it was. See discussion in ch. 3.

Paul believed that God's sovereignty was so extensive that even the evil machinations of his greatest foe, Satan, were sometimes permitted by God. Even though Satan's purposes are for harm, God's purposes ultimately are for the good of his people. Such thoughts are difficult for us—and probably for Paul himself—to fully comprehend, but they are, nonetheless, the direction Paul takes us in 2 Corinthians 12:7, and thereby crack open a window into Paul's thought-world.

An Implication of Criterion 3: Paralleling Job's sufferings (especially Job 1–2), which included skin/flesh

The most important implication of Criterion 3 outside of helping us identify Paul's thorn is the acknowledgment that Paul viewed his personal suffering against the backdrop of the most famous biblical sufferer of all: the person of Job. Paul's comments in 2 Corinthians 12:7 are anchored in the book of Job, and especially chapters 1–2 of that great book. The discussion appearing in our current study (ch. 4) is the most extensive study of intertextual connections between these two passages heretofore undertaken. Consequently, we should understand that when Paul suffered, he looked to the narrative about Job to provide spiritual help. This opens a window into the mind of Paul.

An Implication of Criterion 4: Impacting Paul's physical flesh (also Criterion 18: Involving the ear, and Criterion 19: Involving the eye)

Paul's understanding of Satanic attack was contrary to later interpreters such as Chrysostom, who recoiled at the thought that God would allow Satan to touch Paul's physical body.[2] Paul himself, in contrast, believed—in agreement with Job—not only that Satan could generally oppose God's people, say, through temptations or opposition from people, but could painfully touch someone's physical flesh—even if that person was one of God's chosen apostles.

---

2. See ACCS, 7:305.

An Implication of Criterion 5: Comparable to the jabbing of a sharp-pointed object

If in fact Paul suffered from pain that felt like repeated stabbings of a thorn or stake, that in and of itself expands our understanding of Paul's ministry, and how people would have viewed him. Have you ever observed people who are in pain—who wince, or press a hand against the side of their face, or in other non-verbal ways indicate that they are experiencing momentary physical pain? Such non-verbal actions most often interrupt the flow of a conversation, and, if frequent enough, can hinder a developing relationship. Was this the experience of Paul? Did people experience awkwardness when they personally interacted with Paul? This study would suggest that something like this was at least the occasional reality for Paul during interpersonal interactions.

An Implication of Criterion 6: Excruciating, not simply annoying

Paul seemed to think that we don't have the right to limit the extent of suffering that God might allow. Some modern readers of the Bible acknowledge the possibility that God might allow some (even physical) suffering to train us, but balk when encountering excruciating, long-term suffering. How could more extreme suffering of the kind suggested by Paul be permitted by God? Paul apparently agreed with the theology of the book of Job that even extreme suffering can still be factored into God's ultimate purposes.

An Implication of Criterion 7: Impacting Paul's face (as a part of his head)

If in fact the bodily location of the suffering that Paul labeled "a thorn in the flesh" was his face, this might open for us a way to read 2 Corinthians 3:18–5:12 that factors Paul's own suffering into the reading. For example, think of 2 Corinthians 3:18: "And we all, with unveiled face, beholding the glory of the Lord, are being transformed into the same image from one degree of glory to another." Perhaps we should not merely read Paul's comment about unveiled faces as making a theological point in relation to Moses's face veil (ch. 3); instead, we might also recall as we read this section that Paul's own facial pain would have helped him to gaze more intently at the face of Jesus (4:6), recognize the weakness of his jar-of-clay body (4:7–9), identify with Christ's sufferings (4:10–11), acknowledge the reality of inner renewal despite outward bodily decay (4:16), look beyond his current transitory afflictions (4:17–18) toward the new body that God had prepared for him (5:1–11), all in contrast to those who wanted to take pride in appearance (*en prosōpon*) rather than in heart (5:12). The bodily suffering of Paul that was focused on his face has the potential of adding richness and depth to the way we read this well-known section of an earlier portion of 2 Corinthians.

An Implication of Criterion 8: Viewed by Paul as educational discipline by God

One implication of this study is that Paul becomes a clearer witness to a theme found more explicitly in other parts of the Bible: that God disciplines and trains his children. The idea of God disciplining his people is clear in such diverse passages as Deuteronomy 8:5, 2 Samuel 7:14, Proverbs 3:11–12, Hebrews 12:5–11, and Revelation 3:19. (Paul himself also briefly alludes to the idea in 1 Corinthians 11:32. It may, furthermore, function as a backdrop to the way he sometimes chastises his "children" in the faith.) But Paul's thorn in the flesh, although directly inflicted by an angel of Satan, is viewed by Paul as God disciplining and training him toward humility and dependence upon the God's sufficient grace. This strengthens Paul's role as a witness to God's providential discipline.

An Implication of Criterion 9: Viewed by others as humiliating and weak

An implication of Criterion 9 is that it provides a bit more clarity about Paul's relationship with the Corinthians. Why was Paul so defensive in chapters 10–13? Why did Paul finally decide to explicitly write about his heavenly ascent/vision when other clues in the section suggest his reluctance to do so?

There is no single answer to this question, since it appears that multiple complaints about Paul were circulating in Corinth at the time he wrote 2 Corinthians.[3] But one of the obvious proposed complaints against Paul that helps to explain why Paul was so defensive involves the honor-and-shame world in which Paul lived. The four chapters surrounding 2 Corinthians 12:7 suggest that Paul's thorn in the flesh must have been viewed by others as humiliating and weak. The intertwining themes of humiliation, weakness, and shame are strong in 2 Corinthians 10–13 (see discussion in ch. 7 above). For our understanding of Paul, we need to view him as a full participant in the honor-and-shame cultural setting of the first-century Mediterranean world, while still allowing him to re-theologize honor and shame to fit within a new Christian paradigm of what actually constitutes honor and shame.

An Implication of Criterion 10: Unusual, not like the pains of others

This criterion offers us another peek into the person of Paul. Although Paul was extremely social, at least in the sense that it appears that he almost always chose to be around others (and the couple times we hear of him being alone, he isn't happy, 1 Thess 3:1; 2 Tim 4:11), Paul experienced a different kind of loneliness through his thorn in the flesh. It is possible, but not very likely, that he personally knew someone who shared his same sort of suffering. If we didn't have access to social media in the twenty-first century, most of people suffering from the maladies listed in chapter 14 would have no one with whom to commiserate. This doesn't mean that in Paul's first-century world, just as in ours, others weren't experiencing stabbing facial pain, but in most cases, they probably had never met someone like them. This evokes

---

3. A helpful list is drawn up by Harris, *Second Epistle to the Corinthians*, 69–71 (likely criticisms of Paul) and 71–73 (Paul's criticisms of them).

a type of loneliness-in-suffering that Paul may have experienced, and cracks open another window into the person of Paul.

An Implication of Criterion 11: Long-term, but intermittent

We learn something about the person of Paul from this criterion as well. Since Paul may never have known when his special suffering was going to flare up, it is worthwhile reflecting on what that might have meant for him in practice. Most sufferers of the types of ailments detailed in chapter 14 live in fear both of short-term explosions of pain and longer-term periods when shooting pain is their constant companion. Furthermore, in many such cases (with notable exceptions), people struggling with such afflictions recoil from social situations, and seek isolation away from others. But such was not the case with Paul. He continued pushing through the rigors of active ministry. This means that Paul's trust had gone deep, that minute-by-minute (and year-after-year) he had learned to depend upon God's power in the midst of helplessness and weakness, that he had grown to have faith in God's sovereign wisdom in permitting or holding back flare-ups, and that he had decided to continue to fulfill his God-given calling, despite his likely desire to recoil from public ministry.

An Implication of Criterion 12: Paralleling the sufferings of Jesus

An implication of Criterion 12 is that in Paul's thorn in the flesh, we learn something more about Paul's "in Christ" theology—what theologians usually refer to as union with Christ or participation in Christ. "InChristness" is one of the most important themes in the letters of Paul.[4] Constantine Campbell suggests that union with Christ is like the webbing that holds other themes in Paul together.[5] Paul's physical suffering runs through this theme but is not limited to a spiritual

---

4. As far as I know, I was the first to use the term *inChristness*. See Kenneth Berding, *How to Live an 'In Christ' Life: 100 Devotional Readings on Union With Christ* (Geanies House, Scotland: Christian Focus, 2020), 14–17.

5. Constantine R. Campbell, *Paul and Union with Christ: An Exegetical and Theological Study* (Grand Rapids: Zondervan, 2012), 441–42.

reflection. In Paul's physical suffering, he identified with the suffering of his Lord Jesus. And in this he found comfort, encouragement, and strength to continue.

An Implication of Criterion 13: Exacerbated by stress

A calling of God to do ministry, such as Paul received, does not entail the absence of stress. The weight of responsibility that Paul felt in relationship to the churches he started (2 Cor 11:28–29), including the Corinthian church, is one portion of the backdrop for identifying and understanding Paul's thorn in the flesh in 2 Corinthians 12:7. Non-physical stressors, in addition to physical pain, were an unpleasant reality for the apostle (and very likely exacerbated his physical pain). Paul mentioned open doors three times in his letters (2 Cor 2:12–13; 1 Cor 16:9; Col 4:3), but he was facing stressful situations in all three. Not only physical pain, but also the non-physical stress that intensifies physical pain was a feature of Paul's life indicated by this study.

An Implication of Criterion 14: Negatively impacting Paul's rhetorical ability

One implication of this particular criterion has already been drawn out in this study. Scholars of Paul have struggled to know how to describe Paul in relation to his rhetorical ability. Was he a strong and effective communicator, as his apparent familiarity with rhetorical categories would suggest, or was he a weak speaker, as the apparent criticism of his speaking ability by some in Corinth would suggest? A proposed solution runs through the nature of Paul's thorn as argued more fully in chapter 7 of this book. If Paul's speaking was sometimes interrupted by sudden bouts of face pain that stopped him mid-sentence and caused his face to contort, Paul could be at the same time a strong rhetorician and yet still be criticized for his speaking ability. This could resolve a dilemma that every Pauline scholar has to wrestle with. It also opens up another window into the person of Paul.

An Implication of Criterion 15: Known to the Corinthians, not a secret

I have talked with students of Paul who have apparently thought of Paul as secretive, or at least mysterious. However, except for Paul's use of the word "mystery" (e.g., Eph 3; Col 1), which has nothing to do with being secretive, one of the most likely reasons (ironically!) that someone might deem Paul secretive is because of 2 Corinthians 12 itself. In 2 Corinthians 12, Paul employed third-person pronouns to refer to himself in relation to his heavenly vision/ascent, mentioned things he had heard that he was not permitted to speak, and then dangled in front of his readers a tantalizing description of severe personal suffering—a "thorn" or "stake" in his "flesh." But if, as I have argued in this book, Paul decided to mention his thorn because he was being criticized in some way, and if some of his opponents in Corinth viewed whatever he suffered as humiliating, it is more likely than not that they knew about his suffering. I have already developed this idea in more detail earlier in the book. Consequently, our view of Paul should *not* be that he was secretive—a judgment, I think, that we might make primarily because we are culturally distant and not participants in the correspondence between the Corinthians and Paul. Rather, Paul should be viewed as self-disclosing, open, and inviting. Affirming Paul's open-heartedness and willingness to self-disclose would agree with explicit statements elsewhere in 2 Corinthians (3:18; 4:2; 6:3, 11, 13; 12:6). Viewing Paul as self-disclosing rather than secretive also expands our portrait of the person of Paul.

An Implication of Criterion 16: Analogous to Paul's other sufferings

Criterion 16 was largely derived from observing the important location of Paul's short and generalized list of sufferings in 2 Corinthians 12:10, a list which recapitulates to some degree the sufferings-list found at the end of 2 Corinthians 11. And in 12:10, we observe that Paul claimed to be content with his sufferings. "For the sake of Christ, then, I am content ... for when I am weak, then I am strong." Paul not only had

learned to grit his teeth and endure his suffering. Rather, because of
the spiritual lesson he gained through his thorn ("for my power is
made perfect in weakness" 12:9), he had learned contentment—even
to the point of boasting "all the more gladly" about his weaknesses
(12:9)! What we learn about Paul, then, is that he moved beyond
mere endurance and somehow found a place of contentment in the
midst of his suffering.

An Implication of Criterion 17: Connected to the heavenly ascent

As a result of 2 Corinthians 12:1–10, we need to remind ourselves that
Paul was not simply a missionary or theologian, teacher or evan-
gelist. He, of course, was all of these. But we also need to view him
as the visionary-mystic that he apparently was, and even viewed
himself to be. This characterization of Paul receives support from
the other times in Paul's life when we read about him seeing visions,
receiving revelations, or speaking in tongues (Gal 1:12; 2:2; Eph 3:3;
1 Cor 14:18; Acts 16:9; 18:9; 19:21; 27:23–24). Paul was reluctant to
talk about at least some of his visionary experiences, which hints at
the possibility that he had experienced more mystical experiences
than we know about. In the case of his 2 Corinthians 12 heavenly
ascent (whether in the body or out of the body, he didn't know), he
only wrote about it because he felt that the Corinthians had driven
him to it (2 Cor 12:1). But one implication of this study is that our
portrait of Paul needs to allow space for the mystical dimension of
Paul's life alongside other non-mystical aspects of his life that often
receive greater attention.

[Note to reader: Criterion 18: Involving the ear, and Criterion 19: Involving
the eye, were incorporated into the discussion of implications related to
the physical-flesh Criterion 4 above.]

An Implication of Criterion 20: Visible bodily damage

Finally, even if Criterion 20 is the least well-attested of the twenty criteria, we still perhaps should consider that Paul was disconcerting to look at. This, I think, should be assumed anyway, even apart from connecting to Paul's thorn in the flesh. Since we know that Paul received multiple beatings (2 Cor 11:24–25), and since his face would have been involved on a least some of those occasions, it seems appropriate to assume that Paul's face sported scars and maybe even some deformity from those beatings. (The late second-century *Acts of Paul and Thecla* described Paul's nose as hooked, but it is hard to know whether this in any way reflects Paul's actual appearance—and even if it did, whether the altered appearance of Paul's nose came from it having been formerly broken during beatings.) Regardless, this study reminds us that Paul's face was probably marred in some way, whether the cause was the thorn itself, or only would have been viewed that way by those observing Paul's struggle with facial pain.

Our portrait of the apostle Paul, thus, gets filled out through attentive study of Paul's thorn-in-the-flesh passage (2 Cor 12:1–10), and, in particular, by thinking individually about the twenty criteria that have framed this study. But one of the central conclusions to be drawn from the study of 2 Corinthians 12:1–10—and the primary reason this book was written—is that we can narrow the range of ailments from which Paul could have suffered when he mentioned his thorn in the flesh in 2 Corinthians 12:7. When all the criteria are considered, we must conclude that Paul's thorn in the flesh was unusual, long-term, intermittent, stabbing pain located on his face, viewed by others as shameful and as resulting from black magic attacks, but viewed by Paul as attacks of a demon that God permitted. Paul believed that God used this dreadful suffering as educational discipline, and, particularly, that God wanted him to learn how to rely upon the truth that God's strength is made perfect in weakness.

ACKNOWLEDGMENTS |

I want to thank the many people who have encouraged and supported me during the writing of this book.

Nick Galvan, Jacob Keeth, Barnabas Kwok, and Jane Steel helped me locate relevant books and articles. Thank you so much!

Particular appreciation is due to many learned friends and colleagues who read the manuscript in full or part and offered insightful and sometimes corrective comments. These include Drew Berding, Adam Day, Richard I. Deibert, Alan Hultberg, Michelle Lee-Barnewall, John Makujina, Charlie Trimm, and Matt Williams.

Medical doctors Brian Beck, Phil Lewis, Rosa Lewis, Ken Thompson, and speech specialist Matt Rouse interacted with me on medical issues, as did three of my daughters who serve in medical-related fields: Lydia Lindsay, Grace Ko, and Ana Berding. Ana also drew the diagram of the trigeminal nerve in chapter 14. Thank you to each one.

This book would not exist apart from many conversations with my wife, Trudi, and my friend and colleague at Talbot/Biola, Uche Anizor. I so appreciate their encouragement.

Thanks also are due to the leadership of Biola University for granting a one-semester research leave during the fall of 2019, in part to allow me to start writing this book. In particular, I want to thank my department head, Matt Williams; my division dean, Doug Huffman; the dean of faculty at Talbot School of Theology, Scott Rae; and the dean of Talbot School of Theology, Clint Arnold, for making such a study leave possible.

I am very grateful for the dedicated work of the team at Lexham Press, including Derek Brown, Scott Corbin, Abigail Stocker, Mandi Newell, Jessi Strong, and Katrina Smith.

I dedicate this book to my youngest daughter, Ana. I pray that she will know the sufficiency of God's grace, and that the power of Christ is truly made perfect in weakness.

WORKS CITED

Abernathy, David. "Paul's Thorn in the Flesh: A Messenger of Satan?" *Neot* 35 (2001): 69–79.

Akin, Daniel. "Triumphalism, Suffering, and Spiritual Maturity: An Exposition of 2 Corinthians 12:1–10 in its Literary, Theological, and Historical Context." *CTR* 4 (1989): 119–44.

Aland, Barbara, Kurt Aland, Johannes Karavidopoulos, Carlo M. Martini, and Bruce Metzger, ed. *The Greek New Testament.* 5th revised edition. Stuttgart: Deutsche Bibelgesellschaft, 2014.

Albl, Martin. "'For Whenever I Am Weak, Then I Am Strong': Disability in Paul's Epistles." Pages 145–58 in *This Abled Body: Rethinking Disabilities in Biblical Studies.* Edited by Hector Avalos, Sarah J. Melcher, and Jeremy Schipper. Semeia St 55. Atlanta: Society of Biblical Literature, 2007.

Alexander, Wm. Menzies. "St. Paul's Infirmity." *ExpTim* 10 (1904): 469–73 and 15 (1904): 545–48.

Allo, E. Bernard. *Seconde épître aux Corinthiens.* Paris: J. Gabalda, 1937.

Ambrose. *Selected Works and Letters.* In vol. 10 of *The Nicene and Post-Nicene Fathers*, Series 2. Edited by Philip Schaff and Henry Wace. Translated by H. de Romestin, E. de Romestin, and H. T. F. Duckworth. New York: Christian Literature Company, 1896.

Andersen, Francis I. *Job: An Introduction and Commentary.* TOTC. Downers Grove, IL: InterVarsity Press, 1976.

Ante-Nicene Fathers: Volume 1: The Apostolic Fathers, Justin Martyr, Irenaeus. Edited
by Alexander Roberts and James Donaldson. Revised by A. Cleveland
Coxe. Buffalo, NY: Christian Literature Company, 1885. Reprinted
Peabody, MA: Hendrickson, 2004.

Ante-Nicene Fathers: Volume 3: Latin Christianity: Its Founder, Tertullian I.
Apologetic; II. Anti-Marcion; III. Ethical. Edited by Alexander Roberts and
James Donaldson. Revised by A. Cleveland Coxe. Buffalo, NY: Christian
Literature Company, 1885. Reprinted Peabody, MA: Hendrickson, 2004.

Ante-Nicene Fathers: Volume 4: Tertullian, Part Fourth; Minicius Felix; Commodian;
Origen, Parts First and Second. Edited by Alexander Roberts and
James Donaldson. Revised by A. Cleveland Coxe, 307–578. Buffalo,
NY: Christian Literature Company, 1885. Reprinted Peabody, MA:
Hendrickson, 2004.

Ante-Nicene Fathers: Volume 5: Fathers of the Third Century: Hippolytus, Cyprian,
Novatian, Appendix. Edited by Alexander Roberts, James Donaldson, and
A. Cleveland Coxe. Translated by Robert Ernest Wallis. Buffalo, NY:
Christian Literature Company, 1886.

Aquinas, Thomas. *Commentary on the Letters of Saint Paul to the Corinthians.*
Edited by J. Martensen and E. Alarcon. Translated by F. R. Larcher, B.
Mortensen, and D. Keating. Biblical Commentaries 38. Lander, WY: The
Institute for the Study of Sacred Doctrine, 2012.

Arca, Karissa N. and Rashmi B. Halker Singh. "SUNCT and SUNA: an Update
and Review." *Curr Pain Headache Rep* 22 (2018): 56.

Archer, C. B. and D. J. Eedy. "The Skin and the Nervous System." Pages 63.1–15 in
Rook's Textbook of Dermatology 8th edition, vol. 4. Edited by Tony Burns
and Arthur Rook. Chichester, UK: Wiley-Blackwell, 2010.

Arnold, Clinton E. *Ephesians: Power and Magic: The Concept of Power in Ephesians*
in Light of its Historical Setting. Grand Rapids: Baker, 1989.

———. "'I Am Astonished That You Are So Quickly Turning Away!' (Gal 1:6): Paul
and Anatolian Folk Belief." *NTS* 51 (2005): 429–449.

———. *Powers of Darkness: Principalities & Powers in Paul's Letters.* Downers Grove,
IL: InterVarsity Press, 1992.

Arzt-Grabner, Peter (with Ruth E. Kritzer). *2. Korinther.* PKNT 4. Göttingen:
Vandenhoeck & Ruprecht, 2014.

Baad-Hansen, Lene and Rafael Benoliel. "Neuropathic orofacial pain: Facts and fiction." *Cephalalgia* 37 (2017): 670–79.

Bailey, Kenneth E. "Informal Controlled Oral Tradition and the Synoptic Gospels," *AsJT* 5 (1991): 34–54.

Baldwin, Joyce G. *Haggai, Zechariah, Malachi: An Introduction & Commentary.* TOTC. Leicester: Inter-Varsity Press, 1972.

Bailliot, Magali. "Rome and the Roman Empire." Pages 175–97 in *Guide to the Study of Ancient Magic.* Edited by David Frankfurter. RGRW 189. Leiden and Boston: Brill, 2019.

Barnett, Paul. *The Second Epistle to the Corinthians.* NICNT. Grand Rapids and Cambridge: Eerdmans, 1997.

Barré, M. L. "Qumran and the 'Weakness' of Paul." *CBQ* 42 (1980): 216–27.

Barrett, C. K. *The Second Epistle to the Corinthians.* BNTC. Peabody, MA: Hendrickson, 1973.

Bauer, Walter. BDAG. Revised and edited by Frederick W. Danker. 3rd ed. Chicago: University of Chicago Press, 2000.

Beale, G. K. and D. A. Carson, eds. *Commentary on the New Testament Use of the Old Testament.* Grand Rapids: Baker and Nottingham: Apollos, 2007.

Beale, G. K. and Sean M. McDonough. "Revelation." Pages 1081–161 in *Commentary on the New Testament Use of the Old Testament.* Edited by G. K. Beale and D. A. Carson. Grand Rapids: Baker and Nottingham: Apollos, 2007.

Belleville, Linda L. *2 Corinthians.* IVPNTC. Downers Grove, IL: InterVarsity Press, 1996.

Benoliel, Rafael. "Trigeminal Autonomic Cephalalgias." *BJP* 6 (2012): 106–23.

Benoliel, R., J. Kahn, and E. Eliav. "Peripheral painful traumatic trigeminal neuropathies." *Oral Diseases* 18 (2012): 317–32.

Berding, Kenneth. "God and Paul (in Christ) On Three Visits as the 'Two or Three Witnesses' of 2 Corinthians 13:1." *JSPL* 7 (2017): 5–25.

———. *How to Live an 'In Christ' Life: 100 Devotional Readings on Union with Christ.* Geanies House, Scotland: Christian Focus, 2020.

———. *Polycarp and Paul: An Analysis of their Literary and Theological Relationship in light of Polycarp's Use of Biblical and Extra-biblical Literature.* VCSup 62. Leiden: Brill, 2002.

Berding, Kenneth and Jonathan Lunde, eds. *Three Views on the New Testament Use of the Old Testament*. Grand Rapids: Zondervan, 2008.

Beswick, T. S. L. "The Origin and Use of the Word 'Herpes.'" *MH* 6 (1962): 214–32.

Betz, Hans Dieter. *The Greek Magical Papyri in Translation: Including the Demotic Spells*. Chicago and London: The University of Chicago Press, 1986.

Bickley, Lynn S. and Peter G. Szilagyi. *Bates' Guide to Physical Examination and History Taking*. 12th ed. Philadelphia: Wolters Kluwer and Lippincott Williams & Wilkins, 2017.

Binder, Hermann. "Die angebliche Krankheit des Paulus." *TZ* 32 (1976): 1–13.

Black, David Alan. *Paul, Apostle of Weakness: Astheneia and Its Cognates in the Pauline Literature*. Revised edition. Eugene, OR: Pickwick, 2012.

Bockmuehl, Markus. *Simon Peter in Scripture and Memory: The New Testament Apostle in the Early Church*. Grand Rapids: Baker, 2012.

Boda, Mark J. *The Book of Zechariah*. NICOT. Grand Rapids: Eerdmans, 2016.

Bohak, Gideon. *Ancient Jewish Magic*. Cambridge: Cambridge University Press, 2008.

Bowens, Lisa M. *An Apostle in Battle: Paul and Spiritual Warfare in 2 Corinthians 1:1–10*. WUNT 2. Reihe 433. Tübingen: Mohr Siebeck, 2017.

Bradshaw, William Brandt. "Demonology in Hebrew and Jewish Tradition: A Study in New Testament Origins," Ph.D. thesis, University of St. Andrews, 1963.

Bray, Gerald, ed. *Ancient Christian Commentary on Scripture: New Testament VII: 1–2 Corinthians*. Downers Grove, IL: InterVarsity Press, 1999.

Brown, Derek R. *The God of This Age: Satan in the Churches and Letters of the Apostle Paul*. WUNT 2. Reihe 409. Tübingen: Mohr Siebeck, 2015.

Brown, Jeannine K. *Scripture as Communication: Introducing Biblical Hermeneutics*. Grand Rapids: Baker, 2007.

Bruce, F. F. *The Epistle to the Galatians*. NIGTC. Grand Rapids: Eerdmans; Exeter: Paternoster, 1982.

Burish, Mark J. and Todd D. Rozen. "Trigeminal Autonomic Cephalalgias." *Neurologic Clinics* 37 (2019): 847–69.

Bultmann, Rudolf. *The Second Letter to the Corinthians.* Translated by Roy A. Harrisville. Minneapolis: Augsburg, 1985.

Callimachus: Aetia, Iambi, Hecale and Other Fragments; Musaeus: Hero and Leander. Edited and translated by C. A. Trypanis, T. Gelzer, and Cedric H. Whitman. LCL 421. Cambridge, MA: Harvard University Press, 1973.

Calvin, John. *Commentary on the Epistles of Paul the Apostle to the Corinthians.* Vol. 2. Translated by John Pringle. Grand Rapids: Eerdmans, 1948.

Campbell, Constantine R. *Paul and Union with Christ: An Exegetical and Theological Study.* Grand Rapids: Zondervan, 2012.

Carson, D. A. and Douglas J. Moo. *An Introduction to the New Testament.* 2nd ed. Grand Rapids: Zondervan, 2005.

Casey, Kenneth and George Weigel. *Striking Back: A Layman's Guide to Facial Pain.* 3rd ed. Las Vegas, NV: Kenneth Casey, 2020.

Chakraborti, Chandana, and Shreya Gayen. "An Unusual Journey of a Periocular Date Palm Thorn." *Saudi Journal of Ophthalmology* 33 (2019): 165–67.

Chilton, Bruce. *Rabbi Paul: An Intellectual Biography.* New York: Doubleday, 2004.

Chrysostom, Saint John. *Letters to Saint Olympia.* Translated by David C. Ford. PPS 56. Yonkers, NY: St. Vladimir's Seminary Press, 2016.

Cimosa, Mario, and Gillian Bonney. "The Use of the Septuagint Job in the New Testament and Early Christian Exegesis." *Salesianum* 76 (2014): 645–69.

Clarke, W. K. Lowther. *New Testament Problems: Essays, Reviews, Interpretations.* London: SPCK, 1929.

Clavier, H. "La santé de l'apôtre Paul." Pages 66–82 in *Studia Paulina in honorem Johannis De Zwaan Septuagenarii.* Edited by J. N. Sevenster and W. C. van Unnik. Haarlem: De Erven F. Bonn N.V., 1953.

Cole, Graham A. *Against the Darkness: The Doctrine of Angels, Satan, and Demons.* Wheaton, IL: Crossway, 2019.

Collins, Adela Yarbro. "Paul's Disability." Pages 165–83 in *Disability Studies and Biblical Literature.* Edited by Candida R. Moss and Jeremy Schipper. New York: Palgrave Macmillan, 2011.

Cooper, Stephen Andrew, and Marius Victorinus, eds. *Marius Victorinus' Commentary on Galatians.* Translated by Stephen Cooper. OECS. Oxford: Oxford University Press, 2005.

Correspondence of Erasmus: Letters 2082 to 2203. Translated by Alexander Dalzell, annotated by James M. Estes. Toronto: University of Toronto Press, 2011.

Cousar, Charles B. *A Theology of the Cross: The Death of Jesus in the Pauline Letters*. OBT 24. Minneapolis: Fortress, 1990.

Cox, Claude E. "Iob." Pages 667–96 in *A New English Translation of the Septuagint and the Other Greek Translations Traditionally Included under That Title*. Edited by Albert Pietersma and Benjamin G. Wright. Oxford and New York: Oxford University Press, 2007.

Danker, Frederick W. *II Corinthians*. ACNT. Minneapolis: Augsburg, 1989.

da Vela, Beatrice. "From the Stage to the Court: Rhetorical and Dramatic Performance in Donatus' Commentary on Terence." Pages 157–74 in *The Theatre of Justice: Aspects of Performance in Greco-Roman Oratory and Rhetoric*. Edited by Sophia Papaioannou, Andreas Serafim, and Beatrice da Vela. MNS 403. Leiden: Brill, 2017.

Dawson, Audrey. *Healing, Weakness and Power: Perspectives on Healing in the Writings of Mark, Luke and Paul*. PBM. Eugene, OR: Wipf & Stock, 2008.

Dayan, Roy Rafael and Roni Peleg. "Herpes zoster – typical and atypical presentations." *Postgrad. Med.* 129 (2017): 567–71.

Defrin, Ruth. "Chronic post-traumatic headache: clinical findings and possible mechanisms." *J. Man. Manip. Ther.* 22 (2014): 36–44.

Deibert, Richard I. *Second Corinthians and Paul's Gospel of Human Mortality: How Paul's Experience of Death Authorizes His Apostolic Authority in Corinth*. WUNT 2. Reihe 430. Tübingen: Mohr Siebeck, 2017.

Dell, Katharine J. "What was Job's Malady?" *JSOT* 41 (2016): 61–77.

de Vos, Craig S. "Finding a Charge That Fits: The Accusation against Paul and Silas at Philippi (Acts 16.19–21)." *JSNT* 21 (1999): 51–63.

Dibelius, Martin. *Die Geisterwelt im Glauben des Paulus*. Göttingen: Vandenhoeck & Ruprecht, 1909.

Dickie, June F. "Communicating Biblical Text to Be Heard Well: Lessons from Orality and Performance Studies." *Neot* 52 (2018): 289–311.

Dickie, Matthew W. *Magic and Magicians in the Greco-Roman World*. London and New York: Routledge, 2001.

Dodd, C. H. *New Testament Studies*. New York: Scribner, 1954.

Dunne, John Anthony. *Persecution and Participation in Galatians*. WUNT 2. Reihe
    454. Tübingen: Mohr Siebeck, 2017.

Eadie, John. "Paul's 'Thorn in the Flesh.'" Pages 334–35 in *The Weekly Christian
    Teacher Volume 1: December 2, 1837–November 24, 1838*. Glasgow: A.
    Fullerton and Co., 1838.

Earman, John. *Hume's Abject Failure: The Argument Against Miracles*. Oxford:
    Oxford University Press, 2000.

Eidinow, Esther. "Binding Spells on Tablets and Papyri." Pages 360–87 in *Guide
    to the Study of Ancient Magic*. Edited by David Frankfurter. RGRW 189.
    Leiden and Boston: Brill, 2019.

Elliott, John H. *Beware the Evil Eye (Volume 3): The Evil Eye in the Bible and the
    Ancient World: The Bible and Related Sources*. Cambridge: Lutterworth, 2016.

Erickson, Amy. "'Without My Flesh I Will See God': Job's Rhetoric of the Body."
    JBL 132 (2013): 295–313.

Essick, G. K. "Psychophysical assessment of patients with posttraumatic
    neuropathic trigeminal pain." *J. Oral Facial Pain Headache* 18 (2004):
    345–54.

Faraone, Christopher A. "The Agonistic Context of Early Greek Binding Spells."
    Pages 3–32 in *Magika Hiera: Ancient Greek Magic and Religion*. Edited by
    Christopher A. Faraone and Dirk Obbink. New York and Oxford: Oxford
    University Press, 1991.

———. "Binding and burying the forces of evil: The defensive use of 'voodoo' dolls
    in ancient Greece." *ClAnt* 10 (1991): 165–205.

———. "Magic and Medicine in the Roman Imperial Period: Two Case Studies."
    Pages 135–58 in *Continuity and Innovation in the Magical Tradition*. Edited
    by Gideon Bohak, Yuval Harariand, and Shaul Shaked. Leiden: Brill, 2011.

Facial Pain Association, "What is Trigeminal Neuralgia?" https://fpa-support.org/
    learn/.

Farrar, F. W. "St. Paul's 'Stake in the Flesh.'" Pages 652–61 in *The Life and Work of
    St. Paul*, vol. 1, excursus X. New York: E. P. Dutton & Company, 1879.

Fee, Gordon D. *God's Empowering Presence: The Holy Spirit in the Letters of Paul*.
    Peabody, MA: Hendrickson, 1994.

Gager, John G., ed. *Curse Tablets and Binding Spells from the Ancient World*. Oxford:
    Oxford University Press, 1992.

Gammie, John G. "The Angelology and Demonology in the Septuagint of the Book of Job." *HUCA* 56 (1985): 1–19.

Garland, David E. *2 Corinthians*. NAC. Nashville: Broadman & Holman, 1999.

Garrett, Susan R. *The Demise of the Devil: Magic and the Demonic in Luke's Writings*. Minneapolis: Fortress, 1989.

———. "Paul's Thorn and Cultural Models of Affliction." Pages 82–99 in *The Social World of the First Christians: Essays in Honor of Wayne A. Meeks*. Edited by L. Michael White and O. Larry Yarbrough. Minneapolis: Fortress, 1995.

Geivett, Douglas and Gary R. Habermas, eds. *In Defense of Miracles: A Comprehensive Case for God's Action in History*. Downers Grove, IL: IVP Academic, 1997.

Glancy, Jennifer A. "Boasting of Beatings (2 Corinthians 11:23–25)." *JBL* 123 (2004): 99–135.

Glessner, Justin M. "Ethnomedical Anthropology and Paul's 'Thorn' (2 Corinthians 12:7)." *BTB* 47 (2017): 15–46.

Gooder, Paula R. *Only the Third Heaven? 2 Corinthians 12:1–10 and the Heavenly Ascent*. LNTS 313. London: T&T Clark, 2006.

Gorman, Michael J. "Cruciformity According to Jesus and Paul." Pages 173–201 in *Unity and Diversity in the Gospels and Paul: Essays in Honor of Frank J. Matera*. Edited by Christopher W. Skinner and Kelly R. Iverson. Atlanta: Society of Biblical Literature, 2012.

———. *Cruciformity: Paul's Narrative Spirituality of the Cross*. Grand Rapids: Eerdmans, 2001.

———. "Paul and the Cruciform Way of God in Christ." *J. Moral Theol.* 2 (2013): 64–83.

Goulder, Michael D. "Visions and Revelations of the Lord (2 Corinthians 12:1–10)." Pages 303–12 in *Paul and the Corinthians: Studies on a Community in Conflict: Essays in Honour of Margaret Thrall*. Edited by Trevor J. Burke and J. Keith Elliott. NovTSup 109. Leiden: Brill, 2003.

Graf, Fritz, "Magic and Divination: Two Apolline Oracles on Magic." Pages 119–33 in *Continuity and Innovation in the Magical Tradition*. Edited by Gideon Bohak, Yuval Harariand, and Shaul Shaked. Leiden: Brill, 2011.

———. *Magic in the Ancient World*. Translated by Franklin Philip. Cambridge, MA and London: Harvard University Press, 1997.

Graff-Radford, Steven and Suthipun Jitpimolmard. "Neuropathic Pain." Pages 157–69 in *Orofacial Pain*. Edited by Joanna M. Zakrzewska. Oxford: Oxford University Press, 2009.

Graff-Radford, Steven and Bahareh Safaie. "Diagnosing and Managing Trigeminal Nerve Pain." Pages 26–36 in *Facial Pain: A 21st Century Guide: For People with Trigeminal Neuropathic Pain*. Edited by Jeffrey A. Brown and Anne Brazer Ciemnecki. Facial Pain Association, 2020.

Gregory of Nazianzus. *Select Orations*. In vol. 7 of *The Nicene and Post-Nicene Fathers*, Series 2. Edited by Philip Schaff and Henry Wace. Peabody, MA: Hendrickson, 1984, reprint 2004.

Gren, Conrad R. "Piercing the Ambiguities of Psalm 22:16 and the Messiah's Mission." *JETS* 48 (2005): 283–99.

Güttgemanns, Erhardt. *Der Leidende Apostel und Sein Herr: Studien zur Paulinischen Christologie*. FRLANT 90. Göttingen: Vandenhoeck & Ruprecht, 1986.

Guthrie, George H. *2 Corinthians*. BECNT. Grand Rapids: Baker, 2015.

Habel, Norman C. *The Book of Job: A Commentary*. Philadelphia: Westminster, 1985.

Hadley, Graham R., Julie A. Gayle, Juan Ripoll, Mark R. Jones, Charles E. Argoff, Rachel J. Kaye, and Alan D. Kaye. "Post-herpetic Neuralgia: a Review," *Curr Pain Headache Rep* 20 (2016): 17.

Hafemann, Scott J. *2 Corinthians*. NIVAC. Grand Rapids: Zondervan, 2000.

———. "'Because of weakness' (Galatians 4:13): the role of suffering in the mission of Paul." Pages 131–46 in *The Gospel to the Nations: Perspectives on Paul's Mission*. Edited by Peter Bolt and Mark Thompson. Downers Grove, IL: InterVarsity Press and Leicester: Apollos, 2000.

Hagel, Lukas. "The Angel of Satan: 2 Corinthians 12:7 Within a Social-Scientific Framework." *SEÅ* 84 (2019): 193–207.

Hagler, S., K. Ballaban-Gil, and M. S. Robbins. "Primary Stabbing Headache in Adults and Pediatrics: a Review." *Curr Pain Headache Rep* 18 (2014): 450.

Halbwachs, Maurice. *On Collective Memory*. Edited and translated by Lewis A. Coser. Chicago: University of Chicago Press, 2008.

Hanson, Anthony Tyrrell. *The Paradox of the Cross in the Thought of St. Paul*. JSNTSup 17. Sheffield: JSOT Press, 1987.

Harris, Murray J. *Prepositions and Theology in the Greek New Testament: An Essential Reference Resource for Exegesis*. Grand Rapids: Zondervan, 2012.

————. *The Second Epistle to the Corinthians: A Commentary on the Greek Text.*
    NIGTC. Grand Rapids: Eerdmans and Milton Keynes: Paternoster, 2005.

Hartley, John E. *The Book of Job.* NICOT. Grand Rapids: Eerdmans, 1988.

Harvey, John D. "Orality and Its Implications for Biblical Studies: Recapturing an
    Ancient Paradigm." *JETS* 45 (2002): 99–109.

Hawthorne, Gerald R. and Ralph P. Martin, eds. *Dictionary of Paul and His Letters.*
    Downers Grove, IL: InterVarsity Press, 1993.

Hays, Richard B. *Echoes of Scripture in the Letters of Paul.* New Haven and London:
    Yale University Press, 1989.

————. "Galatians." Pages 181–348 in *The New Interpreter's Bible: Volume XI.*
    Nashville: Abingdon, 2000.

Hazen, Walter A. *Everyday Life: Ancient Times.* Tucson, AZ: Good Year Books,
    2005.

Headache Classification Committee of the International Headache Society (IHS). "The
    International Classification of Headache Disorders, 3rd edition (beta
    version)." *Cephalalgia* 33 (2013): 629–808.

Heckel, Ulrich. "Der Dorn im Fleisch: Die Krankeit des Paulus in 2Kor 12,7 und
    Gal 4,13f." *ZNW* 84 (1993): 65–92.

Heiser, Michael S. *The Unseen Realm: Recovering the Supernatural Worldview of the
    Bible.* Bellingham, WA: Lexham Press, 2015.

Henry, Matthew. *Matthew Henry's Commentary on the Whole Bible: Complete and
    Unabridged in One Volume.* Peabody, MA: Hendrickson, 1994.

Hisey, Alan and James S. P. Beck. "Paul's 'Thorn in the Flesh': A Paragnosis."
    JBR 29 (1961): 125–29.

Hoffmann, Jan. "Diagnosis, pathophysiology, and management of cluster
    headache." *Lancet Neurol.* 17 (2018): 75–83.

Holmes-Gore, V.A. "St. Paul's Thorn in the Flesh." *Theology* 32 (1936): 111–12.

Hood, Jason B. "The Temple and the Thorn: 2 Corinthians 12 and Paul's Heavenly
    Ecclesiology." *BBR* 21 (2011): 357–70.

Hughes, Philip Edgcumbe. *Paul's Second Epistle to the Corinthians: The English Text
    with Introduction, Exposition and Notes.* Grand Rapids: Eerdmans, 1962.

Hume, David. "Of Miracles." Pages 29–44 in *In Defense of Miracles: A
    Comprehensive Case for God's Action in History.* Edited by Douglas Geivett
    and Gary R. Habermas. Downers Grove, IL: IVP Academic, 1997.

Janowitz, Naomi. *Magic in the Roman World: Pagans, Jews and Christians*. London and New York: Routledge, 2001.

Janzen, J. Gerald. "Paul's 'Robust Conscience' and His Thorn in the Flesh." *Canadian Theological Review* 3 (2014): 71–83.

Jegher-Bucher, Verena. "'The Thorn in the Flesh'/'Der Pfahl im Fleisch': Considerations about 2 Corinthians 12.7–10 in connection with 12.1–13." Pages 388–97 in *The Rhetorical Analysis of Scripture: Essays from the 1995 London Conference*. Edited by Stanley E. Porter and Thomas H. Olbricht. JSNTSup 146. Sheffield: Sheffield Academic, 1997.

Jitpimolmard, Suthipun and Steven Graff-Radford. "Neuropathic Pain." Pages 135–55 in *Orofacial Pain*. Edited by Joanna M. Zakrzewska. Oxford: Oxford University Press, 2009.

Jobes, Karen H. and Moisés Silva. *Invitation to the Septuagint*. Grand Rapids: Baker, 2000.

Johnson, Eleanor Anglin. "St. Paul's 'Infirmity.'" *ExpTim* 39 (1927–1928): 428–29.

Johnson, Lee A. "Satan Talk in Corinth: The Rhetoric of Conflict," *BTB* 29 (1999): 145–55.

Jones, Scott. "Corporeal Discourse in the Book of Job." *JBL* 132 (2013): 845–63.

Kandel, S. A. and P. Mandiga. *Cluster Headache*. Treasure Island, FL: StatPearls Publishing, 2019.

Käsemann, Ernst. "The Saving Significance of the Death of Jesus in Paul." Pages 32–59 in *Perspectives on Paul*. Translated by Margaret Kohl. Philadelphia: Fortress, 1971.

Kearsley, R. "Tertullian." Pages 60–65 in *Historical Handbook of Major Biblical Interpreters*. Edited by Donald K. McKim. Downers Grove, IL: InterVarsity Press, 1998.

Keener, Craig S. *Acts: An Exegetical Commentary*. Vol. 3. Grand Rapids: Baker, 2014.

———. *1–2 Corinthians*. NCBC. Cambridge: Cambridge University Press, 2005.

———. *Galatians: A Commentary*. Grand Rapids: Baker, 2019.

———. *Miracles: The Credibility of the New Testament Accounts*. 2 vols. Grand Rapids: Baker, 2011.

———. *The IVP Bible Background Commentary: New Testament*. Downers Grove, IL: InterVarsity Press, 1993.

Kent, Benedict H. M. "Curses in Acts : Hearing the Apostles' Words of Judgment Alongside 'Magical' Spell Texts." *JSNT* 39 (2017): 412–40.

Keyser, Paul T. "Science and Magic in Galen's Recipes (Sympathy and Efficacy)." Pages 175–98 in *Galen on Pharmacology: Philosophy, History and Medicine, Proceedings of the V-th International Galen Colloquium, Lille, 16–18 March 1995.* Edited by Armelle Debru. Leiden: Brill, 1997.

Khazen, Olga and Julie G. Pilitsis. "Motor Cortex Stimulation." Pages 93–95 in *Facial Pain: A 21st Century Guide: For People with Trigeminal Neuropathic Pain.* Edited by Jeffrey A. Brown and Anne Brazer Ciemnecki. N.p.: Facial Pain Association, 2020.

Kidner, Derek. *Psalms 1–72: An Introduction & Commentary.* TOTC. Leicester and Downers Grove, IL: InterVarsity Press, 1973.

Kierkegaard, Soren. "The Thorn in the Flesh." *Edifying Discourses 4.* Minneapolis: Augsburg, 1962.

Kistemaker, Simon J. *New Testament Commentary: Exposition of the Second Epistle to the Corinthians.* Grand Rapids: Baker, 1997.

Kittel, Gerhard, and Gerhard Friedrich, eds. *TDNT.* Translated by Geoffrey W. Bromiley. 10 vols. Grand Rapids: Eerdmans, 1964–1976.

Klauck, Hans-Josef. *Magic and Paganism in Early Christianity: The World of the Acts of the Apostles.* Translated by Brian McNeil. Edinburgh: T&T Clark, 2000.

———. "With Paul in Paphos and Lystra: Magic and Paganism in the Acts of the Apostles." *Neot* 28 (1994): 93–108.

Knapp, Margaret L. "Paul the Deaf." *The Biblical World* 47 (1916): 311–17.

Knight, George W. *The Pastoral Epistles: A Commentary on the Greek Text.* NIGTC. Grand Rapids: Eerdmans and Carlisle: Paternoster, 1992.

Krenkel, Max. *Beiträge zur Aufhellung der Geschichte und der Briefe des Apostels Paulus.* 2nd ed. Braunschweig: C. A. Schwetschke, 1895.

Kruse, Colin G. *The Second Epistle of Paul to the Corinthians: An Introduction and Commentary.* Leicester: Inter-Varsity Press and Grand Rapids: Eerdmans, 1987, repr. 1995.

Kuhn, Thomas S. *The Structure of Scientific Revolutions.* 2nd ed. Chicago: The University of Chicago Press, 1970.

Lahz, Sophia and Richard A. Bryant. "Incidence of chronic pain following traumatic brain injury." *Arch. Phys. Med. Rehabil.* 77 (1996): 889–91.

Lambrecht, Jan. "The Fool's Speech and Its Context: Paul's Particular Way of Arguing in 2 Cor 10–13." *Bib* 83 (2001): 305–24.

Land, Christopher D. *The Integrity of 2 Corinthians and Paul's Aggravating Absence.* NTM 36. Sheffield: Sheffield Phoenix, 2015.

Landsborough, D. "St Paul and Temporal Lobe Epilepsy." *J. Neurol. Neurosurg. Psychiatry* 50 (1987): 659–64.

Lapide, R. P. Cornelii à. *Commentaria in Scripturam Sacram.* Paris: Apud Ludovicum Vivès, Bibliopolam Editorem, 1891.

Lau, Te-Li. *Defending Shame: Its Formative Power in Paul's Letters.* Grand Rapids: Baker, 2020.

Leary, T. J. "A Thorn in the Flesh—2 Corinthians 12:7." *JTS* 43 (1992): 520–22.

Levy, Andrew and Manjit S Matharu. "Short-lasting unilateral neuralgiform headache attacks." *Ann. Indian Acad. Neurol.* 21 (2018): 31–38

Lewin, Thomas. *The Life and Epistles of St. Paul,* vol. 1. 5th ed. London: George Bell and Sons, 1890.

Lewis, Charlton T. *A Latin Dictionary: Lewis and Short.* Oxford: Clarendon, 1998.

Lexico. "Cuff." https://www.lexico.com/en/definition/cuff.

Liang, Xiping, Guomin Ying, Qingqing Huang, Jing Wang, Nan Li, Ge Tan, Tristan R. Zhang, Zhen Huang, and Jiying Zhou. "Characteristics of Primary Stabbing Headache in a Tertiary Neurological Clinic in China." *Pain Medicine* 15 (May 2014): 871–75.

Liddell, Keith. "Skin diseases in antiquity." *Clinical Medicine* 6 (2006): 81–86.

Liddell, Henry George, Robert Scott, and Henry Stuart Jones. LSJ. 9th ed. Oxford: Clarendon, 1996.

Lightfoot, J. B. *Saint Paul's Epistle to the Galatians: A Revised Text with Introduction, Notes, and Dissertations.* London: Macmillan, 1921.

Lim, Kar Young. *The Sufferings of Christ are Abundant in Us: A Narrative Dynamics Investigation of Paul's Sufferings in 2 Corinthians.* TTCLBS 399. London: T&T Clark, 2009.

Litwa, M. David. "Paul the 'God' in Acts 28: A Comparison with Philoctetes." *JBL* 136 (2017): 707–26.

———. "Paul's Mosaic Ascent: An Interpretation of 2 Corinthians 12.7–9." *NTS* 57 (2011): 238–57.

Long, V. Philips. "The Art of Biblical History." Pages 281–428 in *Foundations of Contemporary Interpretation*. Edited by Moisés Silva. Grand Rapids: Zondervan, 1996.

Longenecker, Richard N. *Galatians*. WBC. Dallas: Word, 1990.

Longman III, Tremper. *Job*. BCOTWP. Grand Rapids: Baker, 2012.

Loubser, J. A. "Exegesis and Proclamation: Winning the Struggle (Or: How to Treat Heretics) (2 Corinthians 12:1–10)." *JTSA* 75 (1991): 75–83.

Louw, Johannes P., and Eugene Albert Nida. *Greek-English Lexicon of the New Testament: Based on Semantic Domains*. New York: United Bible Societies, 1996.

Love, Seth and Hugh B. Coakham. "Trigeminal neuralgia: Pathology and pathogenesis." *Brain* 124 (2001): 2347–60.

Lunde, Jonathan. *Following Jesus, The Servant King: A Biblical Theology of Covenantal Discipleship*. BTL. Grand Rapids: Zondervan, 2010.

Luther, Martin. "Heidelberg Disputation (1518)." Pages 14–25 in *Martin Luther's Basic Theological Writings*. Edited by Timothy F. Lull and William R. Russell. Minneapolis: Fortress, 2012.

Maarbjerg, Stine, Giulia Di Stefano, Lars Bendtsen, and Giorgio Cruccu. "Trigeminal neuralgia – diagnosis and treatment." *Cephalalgia* 37 (2017): 648–57.

Malay, Hasan and Georg Petzl. *New Religious Texts from Lydia*. ETAM 28. Wien: Verlag der Österreichischen Akademie der Wissenschaften, 2017.

Maloney, Elliott. "When I Am Weak, Then I Am Strong: Understanding St. Paul's 'thorn in the flesh.'" *The Priest* (2018): 20–26.

Mangan, Edward A. "Was Saint Paul an Invalid?" *CBQ* 5 (1943): 68–72.

Marcus, Dawn A. "Disability and Chronic Posttraumatic Headache." *Headache* 43 (2003): 117–21.

Marshall, Peter. *Enmity in Corinth: Social Conventions in Paul's Relations with the Corinthians*. Tübingen: Mohr Siebeck, 1987.

———. "A Metaphor of Social Shame: ΘΡΙΑΜΒΕΥΕΙΝ in 2 COR. 2:14." *NovT* 25 (1983): 302–17.

Martin, Dale B. *The Corinthian Body*. New Haven: Yale University Press, 1995.

Martin, Ralph P. *2 Corinthians*. WBC. Waco, TX: Word, 1986.

Martyn, J. Louis. *Galatians: A New Translation with Introduction and Commentary*.

AB 33A. New York: Doubleday, 1997.

Mbuvi, Andrew M. "The Ancient Mediterranean Values of 'Honour and Shame' as a Hermeneutical Lens of Reading the Book of Job." *OTE* 23/3 (2010): 752–68.

McCant, Jerry. "Paul's Thorn of Rejected Apostleship." *NTS* 34:4 (1988): 550–72.

McCartney, Dan and Charles Clayton. *Let the Reader Understand: A Guide to Interpreting and Applying the Bible*. Phillipsburg, NJ: P&R, 2002.

McGrath, Alister E. *Paul's Theology of the Cross*. 2nd ed. Oxford: Wiley-Blackwell, 2011.

Menoud, Philippe-H. "The Thorn in the Flesh and Satan's Angel (2 Cor. 12:7)." Pages 19–30 in *Jesus Christ and the Faith: A Collection of Studies*. PTMS 18. Pittsburgh: Pickwick, 1978.

Merrins, Edward M. "St. Paul's Thorn in the Flesh." *BSac* 64 (1907): 661–92.

Metzger, Bruce M. *A Textual Commentary on the Greek New Testament*. London: United Bible Societies, 1971.

Minn, H. R. *The Thorn that Remained: Materials for the Study of St. Paul's Thorn in the Flesh: 2 Corinthians XII. vv. 1–10*. Auckland: Institute, 1972.

Minor, Mitzi L. *2 Corinthians*. SHBC. Macon, GA: Smyth & Helwys, 2009.

Moo, Douglas J. *Galatians*. BECNT. Grand Rapids: Baker, 2013.

Morray-Jones, Christopher R. A. "The Ascent into Paradise (2 Cor 12:1–12): Paul's *Merkava* Vision and Apostolic Call." Pages 245–85 in *Second Corinthians in the Perspective of Late Second Temple Judaism*. Edited by Reimund Bieringer, Emmanuel Nathan, Didier Pollefeyt, and Peter J. Tomson. CRINT 14. Leiden and Boston: Brill, 2014.

Moss, Candida R. "Christly Possession and Weakened Bodies: Reconsideration of the Function of Paul's Thorn in the Flesh (2 Cor. 12:7–10)." *Relig.* 16:4 (2012): 319–33

———. "The Justification of the Martyrs." Pages 104–18 in *Tertullian and Paul*. Edited by Todd D. Still and David E. Wilhite. Pauline and Patristic Scholars in Debate, vol. 1. New York: Bloomsbury, 2013.

Moulton, James Hope. *A Grammar of New Testament Greek: Vol. II: Accidence and Word-Formation*. Edinburgh: T&T Clark, 1919.

Moulton, J. H. and G. Milligan. *Vocabulary of the Greek New Testament*. Peabody, MA: Hendrickson, 1997.

Mullins, Terence Y. "Paul's Thorn in the Flesh." *JBL* 76 (1957): 299–303.

Murray, Danielle and Esma Dilli. "Primary Stabbing Headache." *Curr Neurol Neurosci Rep* 19 (2019): 47.

Nash, Charles Harris. "Paul's 'Thorn in the Flesh' in Its Bearing on his Character and Mission." *RevExp* 28 (1931): 33–51.

Neyrey, Jerome H. "Bewitched in Galatia: Paul and Cultural Anthropology." *CBQ* 50 (1988): 72–100.

Nicolatti, Andrea. "The Scourge of Jesus and the Roman Scourge." *JSHJ* 15 (2017): 1–59.

Nida, Eugene A. *Componential Analysis of Meaning: An Introduction to Semantic Structures.* Approaches to Semiotics 57. The Hague: Mouton, 1975.

Nisbet, Patricia. "The Thorn in the Flesh." *ExpTim* 80 (1969): 126.

Nummenmaa, Lauri, Enrico Glerean, Riitta Hari, and Jari K. Hietanen. "Bodily maps of emotions." *PNAS* 111 (2014): 646–51.

Oakes, Peter. *From People to Letter.* SNTSMS 110. Cambridge: Cambridge University Press, 2000.

Ogden, Daniel. *Magic, Witchcraft, and Ghosts in the Greek and Roman Worlds: A Sourcebook.* Oxford: Oxford University Press, 2002.

Omerzu, Heike. "The Portrayal of Paul's Outer Appearance in the Acts of Paul and Thecla: Reconsidering the Correspondence between the Body and Personality in Ancient Literature." *R&T* 15 (2008): 252–79.

Oropeza, B. J. *Exploring Second Corinthians: Death and Life, Hardship and Rivalry.* RRA 3. Atlanta: SBL Press, 2016.

Osborne, Grant R. *The Hermeneutical Spiral: A Comprehensive Introduction to Biblical Interpretation.* Downers Grove, IL: IVP Academic, 2006.

Page, Sydney H. T. "Satan: God's Servant." *JETS* 50 (2007): 449–65.

Park, David M. "Paul's ΣΚΟΛΟΨ ΤΗ ΣΑΡΚΙ: Thorn or Stake? (2 Cor. XII 7)." *NovT* 22 (1980): 179–83.

Pascual, Antonio Macaya, Ignacio Manresa Lamarca, and Jaime Piquero Casals. "Saint Paul's Thorn in the Flesh: A Dermatological Weakness?" *SetF* 10 (2022): 9–27.

Parsons, Mikeal C. and Michael Wade Martin. *Ancient Rhetoric and the New Testament: The Influence of Elementary Greek Composition.* Waco, TX: Baylor University Press, 2018.

Patel, Smruti K. and James K. Liu. "Overview and History of Trigeminal Neuralgia." *Neurosurg. Clin. N. Am.* 27 (2016): 265–76.

Patient Guide: Understanding Trigeminal Neuralgia & Neuropathic Face Pain. Gainesville: Facial Pain Association. https://fpa-support.org/support-network/guide/.

Perseus Digital Library. https://www.perseus.tufts.edu.

Peterson, David G. *The Acts of the Apostles.* PNTC. Grand Rapids and Cambridge: Eerdmans and Nottingham: Apollos, 2009.

Philo. *The Works of Philo: Complete and Unabridged.* Translated by Charles Duke Yonge. Peabody, MA: Hendrickson, 1993.

Piovesan, Elcio Juliato, Pedro André Kowacs, Marcos Cristiano Lange, Carlos Pacheco, Liciane do Rocio Maia Piovesan, Lineu Cesar Werneck. "Prevalence and semiologic aspects of the idiopathic stabbing headache in a migraine population." *Arquivos de Neuro-Psiquiatria* 59 (2001): 201–5.

Plummer, Alfred. *A Critical and Exegetical Commentary on the Second Epistle of St. Paul to the Corinthians.* ICC. Edinburgh: T&T Clark, 1915.

Plumptre, E. H. *The Second Epistle to the Corinthians.* Edited by Charles John Ellicott. London: Cassell, 1883.

Prakash, Sanjay and Rushad Patell. "Paroxysmal Hemicrania: An Update." *Curr Pain Headache Rep* 18 (2014): 407.

Preisendanz, Karl, ed. *PGM.* 2 Vols. Leipzig: Teubner, 1928 and 1931.

Price, Robert M. "Punished in Paradise (An Exegetical Theory on II Corinthians 12:1–10)." *JSNT* 7 (1980): 33–40.

Ramsay, William M. *St. Paul the Traveler and Roman Citizen.* Revised by Mark Wilson. Grand Rapids: Kregel, 2001.

Reece, Steve. *Paul's Large Letters: Paul's Autographic Subscriptions in the Light of Ancient Epistolary Conventions.* LNTS 561. London: Bloomsbury T&T Clark, 2017.

Renan, Ernest. "The Portraits of Saint Paul: Letter to M. Mézmièrez of the French Academy." Pages 146–56 in *Recollections and Letters of Ernest Renan.* Translated by Isabel F. Hapgood. New York: Cassell, 1892.

Rescher, Nicholas and Carey B. Joynt. "Evidence in History and in the Law." *J. Philos.* 56 (1959): 561–78.

Richards, E. Randolph. *Paul and First-Century Letter Writing: Secretaries, Composition and Collection*. Downers Grove, IL: InterVarsity Press, 2004.

Robertson, A. T. *A Grammar of the Greek New Testament in the Light of Historical Research*. Nashville: Broadman, 1934.

Rodríguez, Rafael. *Oral Tradition and the New Testament: A Guide for the Perplexed*. Guides for the Perplexed. London: T&T Clark, 2014.

Roetzel, Calvin J. *2 Corinthians*. ANTC. Nashville: Abingdon, 2007.

Rouse, Matthew H. *Neuroanatomy for Speech-Language Pathologists and Audiologists*. Burlington, MA: Jones & Bartlett Learning, 2016.

Russell, Ronald. "Redemptive Suffering and Paul's Thorn in the Flesh." *JETS* 39 (1996): 559–70.

Ryken, Leland, James C. Wilhoit, and Tremper Longman III, eds. *DBI*. Downers Grove, IL: InterVarsity Press, 1998.

Jerome. *Letters and Select Works*. In vol 6 of *The Nicene and Post-Nicene Fathers*, Series 2. Edited by Philip Schaff and Henry Wace. Translated by W. H. Fremantle, G. Lewis, and W. G. Martley. New York: Christian Literature Company, 1893.

———. *St. Jerome's Commentaries on Galatians, Titus, and Philemon*. Translated by Tomas P. Scheck. Notre Dame: University of Notre Dame Press, 2010.

Savage, Timothy B. *Power through Weakness: Paul's Understanding of the Christian Ministry in 2 Corinthians*. Cambridge: Cambridge University Press, 1996.

Schellenberg, Ryan S. *Rethinking Paul's Rhetorical Education: Comparative Rhetoric and 2 Corinthians*. ECL. Atlanta: Society of Biblical Literature, 2013.

Schipper, Jeremy. "Healing and Silence in the Epilogue of Job." *Word & World* 30 (2010): 16–22.

Schlatter, Adolf. *Paulus, der Bote Jesu: Eine Deutung seiner Briefe an die Korinther*. 2nd ed. Stuttgart: Calwer Verlag, 1956.

Schmader, Kenneth. "Herpes Zoster." *Clin. Geriatr.* 32 (2016): 539–53.

Schreiner, Thomas R. *Galatians*. ZECNT. Grand Rapids: Zondervan, 2010.

Schweitzer, Albert. *The Mysticism of Paul the Apostle*. 2nd ed. Translated by William Montgomery. London: Black, 1953.

Schwemer, Daniel. *Abwehrzauber und Behexung: Studien zum Schadenzauberglauben im alten Mesopotamien*. Wiesbaden: Harrassowitz Verlag, 2007.

Scott, James M. 2 Corinthians. NIBC. Peabody, MA: Hendrickson, 1998.

Seifrid, Mark A. The Second Letter to the Corinthians. PNTC. Grand Rapids: Eerdmans, 2014.

Shantz, Colleen. Paul in Ecstasy: The Neurobiology of the Apostle's Life and Thought. Cambridge: Cambridge University Press, 2009.

Shi, Wenhua. Paul's Message of the Cross as Body Language. WUNT 2. Reihe 254. Tübingen: Mohr Siebeck, 2008.

Silva, Anna M. The Asketikon of St Basil the Great. Oxford: Oxford University Press, 2005.

Silzer, Peter James, and Thomas John Finley. How Biblical Languages Work. Grand Rapids: Kregel Academic, 2004.

Smith, Neil Gregor. "The Thorn that Stayed: An Exposition of II Corinthians 12:7–9." Int 13 (1959): 409–16.

Sophocles, E. A. Greek Lexicon of the Roman and Byzantine Periods (From B.C. 146 to A.D. 1100). Volume 2. New York: Frederick Ungar, 1957.

Spittler, Russell P. "The Limits of Ecstasy: An Exegesis of 2 Corinthians 12:1–10." Pages 259–66 in Current Issues in Biblical and Patristic Interpretation: Studies in Honor of Merrill C. Tenney presented by his Former Students. Edited by Gerald F. Hawthorne. Grand Rapids: Eerdmans, 1975.

Stegman, Thomas. The Character of Jesus: The Linchpin to Paul's Argument in 2 Corinthians. AnBib 158. Rome: Editrice Pontificio Istituto Biblico, 2005.

Stokes, Ryan E. The Satan: How God's Executioner Became the Enemy. Grand Rapids: Eerdmans, 2019.

Strelan, Rick. Paul, Artemis, and the Jews in Ephesus. BZNW 80. Berlin and New York: Walter de Gruyter, 1996.

Taber's Cyclopedic Medical Dictionary: Edition 23. Philadelphia: F. A. Davis, 2013.

Tabor, James D. Things Unutterable: Paul's Ascent to Paradise in Its Greco-Roman, Judaic, and Early Christian Contexts. London: University Press of America, 1987.

Taurig, H. H. and B. E. Maley. "The trigeminal system." Pages 239–48 in Neuroscience in Medicine. Edited by P. M. Conn. Philadelphia: J. B. Lippincott, 1995.

Tertullian: Adversus Marcionem: Books 4 and 5. Edited and translated by Ernest Evans. Oxford: Clarendon, 1972.

Thesaurus Linguae Graecae Digital Library. http://stephanus.tlg.uci.edu/index. php.

Thierry, J. J. "Der Dorn im Fleische (2 Kor. Xii 7–9)." *NovT* 5 (1962): 301–10.

Thiselton, Anthony C. *The Two Horizons: New Testament Hermeneutics and Philosophical Description with Special Reference to Heidegger, Bultmann, Gadamer, and Wittgenstein.* Grand Rapids: Eerdmans, 1980.

Thomas, John Christopher. "'An Angel from Satan': Paul's Thorn in the Flesh (2 Corinthians 12.7–10)." *JPT* 9 (1996): 39–52.

———. *The Devil, Disease and Deliverance: Origins of Illness in New Testament Thought.* London: Continuum, Sheffield University Press, 1998, reprinted, 2005.

Thompson, James W. *Apostle of Persuasion: Theology and Rhetoric in the Pauline Letters.* Grand Rapids: Baker, 2020.

Thornton, Dillon T. "Satan as Adversary and Ally in the Process of Ecclesial Discipline: The Use of the Prologue to Job in 1 Corinthians 5:5 and 1 Timothy 1:20." *TynBul* 66 (2015): 137–51.

Thrall, Margaret E. *2 Corinthians 8–13: Volume 2.* A Critical and Exegetical Commentary on The Second Epistle to the Corinthians. ICC. London and New York: T&T Clark, 2000.

Togarasei, Lovemore. "Paul's 'Thorn in the Flesh' and Christian Mission to People with Disabilities." *IRM* 108 (2019): 136–47.

Towner, Philip H. *The Letters to Timothy and Titus.* NICNT. Grand Rapids: Eerdmans, 2006.

Trimm, Charlie. *Fighting for the King and the Gods: A Survey of Warfare in the Ancient Near East.* RBS 88. Atlanta, GA: SBL, 2017.

Twelftree, Graham H. "The Historian and the Miraculous." *BBR* 28 (2018): 199–217.

Versnel, H. S. "Beyond Cursing: The Appeal to Justice in Judicial Prayers." Pages 60–106 in *Magika Hiera: Ancient Greek Magic and Religion.* Edited by Christopher A. Faraone and Dirk Obbink. New York and Oxford: Oxford University Press, 1991.

Wallace, James Buchanan. *Snatched into Paradise (2 Cor 12:1–10): Paul's Heavenly Journey in the Context of Early Christian Experience.* BZNW 179. Berlin: Walter de Gruyter, 2011.

Walton, John H. and J. Harvey Walton. *Demons and Spirits in Biblical Theology: Reading the Biblical Text in Its Cultural and Literary Context.* Eugene, OR: Cascade, 2019.

Watson, Duane F. "Paul and Boasting." Pages 90–112 in *Paul in the Greco-Roman World: A Handbook.* Edited by J. Paul Sampley. 2nd ed. London: Bloomsbury, 2016.

Weaver-Agostoni, Jacqueline. "Cluster Headache." *AFP* 88 (2013): 122–28.

Whitby, Daniel. *A Paraphrase and Commentary on the New Testament,* vol. 2. London: Black Swan, 1703.

Wilburn, Andrew T. "Figurines, Images, and Representations Used in Ritual Practices." Pages 456–506 in *Guide to the Study of Ancient Magic.* Edited by David Frankfurter. RGRW 189. Leiden and Boston: Brill, 2019.

Wilkinson, John. *The Bible and Healing: A Medical and Theological Commentary.* Grand Rapids: Eerdmans, 1998.

Wilson, Mark. "Galatia in Text, Geography, and Archaeology." *BAR* (2020): 54–56.

Windisch, Hans. *Der Zweite Korintherbrief.* MeyerK 6. Göttingen: Vandenhoeck & Ruprecht, 1924.

Wiseman, Donald J. *1 & 2 Kings: An Introduction & Commentary.* TOTC. Downers Grove, IL: InterVarsity Press, 1993.

Witherington III, Ben. *Conflict & Community in Corinth: A Socio-Rhetorical Commentary on 1 and 2 Corinthians.* Carlisle: Paternoster, 1995.

———. *Grace in Galatia: A Commentary on Paul's Letter to the Galatians.* Grand Rapids: Eerdmans, 1998.

———. *New Testament Rhetoric: An Introductory Guide to the Art of Persuasion in and of the New Testament.* Eugene, OR: Cascade, 2009.

Wood, John E. "Death at Work in Paul." *EvQ* 54 (1982): 151–55.

Woods, Laurie. "Opposition to a Man and His Message: Paul's 'Thorn in the Flesh' (2 Cor 12:7)." *ABR* 39 (1991): 44–53.

Wrede, William. *Paul.* Translated by E. Lummis. London: Philip Green, 1907.

Yawn, Barbara P., Peter C. Wollan, Marge J. Kurland, Jennifer L. St. Suaver, Patricia Saddier. "Herpes Zoster Recurrences More Frequent Than Previously Reported." *Mayo Clin. Proc.* 86:2 (2011): 88–93.

Yong, Amos. *The Bible, Disability, and the Church: A New Vision of the People of God.* Grand Rapids: Eerdmans, 2011.

Yoon, David I. "Paul's Thorn and His Gnosis: Epistemic Considerations." Pages 23–43 in *Paul and Gnosis*. Edited by Stanley E. Porter and David I. Yoon. Leiden: Brill, 2016.

Zakrzewska, Joanna M. "Facial Pain: Neurological and Non-Neurological." *J. Neurol. Neurosurg. Psychiatry* 72 (2002): 27–32.

Zakrzewska, Joanna M. and Mark E. Linskey, "Trigeminal Neuralgia." Pages 119–33 in *Orofacial Pain*. Edited by Joanna M. Zakrzewska. Oxford: Oxford University Press, 2009.

Ziegler, Joseph. *Septuaginta: Vetus Test-amentum Graecum Auctoritate Academiae Scientiarum Gottingensis editum XI.4: Iob*. Göttingen: Vandenhoeck & Ruprecht, 1982.

Ziegler, W. C. L. *Theologische Abhandlungen*, vol. 2. Göttingen: H. Dieterich, 1804.

Zucconi, Laura M. *Ancient Medicine: From Mesopotamia to Rome*. Grand Rapids: Eerdmans, 2019.

SUBJECT & AUTHOR INDEX |

faces and, 100–101, 127–29, 200–201
language of, 82–83, 100
Paul's defense in 2 Cor, 121–25, 232
Hood, Jason B., 31
humiliation
dramatization of Paul's, 1–2, 230
facial pain and, 100–101, 125, 131
in Galatians, 171
parallels of Jesus and Paul, 143–44,
146–47, 146n16, 151n26
parallels in Job and Paul, 82–83, 196,
201
physical weakness and, 121–25, 123n5,
200–201
thorn as discipleship, 102–4, 200,
209–12, 231
Hughes, Philip Edgcumbe, 14, 28, 92n7
Hume, David, 17n20

I

Index of Quotations, 72
interpretation
evaluating influences, 8, 18–19, 19n23
intertextuality, 17, 22, 37, 72–73,
86–87, 185
methodology, 15
presuppositions, 5, 11–12, 34–35
intertextuality, 17, 22, 37, 72–73, 86–87,
185
Irenaeus, 7, 18, 24, 153, 155–59, 197

J

Jacob (biblical figure), 67n66
Janowitz, Naomi, 40–41, 52n32
Janzen, J. Gerald, 31
Jegher-Bucher, Verena, 31, 101, 173n11
Jerome, 25, 25n19, 155
Jesus Christ
baptism into, 149
crown of thorns, 143–44
crucifixion, 144–45
humiliation, 146–47, 146n16, 201

sharing in his sufferings, 7, 130,
139–52, 180, 184, 199, 201, 202,
231, 233–34
struck in the face, 145–46
his trial, 99, 101, 142n14
Job (book of)
demonic activity in, 66
subtext for thorn, 6, 18, 71–88, 184,
195–96, 198, 209–12, 229
theology of suffering, 80–82
Johnson, Eleanor Anglin, 25
Johnson, Lee A., 54n37, 80n24
Joynt, Carey B., 19n23

K

Käsemann, Ernst, 140, 141n9
Kearsley, R., 163n15
Keener, Craig S., 30, 30n77, 80n24
khtsy (Heb.), 79
Kidner, Derek, 149n18
Kierkegaard, Søren, 24
Kistemaker, Simon J., 14–15
Klauck, Hans-Josef, 57n43, 58n47,
60n51
kolossoi, 44–45, 49, 50–51
Knapp, Margaret L., 27
kolaphizō, 6, 96–102, 97n21, 98n23,
99n25, 99n26, 101n32, 102n33,
145, 162, 199, 204, 205
Krenkel, Max, 26
Kruse, Colin G., 13, 109n10
Kuhn, Thomas, 12

L

Landborough, D., 26
à Lapide, R. P. Cornelii, 30
Leah (biblical figure), 67n66
Leary, T. J., 26
Lewin, Thomas, 26
Lewis, Charlton E., 102n33
Libanius, 53
Liddell, Keith, 172n10

SCRIPTURE INDEX |

OLD TESTAMENT

NEW TESTAMENT

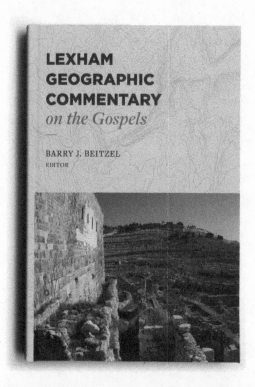